EAST AFRICA
AND THE HORN

INTERNATIONAL PEACE ACADEMY
OCCASIONAL PAPER SERIES

EAST AFRICA AND THE HORN

Confronting Challenges to Good Governance

edited by
Dorina A. Bekoe

LYNNE
RIENNER
PUBLISHERS

BOULDER
LONDON

Published in the United States of America in 2006 by
Lynne Rienner Publishers, Inc.
1800 30th Street, Boulder, Colorado 80301
www.rienner.com

and in the United Kingdom by
Lynne Rienner Publishers, Inc.
3 Henrietta Street, Covent Garden, London WC2E 8LU

Library of Congress Cataloging-in-Publication Data
East Africa and the Horn : confronting challenges to good governance /
    edited by Dorina A. Bekoe.
    p. cm. — (An International Peace Academy occasional paper)
    Includes bibliographical references and index.
    ISBN 1-58826-379-7 (pbk. : alk. paper)
    1. Africa, East—Politics and government. 2. Democratization—Africa, East.
3. Conflict management—Africa, East. 4. Gun control—Africa, East. 5. Africa,
East—Foreign relations—United States. 6. United States—Foreign relations—
Africa, East. I. Bekoe, Dorina Akosua Oduraa. II. Series: International Peace
Academy occasional paper series.
JQ2945.A58E23 2006
320.9676'09'0511—dc22   2005018303

British Cataloguing in Publication Data
A Cataloguing in Publication record for this book
is available from the British Library.

Printed and bound in the United States of America

    The paper used in this publication meets the requirements
∞ of the American National Standard for Permanence of
    Paper for Printed Library Materials Z39.48-1992.

5 4 3 2 1

Contents

Foreword

Terje Rød-Larsen
President, International Peace Academy

It is with great pleasure that the International Peace Academy (IPA) presents this scholarly volume on governance challenges in East Africa and the Horn. The volume is edited by Dorina Bekoe, a former member of IPA's Africa Program and currently program officer in the Research and Studies Department at the US Institute of Peace. She has worked closely with the eight contributors in assessing the important issues of good governance as they affect the member states of the Intergovernmental Authority on Development and the East African Community. The book is the outcome of a joint policy seminar organized by the International Peace Academy in cooperation with Makerere University and the Africa Peace Forum in Entebbe, Uganda, in December 2002. The authors have also incorporated into their chapters reflections on new developments since the seminar took place.

Since its inception in 1992, the International Peace Academy's Africa Program has focused on strengthening African capacities to manage conflict, reduce sources of tension, and prevent violence. Successive directors of the Africa Program—Margaret Vogt, Adekeye Adebajo, and Ruth Iyob—developed extensive networks of African policy experts and practitioners, and contributed significantly to the growing scholarly output on African conflict management. In the 1990s, much of this work focused on supporting the Organization of African Unity in the creation of the Mechanism for Conflict Prevention, Management, and Resolution, which was adopted in Cairo in June 1993, and its accompanying Conflict Management Centre in Addis Ababa. In the years 2000–2003, the program focused on assessments of conflicts in Africa's subregions and sought to strengthen the capacity of Africa's subregional organizations to prevent and more effectively manage the resolution of conflicts. Major policy conferences were held in Botswana (December 2000), Nigeria (September 2001), Uganda (December 2002), and Tanzania (December 2003). The Tanzania conference focused on the dynamics of conflict in the Great Lakes region. In October 2003, the IPA also convened a strategic brainstorming meeting at the request of the secretary-general of the newly instituted African Union (AU) in Addis Ababa, to facilitate the AU's articulation of its vision and framework.

Against this backdrop, the publication of this volume is most timely, given the current international focus on the North-South peace agreement in Sudan, the dispatch of a UN peacekeeping operation to monitor and implement the agreement, and the deployment of African Union peacekeepers to Darfur. These developments constitute a major international and continental undertaking. Yet, prospects for success hinge to a large extent on whether the Sudanese state, provincial governments, and civil society can implement good governance and provide tangible social and economic benefits for their communities in the coming years.

The dynamics in East Africa and the Horn hold valuable lessons for countries, such as Sudan, that are transitioning out of conflict. The book looks closely at the subregion's past and present geostrategic importance, its large displaced populations, and the difficulties in resolving some of Africa's longest-running conflicts. Among other issues the authors address are Kenya's civil society efforts to resolve the problem of internally displaced people; the need for more effective policy to confront small arms and light weapons; the urgent need for improved policy and practice on refugees, especially with regard to long-term solutions; and the tension between federalism and the pursuit of national identity in Ethiopia and Eritrea. The complex legacy of US policy toward democratization and development in the Horn of Africa is given special attention.

It is our hope that this volume, together with earlier volumes from the Botswana and Nigeria conferences, will contribute to a deeper understanding of the challenges facing African governments and civil society in moving forward. The new initiatives of the African Union and the New Partnership for Africa's Development hold out promise for a better future for Africa's citizens. This will require a new and energetic commitment to the principles of good governance discussed in this book. We are profoundly grateful to our donors for their support, particularly the governments of Denmark, Finland, Germany, the Netherlands, and the United Kingdom.

Acknowledgments

I am very grateful to the International Peace Academy for providing me with the opportunity and challenge to learn about the issues facing East Africa and the Horn. Through editing this book, I have worked with a number of exceptional scholars who have conducted original research into important issues facing the subregion. Their contributions are valuable additions to the field of African studies specifically and conflict resolution in general. My interaction with them has been enriching.

No project is successful without significant help from others. This book is no exception. The donors that support the Africa program—the governments of Denmark, Finland, Germany, the Netherlands, and the United Kingdom—made it possible to travel and retain some of the most knowledgeable researchers on the critical issues facing East Africa and the Horn. Our donors' commitment to furthering scholarship on Africa makes them true partners in fulfilling a core component of the International Peace Academy's mission of bringing to the fore voices and points of view that are not often heard. Several people at the International Peace Academy—Terje Rød-Larsen, Neclâ Tschirgi, Elizabeth Cousens, John Hirsch, Mashood Issaka, Kapinga Ngandu, Batabiha Bushoki, Zelia Herrera, Clara Lee, and Beatrice Agyarkoh—have also lent invaluable support. I have also relied on the intellectual contributions of others outside the IPA—Gilbert Khadiagala, Ruth Iyob, and two anonymous reviewers.

Finally, I am most indebted to the continuing support of my family—Seth and Mirta Bekoe, Nicoletta, Francis, and Isabella Fynn-Thompson—and Kwaku Nuamah, who make all endeavors worthwhile.

—*Dorina A. Bekoe*

East Africa
and the Horn

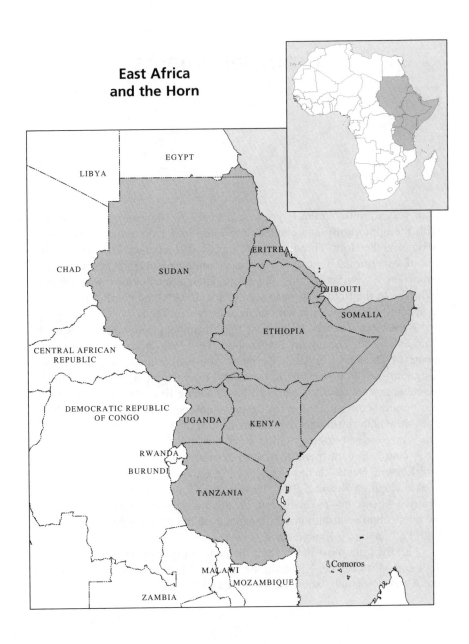

1

Governance in East Africa and the Horn: Confronting the Challenges

Dorina A. Bekoe

Good governance—accepted by most scholars and practitioners as essential to peace, economic growth and development, efficient public administration, strong civil society development, and progressive socioeconomic investment—has been defined fundamentally as the ability of a ruling body to deliver political and economic goods to those under its jurisdiction.[1] More concretely, to policymakers, good governance refers to the ability of governments to administer policies effectively and transparently, honor human rights and the rule of law, and adopt democratic principles.[2] By all accounts, many modern African states, for a variety of endogenous and exogenous reasons, are failing at governance. In other words, governments are not willing or able to make the decisions or adopt the policies necessary to engender economic growth, ensure political stability, improve socioeconomic standings, and foster democratization and respect for human rights.

The willingness and ability of African governments to provide good governance, as the chapters in this book demonstrate, are affected by conflict, political insecurity, weak institutions, and the global political environment. These factors have generated refugees, sped the proliferation of small arms and light weapons (firearms), delayed democratization, suppressed human rights, and pushed the continent further into poverty. These consequences impede good governance: refugees incite fear and discrimination in the host country; the easy availability of weapons exacerbates insecurity; poverty at the state and individual levels precludes investments in socioeconomic improvement; and weak democratization hinders the development of civil society and the attention of governments to the concerns of its citizens. How can governments overcome these obstacles in order to stop the cycle of poor governance and provide economic and political benefits to their citizens? To answer this question, this book looks to the experience of East Africa and the Horn.

As in other regions in Africa, governance in East Africa and the Horn has been hampered by conflict, the repression of human rights to dampen political expression, and the external pressures and incentives of international relations. However, unlike other regions, these states are also caught in the crossfire of a changing international political environment. The attention of the international community has returned to the subregion due to the US war on terrorism—with a renewed attention in general to the indispensability of democracy as a tool against terrorism and a revived interest in ending the conflict in Sudan. In addition, the subregion has been more active than others in curbing the proliferation of weapons—for example, with the Nairobi Declaration[3] and its follow-up efforts[4]—and has a stronger history of progressive refugee policy. As a whole, the subregion highlights the difficulties of democratic transitions, points to the need for improved approaches to address the flow of refugees and weapons in the area; demonstrates the effects of suppressing ethnic groups, and draws attention to the effects of Cold War politics on the pace of democratization and on intraregional relations among states in East Africa and the Horn.[5]

The Spillover of Bad Governance

Conflict has been the most pronounced and visible evidence of the weakness of the state and a central aspect of Africa's modern history. Since 1948, African states have faced armed opposition ranging from minor intensity to war more than 100 times. Of those conflicts, approximately 25 percent have occurred in East Africa and the Horn.[6] Among their most destabilizing effects, the conflicts have generated large flows of refugees and the proliferation of firearms in the subregion—transporting the effects of bad governance over national borders. As the number of firearms spread across borders, their easy availability highlights weak state administration and human insecurity, whereas flows of displaced people pose unique challenges to governance in refugee-hosting states by bringing to the fore issues of political, social, and economic equity; human rights; and citizenship.

Small arms and light weapons are abundantly available in East Africa and the Horn, finding their way to the hands of private citizens and criminals alike. The number of firearms available in the region is difficult to estimate. Some empirical work places the number of firearms in Africa at 30 million and in Kenya, Tanzania, and Uganda, specifically, between 1.5 million and 3 million.[7] The number of firearms for the other countries in the subregion is difficult to establish, but Kiflemariam Gebrewold and Siobhan Byrne estimate from fieldwork that the subregion as a whole has approximately 3 million firearms. Many of the policies adopted by East Africa and the Horn and countries outside the subregion on controlling and accounting for small arms focus on the options available to the state—controlling borders, establishing registration methods, and improving collection practices during demobilization and disarmament.[8] By and large, these policies have not stemmed the illicit trade in firearms. The easy availability of small arms and light weapons, Gebrewold and Byrne explain in Chapter 2, accounts for the high crime rates in urban areas and at the borders, where many pastoralists clash with each other over cattle and land.[9] Conflicts between pastoralists have resulted in interstate conflicts among Kenya, Uganda, Ethiopia, and Sudan (the Elemi Triangle), and worsen human and food security—which in turn fuels conflicts.[10] Indeed, a 2003 study estimated that over 160,000 people were displaced in northern Kenya as a result of pastoral conflicts.[11]

Part of the reason for the failure of the current policy instruments, Gebrewold and Byrne argue, is their failure to address the *demand* for firearms in the region. The demand for firearms exists, Gebrewold and Byrne argue, because citizens perceive the need to acquire arms due to the government's inability to protect its citizens, the lack of economic opportunities, and the tradition of a violent and vendetta culture. The resulting proliferation of firearms does not increase security, but rather exacerbates insecurity in urban areas, rural communities, and border towns. Focusing on demand-side factors that aid the spread of firearms is not new.[12] However, Gebrewold and Byrne enrich the extant literature by providing specific examples from the field and from meetings with community-based organizations. In Chapter 2, Gebrewold and Byrne's focus on the demand for small arms and light weapons shows how the weapons have become institutionalized in rural and urban communities. Their findings demonstrate that addressing the issue of firearms requires the alteration of the vested interests that support their availability and removes the community's perceived need for arms.

In addition to small arms and light weapons, the influx of refugees is a direct consequence of conflict and another example of the spillover of bad governance. The challenge that refugees present to host countries lies in changing existing practices of managing the flow and settlement of displaced people and compliance with the 1951 UN Convention Relating to the Status of Refugees, as Zachary Lomo elaborates in Chapter 3. East Africa and the Horn host nearly 1.4 million displaced people—with almost 600,000 in Tanzania, over 230,000 in Kenya, and about 250,000 in Uganda.[13]

Today, refugees are considered problematic and a source of insecurity, but this has not always been the case. For example, in the aftermath of influx of Rwandan refugees to Tanzania from 1959 to 1961, the Tanzanian government's goal was to integrate refugees into Tanzanian economic and social life. To this end, the Julius Nyerere government provided land to the refugees and in the 1980s offered Tanzanian citizenship to Rwandans.[14] Tanzania's actions addressed a fundamental need of refugees: How do they acquire the tools to begin life again and what rights do they have in the host country? Thus, Tanzania's actions provided refugees with hope and stability. Yet, over the past several years, as the refugee population has grown and Tanzania has faced increasingly difficult economic times and demands on its public funds, its policy toward refugees has not been replicated.[15] Similarly, whereas other countries in Africa have been generally open to receiving refugees, such receptivity has declined.[16] The policy reversals stem from the belief by policymakers and society at large that refugees and internally displaced people (IDPs) pose security risks, drain the public coffers of the host country, and are short-term "problems." As a result, the policies managing displaced people tend to restrict their movements to camps, and few provisions are made to fully integrate refugees into the host country; they are treated and considered as permanent outsiders.[17] A manifestation of these beliefs is the predominance of settlement camps in "managing" the population of displaced people.[18] The change in policies by African states also arises from declining institutional and financial support from international agencies to address the maintenance and environmental effects for large populations of refugees.[19]

In fact, Lomo argues, such negative attributes toward displaced people and their accompanying policies are neither accurate nor productive. While some refugees and IDPs can create insecurity—by threatening the nation's ability to defend itself from internal and external threats and strains on its resources[20]—incur public expenses, and remain in camps for short periods, many refugees and IDPs do not fit this description. Ironically, Lomo demonstrates, because of such exclusionary and state-centric policies that restrict displaced people to settlement camps, displaced people face increased security risks and face higher than necessary hurdles to attain self-sufficiency.

Lomo's timing is propitious. As experts on displaced people are increasingly emphasizing, countries must find more permanent solutions to refugees. More specifically, host states must take a longer-term view of humanitarian crises and employ a more positive view of refugees. The need for more permanent solutions, such as integration, is simple: for many refugees (for example, Congolese, Burundian, and Somali), repatriation is not an immediate option because of persistent instability.[21] As governments in the subregion move forward, they must balance the demands from domestic groups with the need to address the issues facing a significantly large but relatively voiceless group. The status quo simply increases overall insecurity and disrespects human rights.

The Cost of Democratic Transitions

Most of the states in East Africa and the Horn, like the states in other regions, have failed their citizens in the development of political and civil liberties. Using Freedom House's assessment of political and civil rights as one measurement, the states in East Africa and the Horn scored an average of 5.8 on political rights and 5.6 on civil rights in 1972 (the first year this survey was conducted). Since the ratings range from 1 to 7, with 7 representing countries with the most restricted rights, the subregion ranked near the bottom. In 2004, the states in East Africa and the Horn averaged 5.3 and 5.1 for political and civil rights, respectively.[22] Hence, in more than thirty years, the political environment for the subregion has improved only slightly. Today, a key policy recommendation for establishing good governance is the assurance of political and civil rights: holding multiparty elections and creating transparency and accountability in government.[23] This makes Jacqueline M. Klopp's observation in Chapter 4, on internally displaced persons that resulted from the democratic transition in Kenya, all the more important; even after the democratic transition, the issues concerning the internally displaced were not addressed.

In Chapter 4, Klopp documents the creation of IDPs in Kenya by the government of Daniel arap Moi, which used violence to discourage the Kikuyu from participating in elections, and the inability of the newly elected, democratically oriented government of Mwai Kibaki to address and remedy the issue. In 2002, after almost a decade of opposition, the National Rainbow Coalition (NaRC), a union of opposition parties, defeated the Kenya African National Union (KANU), the party of former president Moi that had ruled since 1978, and brought President Kibaki to power. However, the long road to democratic reform was costly, as Klopp demonstrates: violence accompanied the transition to democracy—a fact little acknowledged—which caused approximately 350,000 IDPs. The irony in Kenya's situation, Klopp writes, was the restricted ability of human rights organizations, key actors in the push for multiparty democracy, to prevent the displacement, and then under the more democratic regime of NaRC, to help to bring resolution to the issue. Rather than prevent future violence, Klopp shows that because of restrictions by both the government and their own organizational structure, civil society groups were only able to offer relief.

Although today the issue of Kenya's IDPs appears to be gaining attention and has fostered a group of advocacy organizations, the lesson from Kenya goes beyond understanding the internal dynamics of civil society organizations in democratic transitions. As Klopp alludes, the inaction of civil society in Kenya teaches that good governance does not automatically result from democratic reforms—the new regime in Kenya brought no relief to IDPs. In many cases, civil society organizations can be instrumental in filling the gaps created by poor or weak governments. However, to do so effectively, the international community must assist civil society in overcoming their constraints. Importantly, Kenya's transition from Moi's long-term rule holds lessons about the difficulties faced by civil society and potential for violence that even democratic countries experience as long-serving leaders leave power—particular attention should be given to the political future in Uganda, Guinea, and Zimbabwe.

Governance in Diverse Communities

The inability and unwillingness to recognize multiple ethnic groups, along with the fear that groups will press for secession, have also resulted in bad governance, manifested by political repression and the outbreak of war. States' responses to managing in multiethnic societies include instituting power-sharing arrangements between competing ethnic groups, civil war, and the radical notion of secession.[24] The fight for secession in the Biafra region of Nigeria resulted in civil war and the defeat of the Biafran insurgents and their secessionist ambitions. In Somalia, the northwest territory of Somaliland broke away in 1994; in Ethiopia, the case addressed by Dominique Jacquin-Berdal and Aida Mengistu, the thirty-year war with Eritrea ended in its secession.

Multiple ethnic groups present a challenge to good governance because, as Jacquin-Berdal and Mengistu show in Chapter 5 on the development of nationalism in Ethiopia and Eritrea, states may seek to consolidate authority by suppressing the representation of particular ethnic groups. To this end, Jacquin-Berdal and Mengistu explore the rationale behind the Ethiopian government's policies of suppressing ethnic groups in the name of developing a national identity and the eventual secession of Eritrea. Chapter 5 also touches on the governance challenges of newly independent Eritrea, which ironically must manage its own pressures from multiple ethnic groups, especially non-Tigrinya. In fact, both Eritrea and Ethiopia have violated human rights and disregarded the rule of law as they rebuild their states following the war for independence and the subsequent border war that took place from 1998 to 2000.[25]

Equally important, the chapter holds particular importance for the implementation of the January 2005 Comprehensive Peace Agreement, signed between the government of Sudan and the Sudan People's Liberation Army (SPLA). As part of the peace agreement, the SPLA has been granted a six-year period by which to decide whether to remain part of Sudan or secede. The choices made by each side in the intervening six years will greatly determine the likelihood and consolidation of peace in Sudan. The international and regional organizations can play a watchdog role over governments facing charges of human rights abuses toward particular groups, advocate for sanctions against such governments, and assume a more active role in planting the seeds for democratization.

From the internal forces of marginalization, this book then shifts its focus to external forces that may marginalize domestic groups and delay democratization. Chapter 6, contributed by Ruth Iyob and Edmond J. Keller, traces the impact of Cold War politics on governance and development in the Horn of Africa. During the Cold War, the geostrategic location of the subregion increased the importance of the Horn to both the United States and the Soviet Union. Iyob and Keller document that the result for the Horn of Africa was a tremendous growth in the military-industrial complex in these countries, the ignition of an arms race in the subregion, the support of authoritarian regimes, and a stalling of the development of state institutions. After a disengagement in the 1990s, the region once again regained importance to the United States in the wake of the US Embassy bombings in Kenya and Tanzania in 1998 and the September 11, 2001, attacks on the World Trade Center in New York and the Pentagon in Washington, D.C.

Though Chapter 6 focuses on the Cold War era and its effect on the Horn of Africa, it holds important lessons for the present and suggests opportunities to resolve some of the region's enduring governance challenges. Even though the most visible reengagement by the United States in the subregion has been a military presence in Djibouti, the renewed attention to the region reignited efforts in the United States to end the civil wars in Sudan and Somalia.[26] The conflicts in Sudan and Somalia and its resulting chaos have long been feared to contribute to the creation of an environment conducive to terrorist organization.[27] Indeed, while the US Agency for Development (USAID) has democracy and governance assistance programs in most of the countries of the subregion,[28] a specific US objective in Ethiopia, Sudan, and Somalia is to implement counterterrorism efforts.[29] The challenge lies in how to harness external assistance to further democratization. Although using external assistance to compel reforms in developing countries has been a stated goal of donor policies in the past, the actual record of achieving consolidated and credible policy reforms has been less successful.[30] In particular, many assistance packages have not resulted in reform because they have not ensured that there is an adequate level of political and institutional development to sustain reform.[31] In light of the past record, for the reengagement with the West to prove fruitful, any intervention must account for the level of development of political institutions and the state's capacity for reform. In this regard, we may extract from Iyob and Keller in Chapter 6 that the governance challenge lies with both the states of East Africa and the Horn, as well as the international community.

Conclusion

The cases in this volume discuss the governance challenges facing the countries in East Africa and the Horn. Particularly difficult for the states in the subregion is their ability to foster an effective engagement between civil society and government, enact more progressive policies toward refugees and internally displaced people, reduce the flow of small arms and light weapons, and develop more effective strategies for governing in multiethnic societies. Equally important in addressing the challenges of governance, though not directly addressed by the cases, are the economic policies and options of the subregion. A critical conclusion from these case studies is that the key to effectively resolving these challenges to good governance requires an understanding of their regional implications and the corresponding regional solutions. Framing problems within a regional perspective does not simply entail a listing of similar problems faced by countries within a particular region—although that is often the case. Instead, it requires an understanding that the presence of mutually reinforcing factors—poverty, weak institutions, and competing foreign relations—facilitate the seeming intractability of problems.[32]

Notes

1. There are many sources that define governance: Robert I. Rotberg and Deborah L. West, "The Good Governance Problem: Doing Something About It," *The World Peace Foundation* (July 2004), pp. 1, 5; Goran Hyden, "Governance and the Reconstitution of Political Order," in *State, Conflict, and Democracy in Africa,* ed. Richard Joseph (Boulder: Lynne Rienner Publishers, 1999), p. 186; Carlos Santiso, "Good Governance and Aid Effectiveness: The World Bank and Conditionality," *Georgetown Public Policy Review* 1, no. 1 (Fall 2001): 1–22 (electronic version).

2. Canadian International Development Agency, "Governance in Africa," *CIDA, Africa & the G8* (available online at http://www.acdi-cida.gc.ca, accessed March 11, 2005); World Bank Institute, *Governance Indicators: 1996–2002* (available online at http://www.worldbank.org/wbi/governance/govdata2002, accessed March 11, 2005); US Agency for International Development, "Office of Democracy and Governance" (available online at http://www.usaid.gov/our_work/democracy_and_governance/ technical_areas/dg_office/gov.html, accessed March 12, 2005).

3. The full reference of the March 2000 protocol is the Nairobi Declaration on the Problem of the Proliferation of Illicit Small Arms and Light Weapons in the Great Lakes Region and the Horn of Africa, Nairobi, March 15, 2000. Reproduced by SaferAfrica.org (available online at http://www.saferafrica.org/DocumentsCentre/ Books/Matrix/NairobiDeclartion.asp, accessed November 22, 2004).

4. These efforts include the November 2000 Co-ordinated Agenda for Action on the Problem of the Proliferation of Small Arms and Light Weapons in the Great Lakes Region and the Horn of Africa and The Nairobi Protocol for the Prevention, Control and Reduction of Small Arms and Light Weapons in the Great Lakes Region and the Horn of Africa, signed in April 2004.

5. There are many definitions of this subregion. In this volume, East Africa and the Horn comprise Djibouti, Eritrea, Ethiopia, Kenya, Somalia, Sudan, Tanzania, and Uganda.

6. The dataset used for these figures begins at 1948. This number includes conflicts that resulted in at least twenty-five battle-related deaths. These data were obtained from the 2005 Uppsala Conflict Data Program established by the Department

of Peace and Conflict Research at Uppsala University (available online at http://www.pcr.uu.se/database/index.php). I counted conflicts in the following manner: If the data showed that conflict occurred within a contiguous span of years (for example, 1973 to 1978), it was counted as *one* incident of conflict in the country. A break in the years was counted as multiple conflicts (for example, conflict from 1973 to 1978 and again from 1983 to 1985 was counted as two incidents of conflict). Various factions fighting the government, but during the same span of years, was counted as one incident of conflict (thus, faction X and faction Y fighting between 1985 and 1989 was counted as one incident of conflict).

7. Graduate Institute of International Studies, Geneva, *Small Arms Survey 2003: Development Denied* (Oxford: Oxford University Press, 2003, electronic version), pp. 80, 85.

8. Nairobi Declaration; Organization of African Unity, Bamako Declaration of an African Common Position on the Illicit Proliferation, Circulation and Trafficking of Small Arms and Light Weapons, Bamako, December 2000 (available online at http://www.saferafrica.org/DocumentsCentre/Books/Matrix/BamekoDeclaration.asp); Taya Weiss, "A Demand-Side Approach to Fighting Small Arms Proliferation," *African Security Review* 12 (2003) (electronic version); Catherine Flew and Angus Uruquhart, *Strengthening Small Arms Controls: An Audit of Small Arms Control Legislation in the Great Lakes Region and the Horn of Africa* (SaferAfrica and SaferWorld, February 2004; available online at http://www.saferworld.org.uk/publications/Horn%20narrative%20report.pdf, accessed March 14, 2005), especially Chapter 2, "Regional Overview of Existing Legislation."

9. For more on the subregion's pastoral conflicts, see Kennedy Mkutu, "Pastoral Conflicts and Small Arms: The Kenya-Uganda Border Region," *SaferWorld* (November 2003), p. 11 (electronic version).

10. Mkutu, "Pastoral Conflict and Small Arms," pp. 5–6, 22; Intermediate Technology Development Group-East Africa (ITDG-EA), "Elemi Triangle: A Theatre of Armed Cattle Rustling," *Peace Bulletin* (January 2005) (available online at http://www.itdg.org/print.phpd?id=peace6_elemi, accessed February 1, 2005).

11. ITDG-EA, "Displacements: Resettle Cattle Rustling Victims Too," *Peace Bulletin* (September 2004) (available online at http://www.itdg.org/print.php?id-peace5_displacements, accessed February 1, 2005).

12. See Weiss, "A Demand-Side Approach"; Robert Muggah and Peter Bachelor, *Development Held Hostage: Assessing the Effects of Small Arms on Human Development* (New York: United Nations Development Program, April 2002), pp. 39–40 (electronic version).

13. United Nations High Commissioner for Refugees (UNHCR), *Global Report 2004* (Bucharest: RA Monitorul Oficial, 2004, electronic version), pp. 165–171; 179–237. Tanzania hosts the most number of refugees in Africa (p. 166).

14. Saskia Van Hoyweghen, "Mobility, Territoriality and Sovereignty in Post-Colonial Tanzania," *New Issues in Refugee Research*, Working Paper No. 49 (Geneva: Evaluation and Policy Unit, UNHCR, October 2001), pp. 13–17 (electronic version).

15. Hoyweghen, pp. 17–18.

16. Jeff Crisp, "Africa's Refugees: Patterns, Problems, Policy Changes," *New Issues in Refugee Research*, Working Paper No. 28 (Geneva: Evaluation and Policy Unit, UNHCR, October 2001, electronic version), p. 5.

17. Reg Whittaker, "Refugees: The Security Dimension," *Citizenship Studies* 2, no. 3 (1998, electronic version): 413–434; Karen Jacobsen, "Factors Influencing the Policy Responses of Host Governments to Mass Refugee Influxes," *International Migration Review* 30, no. 3 (Autumn 1996): 666–674 (electronic version).

18. A case in point is Tanzania's decision to restrict the movement of Burundian and Rwandan refugees from the settlement camps, arguing that they represented a security risk to urban areas and the host community (UNHCR, *Global Report 2003* (Bucharest: RA Monitorul Oficial, 2004, electronic version), p. 116.

19. Crisp, "Africa's Refugees," pp. 6–9.

20. Karen Jacobsen, "Factors Influencing the Policy Responses," pp. 671–674.

21. UNHCR, *Global Appeal 2005* (Bucharest: RA Minitorul Oficial, 2004, electronic version), p. 98.

22. Freedom House, *Freedom in the World,* Country Ratings Database (from 1972 to 2003, available at http://www.freedomhouse.org/ratings/allscore04.xls, accessed March 11, 2005).

23. USAID, "Promoting More Transparent and Accountable Governance Institutions," *USAID Democracy and Governance Program* (available online at http://www.usaid.gov/our_work/democracy_and_governance/technical_areas/governance/, accessed March 17, 2005); World Bank, *Governance Matters II: Governance Indicators for 1996–2002* (available online at http://www.worldbank.org/wbi/governance/govdata2002/, accessed March 11, 2005).

24. For more on the management of ethnic groups in conflict see Timothy D. Sisk, *Power Sharing and International Mediation in Ethnic Conflicts* (Washington, DC: United States Institute of Peace, 1996); Arend Lijphart, *Democracy in Plural Societies: A Comparative Exploration* (New Haven, CT: Yale University Press, 1972); and Donald L. Horowitz, *Ethnic Groups in Conflict* (Los Angeles: University of California Press, 2000).

25. Human Rights Watch, *World Report 2005,* "Eritrea" (New York: Human Rights Watch, 2005) and "Ethiopia" (New York: Human Rights Watch, 2005).

26. USAID, "Democracy and Governance in Djibouti" (available online at http://www.usaid.gov/our_work/democracy_and_governance/regions/afr/djibouti.html, accessed March 11 2005).

27. J. Stephen Morrison, "Somalia and Sudan's Race to the Fore in Africa," The Center for Strategic and International Studies and the Massachusetts Institute of Technology, *The Washington Quarterly* 25, no. 2 (Spring 2002): 191–205.

28. Eritrea does not have a USAID "Democracy and Governance" program.

29. USAID, "Democracy and Governance in Ethiopia" (available online at http://www.usaid.gov/our_work/democracy_and_governance/regions/afr/ethiopia.html, accessed March 11 2005); USAID, "Democracy and Governance in Somalia" (available online at http://www.usaid.gov/our_work/democracy_and_governance/regions/afr/somalia.html, accessed March 11 2005); USAID, "Democracy and Governance in Sudan" (available online at http://www.usaid.gov/our_work/democracy_and_governance/regions/afr/sudan.html, accessed March 11, 2005).

30. Paul Collier, "Learning from Failure: The International Financial Institutions as Agencies of Restraint in Africa," in Andreas Schedler, Larry Diamond, and Marc F. Plattner, eds., *The Self-Restraining State: Power and Accountability in New Democracies* (Boulder: Lynne Rienner Publishers, 1999); John W. Harbeson, "Externally Assisted Democratization: Theoretical Issues and African Realities," in John W. Harbeson and Donald Rothchild, eds., *Africa in World Politics: The African State System in Flux,* 3rd edition (Boulder: Westview Press, 2000).

31. Harbeson, "Externally Assisted Democratization," p. 243.

32. Charles Cater, *The Regionalization of Conflict and Intervention* (New York: International Peace Academy, 2003).

2

Small Arms and Light Weapons in the Horn: Reducing the Demand

Kiflemariam Gebrewold and Siobhan Byrne

Like other subregions in Africa, the Horn has a proliferation of small arms and light weapons (SALWs).[1] Fieldwork and interviews with military and intelligence officers conducted from 2000 to 2002 for the Small Arms and Light Weapons Project in the Intergovernmental Authority on Development (IGAD) Countries (SALIGAD project) at the Bonn International Center for Conversion (BICC)[2] place the number of firearms in the Horn of Africa at 3 million.[3] The ramifications of such proliferation are evident in the high incidence of violent robberies in city centers like Nairobi, armed liberation movements operating in southern Sudan and Somalia, and cattle-raiding pastoralists in isolated regions like northern Uganda. Who controls these weapons? As is reflected in global and other trends in Africa, most of the small arms—almost 80 percent—are in the hands of civilians.[4]

Countries have taken a supply-centric approach to control the flow of SALWs—prescribing policies to address how weapons enter a country, how they are distributed, and how they may be controlled through efforts like registration. These regional efforts to control the illicit trade of SALWs, which include the Bamako Declaration (2000), the Nairobi Declaration (2000), and related protocols, have not been properly conceived or implemented.[5] The Nairobi Declaration, the most relevant for the Horn of Africa given its accession by Burundi, the Democratic Republic of the Congo, Djibouti, Eritrea, Ethiopia, Kenya, Rwanda, Somalia, Sudan, Tanzania, and Uganda, has not resulted in the subregion's implementation of its main feature, the National Focal Points (NFPs). The signatories to the Nairobi Declaration envisioned that the NFPs would serve as clearinghouses for information on violent conflicts in the region, share strategies for curbing the flow and stockpiling of weapons in the region, raise awareness of SALWs, and lead to legislative and other reforms to control and manage SALWs in a given country.[6] However, the NFPs have cultivated neither the clout nor the mandate to fulfill their functions because the existing core ministries—

such as the Ministries of Home Affairs and Defence—are not prepared to transfer power to the NFPs and corresponding national-level legislation was not passed. Thus, the relevant ministries at the state level do not feel under any obligation to cooperate with the NFPs. An important reason behind the weakness of the NFPs has been its failure to connect with civil society— hence not acquiring information on the *demand* for small arms and light weapons.

This chapter, which reports on the findings of the SALIGAD project, addresses the demand for SALWs. Focusing on the demand for SALWs is essential for three main reasons. First, demand-centric approaches identify endogenous factors that remain outside the purview of existing institutions and, therefore, not addressed by policymakers. Second, understanding demand for small arms and light weapons allows the construction of different policies that consider varying economic and social strata. Third, focusing on the demand for SALWs highlights the need to reform judicial institutions and means by which grievances are resolved. Concentrating on demand underscores that small arms are "socially embedded"—meaning that they have become part of practiced social and cultural norms and behaviors among divergent communities. Thus, the spread of small arms cannot be tackled from a purely disarmament perspective by police and governments. Instead, open dialogue among local stakeholders, representatives from nongovernmental organizations (NGOs), the academic community, and government officials, as well as having a clear understanding of the mechanisms that embed small arms within the Horn of Africa's culture, are the keys to eradicating the demand for weapons.

Both BICC and the International Resource Group on Disarmament and Security in the Horn of Africa (IRG) jointly initiated the SALIGAD project, believing that to engage effectively in small arms reduction, one needs to understand their demand—in other words why do people want to take up arms? The evidence from the field indicates that an effective approach to curbing small arms proliferation needs to consider the historical, structural, and cultural context of small arms acquisition—a strategy that is buttressed by uncovering the demand for small arms. This chapter's conclusions stem from SALIGAD's fieldwork in the Horn of Africa, facilitation of dialogue among stakeholders, and the development of training workshops. In the end, however, although a supply and demand analysis will help to push the small arms debate forward, it is time to move beyond that dualism. Policymakers must work toward collapsing the rigid distinctions between supply and demand analyses, thereby redefining the debate.

Three sections follow this introduction. The following section provides a definition of SALWs and outlines the methodology used by SALIGAD field researchers to uncover demand for SALWs. The next section presents the empirical data acquired that illustrate the sources of demand for small arms and light weapons. In the final section, policy recommendations are offered to help to curb the demand for SALWs.

Defining Small Arms and Light Weapons

Several unique characteristics of small arms and light weapons make them a significant threat to civilians and therefore a particular concern for development and humanitarian organizations. These weapons do not require extensive logistical capabilities and are thus convenient for highly mobile operations. In fact, small arms and light weapons are often so easy to operate that even young children can use them with minimal training. Due to the enormous firepower of light weapons such as mortars, rockets, and grenade launchers, individuals or armed groups can cause heavy civilian casualties even with limited financial means and technical support. Furthermore, their relatively low cost, in comparison with other conventional arms, makes them accessible to many nonstate actors.

According to the definition drafted by the UN Panel of Experts on Small Arms and approved by the United Nations General Assembly in 1997, small arms and light weapons fall into three categories. The first category includes revolvers and self-loading pistols, rifles, carbines, submachine guns, assault rifles, and light machine guns. These small arms require little, if any, maintenance. In contrast to small arms, which an individual can carry on his person, light weapons refer to a category of armaments that must be transported either by two or more people serving as a crew, by a pack animal, or by a light vehicle.[7] Thus, the second category—light weapons—comprises heavy machine guns, handheld under-barrel and mounted grenade launchers, portable antiaircraft guns, portable antitank guns and recoilless rifles, portable launchers of antitank missile and rocket systems, portable launchers of antiaircraft missile systems, and mortars of less than 100-mm caliber. Another category of light weapons comprises ammunition and explosives: cartridges for small arms, shells and missiles for light weapons, antipersonnel and antitank grenades, landmines, mobile containers with missiles or shells for single-action antiaircraft and antitank systems, and explosives.[8]

Methodology

Researchers for the SALIGAD project conducted fieldwork in Kenya, Somaliland, Ethiopia, Eritrea, and Sudan. In Kenya, three cases were studied: indigenous weapons control in the Kuria region, gun-related violence in Nairobi, and the monitoring of gun prices and demand in Garissa. Research in Somaliland focused on how to get the guns off the street. In

Ethiopia, a study in the regional state of Gambella examined the trafficking of small arms in relation to a territorial conflict between the Anyuak and the Nuer. In Eritrea, the SALIGAD project undertook an exploratory study of small arms in the Gashbarka region of Eritrea. Finally, in Sudan, the SALIGAD project focused on the role of gender and small arms.[9] Because the fieldwork did not examine the same issues in the different locales, the results are not readily generalized. However, the value of the diverse data obtained provides insights into the factors underpinning demand for SALWs, highlights avenues for further research, and points to the need for policy changes in addressing SALWS. Importantly, the methodology—discussed next—which was uniform across locales, underscores the need for greater civil society involvement in curbing the proliferation of SALWs.

The methodology of the SALIGAD project differed from the existing research on SALWs. The project not only aggregated important operational knowledge like numbers of arms, their circulation, and supply routes in the IGAD region, but also brought together local, regional, and international stakeholders—such as local chiefs, security-sector representatives, and the NGO community—for the first time through *facilitating dialogue* and organizing *training workshops*. Although this approach proved more demanding and time consuming than the methodology for the supply-side approach, it has produced information that would otherwise not have been generally available. This intensive approach contributes to an informed discussion about the dangers of small arms in the Horn and encourages people who are directly affected to discuss these dangers and the means to tackle them.

The SALIGAD project has found that the *facilitation of dialogue* among governments, nongovernmental organizations, and grassroots initiatives allows stakeholders to understand why individuals and communities feel they need arms—integral to building steps to curbing such demand. The dialogue forums organized by the SALIGAD project facilitated cooperation between the security sector and civil society. These dialogue forums were all the more important because neither the government nor civil society can effectively tackle the spread and misuse of firearms alone. Each side has an important role, and only when they cooperate can they find success. By the same token, cooperation is needed among the countries of the region. However closely government and civil society work together within each country, they cannot tackle the problems of porous borders, cross-border crime, and illicit international arms trafficking unless they work closely with their neighbors.

The promotion and facilitation of *training workshops* in the Horn also provided critical insights.[10] Community leaders developed ideas on how to limit proliferation in their districts.[11] A workshop on gender and small arms, held in 2002 in Jinja, Uganda, further provided women participants with the opportunity to voice their concerns and share their experiences with SALWs. Some of the meetings our project held explored traditional and informal ways to control weapons. Even though the influence of chiefs and elders is declining, traditional leaders can still exercise some control over who holds which kinds of weapons and how they are used. The same sometimes applies to churches and other civil society organizations. This approach to weapons control has obvious limitations and drawbacks, but in the absence of effective state institutions, it may be the only option.

Understanding Demand for Small Arms and Light Weapons

Through these three core areas of activity—fieldwork, dialogues, and training workshops—the project has identified important structural and cultural impediments to curbing the misuse of SALWs that need to be turned into strategies for preventing the uncontrolled accumulation and misuse of weapons. The following section details the threats to human security, the politics of exclusion, refugee crises, lack of opportunities for youth, and resource scarcity that underpin structural causes and impediments to curbing SALW proliferation and misuse throughout the Horn of Africa. These elements reveal that demand for SALWs hinges on the failure of government to provide adequate security, the competition for land, the rise in urban crime, inadequate remuneration for security forces, high unemployment, and competing cultural traditions.

Threats to Human Security

Many states in the Horn of Africa fail to ensure the security of communities within their borders because they often lack the capacity to provide adequate policing and an impartial judicial system. Though both urban and rural areas grapple with insecurity, the threat is particularly acute in rural areas. For centuries, people living in the rural regions have taken security into their own hands because the state has been unable to do so. Even today, the police who are supposed to provide security do not have a visible presence in most rural areas. Those police officers that are available lack even the most basic provisions—like fuel to operate their vehicles. Therefore, they cannot reach remote communities that do not have their own police station.

As one consequence of the state's inability to extend its administration, many states in the region have, overtly or covertly, opted to arm groups in rural areas so that they can protect themselves. This has happened extensively in Kenya and, to a lesser extent, in other IGAD member states at different stages. The previous government in Kenya—the administration of President Daniel arap Moi—at different stages armed ethnic groups living in remote areas, with the intention that they would protect themselves from outsiders coming across the border from, for example, Uganda. The government singled out the Pokots, in particular during the 1990s, providing arms when it proved politically propitious or when the government sought to oppress other ethnic groups not loyal to the ruling party. In fact, the Moi government did not intervene when Pokots evicted non-Pokots. However, when the predatory raids and assaults by Pokots against neighboring tribes or even across the border—mainly in Uganda—became politically unbearable or when the cattle stealing became a massive sustained and prolonged raid, the groups disarmed. The government also armed the Kalenjin groups prior to the 1997 elections. (This is more extensively addressed in Chapter 4 by Jacqueline M. Klopp.) Similarly, in Uganda, the Teso ethnic group was armed against the Karamajong.[12]

Over the years, this practice by government has signaled to rural communities that they should take care of their own security, thus solidifying the belief among opinion leaders and heads of ethnic groups that the government itself is unable to take care of their basic security needs. During different interactions with elders and youth groups in Garissa, in northeastern Kenya, the SALIGAD project team was made to understand by the rural communities that they did not feel that they could rely on protection by the government. Hence they opted to take security into their own hands, which had been done traditionally in nomadic communities. Furthermore, the shifting policy of the government to arm, disarm, and then rearm groups at will indicated to the Garissa community that they would fare better on their own. The practice thus provides another key to understanding the dynamics of demand in the region.

Urban communities are also unsafe. Though the exact number of arms in the cities of the Horn of Africa may not be known, in urban centers, police officers, nongovernmental organizations (NGOs), and faith-based organizations have repeatedly warned that individuals often obtain small arms by illegal means. During a workshop co-organized by the SALIGAD project with the National Council of Churches of Kenya (NCCK) in November 2003 in Limuru, Kenya, several speakers highlighted the pervasiveness of weapons in urban areas; the former chief firearms licensing officer of Kenya, Ole Empesha, estimated that "75 percent" of the country was awash with illegal arms.[13] In urban centers, such as Nairobi, people arm themselves to avoid being victims of crime. This, in turn, increases the number of small arms in the hands of civilians, which worsens the problem of uncontrolled availability and weapons misuse. A survey supervised by the Safer Cities Programme of the United Nations Human Settlements Programme found that more than 35 percent of respondents have been victims of robbery and nearly 20 percent have been assaulted. The data collected indicate that at such a rate of crime, one in five people living in Nairobi will become a victim of assault, one in five will become a victim of a snatch-ing on the street, and two in five will likely become victims of robbery.[14]

Threats to Economic Security

The uncertainties of economic conditions in rural areas, poorly paid law enforcement, and scarce opportunities for youth play critical roles in the demand for small arms and light weapons. In some cases, small arms have become new means to fight old battles, as indicated by the competition for scarce agricultural resources and the struggle to overcome the conse-quences of poor land use policies. In other cases, the sale and rental of small arms can be used to supplement income or acquire goods. Still other reasons for possessing weapons include the need to protect single sources of income, such as livestock.

Isolated regions, where ethnic groups compete for the same fertile land and cattle, have become flashpoints for violence—as the fieldwork in Garissa demonstrated. The competition for agricultural land over pasture is driven by scarcity or poor land management—such as the transformation of large tracts of land in the Awash Valley of Ethiopia into huge plantations—which leads to depletion of available resources, unsustainable land use pat-terns, or land degradation. The rural pastoral economy, which is based on the number of herds, subsequently suffers from overgrazing, leaving pas-tures depleted and worsening pressure on the ecosystem. In colonial times, for example in Kenya, the periodicity and routes the pastoralists would take within Kenya and beyond were defined and followed a pattern that would allow the grazing land to rehabilitate. Today, however, the more that land is transformed to agricultural land—for export crops and staple food—the less land is available for pastoral communities.

Even before the influx of small arms to pastoralist areas in the late 1970s, pastoralists still competed for land and cattle and still faced inade-quate state security, but they relied on less lethal weapons to protect them-selves from external threats. In more recent years, the threats have not abated, but with the easy availability of small arms, pastoralist communities go to great expense to acquire small arms. In Somaliland, we came across ex-combatants and elders, who confirmed that in rural communities almost half the households had some sort of functioning rifle—whether a carbine rifle, a semiautomatic rifle, or an assault rifle. The same applies in south-eastern Ethiopia; local communities stated during a workshop in mid-2002 in the town of Dire Dawa that household heads—who are usually men—use the available family income to purchase a gun or ammunition for an exist-ing gun. Paradoxically, the proliferation and availability of small arms have exacerbated the threat to human and economic security—creating deadly zones of cattle-raiding violence and a growing environment of insecurity.

Pastoralists require freedom of movement and large areas for grazing. Through population growth and the limited land-carrying capacity of this extensive system of grazing, armed conflicts have erupted between sedentarists and pastoralists competing for the same resource, namely land. Since agricultural land, grazing land, and water sources cannot be increased, competition over grazing land and water rights, among others, is therefore built into the rural political economy that predominates in the IGAD region. One has to distinguish that not all land is—from an agronomic point of view—suitable for agriculture and/or grazing. A well-thought-out land use system, allocating land according to its suitability, is the role of governments in the Horn of Africa. Without cooperation between the pastoralists and farming communities to develop viable strategies to address each other's land requirements, the governments of the Horn will not have peace in the rural areas.

Improving Law Enforcement's Economic Standing

Economic conditions in the Horn of Africa, where police and armed forces often live and work in appalling conditions, exacerbate the proliferation of small arms. Police officers are paid low and irregular wages, and sometimes funds allocated to the forces are criminally diverted. In addition, there is a lack of promotion and training opportunities and equipment is poor. In Nairobi, the SALIGAD team learned that some individual police officers rent their arms to gangsters and bandits as a means of generating income. The SALIGAD project's research revealed that the police in Nairobi rent a gun for a few hours at $20 to $40 per "action" or night. This feeds the demand for small arms, as citizens, who cannot rely on the police in these circumstances, arm themselves for self-defense purposes. Although it is little studied, our field observations and interviews indicated that income generation through selling or renting official weapons is widespread. Only an independent inquiry or internal study can unveil the proportion of police officers who rent arms to others. To our knowledge this has not been attempted in the Horn of Africa, but it would be a vital component in the framework of assessing good governance.

Despite the inadequate police presence, addressing the demand for small arms by simply providing additional police or engaging community leaders in disarmament programs is not a straightforward solution. First, the history of militarized politics cautions that measures taken to strengthen police forces are not necessarily desirable if they are not accompanied by human rights training and improved civilian controls. Professionalizing the police force can only be effective in providing human security if conditions can assure citizens that a greater number and well-armed police are also accompanied by greater accountability to the public and respect for human rights. Without an established relationship between civilians and uniformed forces, security forces will not be able to mitigate the misuse of small arms. Second, civilians may also be equally distrustful of community leaders that urge disarmament. Indeed, once the government's credibility has been damaged, community leaders face a difficult task in convincing members of the community to hand over small arms or to support a destruction program to get rid of obsolete or surplus weapons. In this situation, only a plan that includes the participation of the communities concerned would work.

Poverty and Income Disparity

Fieldwork conducted by SALIGAD showed that many groups in the Horn of Africa—such as civil servants, academics, and church leaders—believe that lack of economic opportunities has led to a growing demand for small arms in their region.[15] According to community groups, pastoralists arm themselves because they lack the ability to protect their meager resources—frequently from a single source of income—from theft, disease, or the environment. The wealth they have accumulated, often measured by the number of heads of cattle, camels, or other livestock, is their only resource. When droughts decimate their animals or other events reduce their resources, the absence of alternative income-generating options makes it necessary to defend the single source of income they have. As community groups noted during a workshop in Dire Dawa in southeastern Ethiopia in 2001, many sell animals to buy guns and ammunition to protect their livelihood.

The paucity of opportunities for youth in the Horn of Africa also feeds the demand for SALWs. Young men face particularly acute dangers. In Yei County in south Sudan, for example, fieldwork revealed that young men without job opportunities, access to education, and training are unrestrained and use their guns to get respect, force cash or income in kind, and take girls at their will.[16] In Hargeisa, Somaliland, stakeholders pointed to the link between the youths' lack of opportunities for income and arms. Here, too, guns enabled these young men—in many instances coached and controlled by the elders—to obtain income in various forms.[17] Indeed young males are frequently recruited, by force or voluntarily, to serve in criminal gangs and organized groups of cattle rustlers.

Still, despite the connection between poor economic prospects and arms acquisition, it is equally important to note that poverty and social injustices cannot be eliminated overnight, and poverty reduction[18] programs may not automatically lead to a decrease in the desire to acquire weapons for protection of self and property. Rather, the fieldwork conducted by SALIGAD indicates that governments must use caution when implementing poverty reduction programs. In a rural setting, development projects can lead to uneven wealth distribution, as only selected communities are targeted for assistance. Thus, ironically, improving the economic situation for some communities might lead to an increased demand for small arms, as people clash over the new and meager wealth created in small pockets throughout the region. Moreover, if cultural practices improve men's social standing with the acquisition of a weapon, then improvements in the living conditions may not reduce armed conflicts.

Cultural Factors

In addition to the above-mentioned structural conditions that continue to impede efforts to curb the misuse of small arms, traditional practices such as cattle rustling, to fulfill bride-prices, and warrior cultures, which once included the use of traditional weapons, now attract SALWs. The replacement of traditional weapons with SALWs in cultural practices demonstrates further how SALWs have become rooted in individual and community identities, behavioral norms, and indigenous values. This section briefly outlines the results of fieldwork that illustrate the misuse of small arms in the traditional practices of cattle rustling and the payment of bride-prices and remnants of vendetta and warrior cultures.

Cattle rustling and bride-prices. Cattle are considered precious commodities in East Africa. Cattle are used for bride-prices, serve as an indication of wealth, and are also used to settle debts. Those without sufficient cattle to meet such needs may engage in cattle rustling. Traditionally, cattle rustling was done with *pangas* (a wooden stick) or poisoned sticks, but the wide availability of small arms has made cattle rustling easier and more profitable. In fact, evidence suggests that predatory cattle rustling is on the increase and outsiders, who are professional raiders, engage in cattle rustling for commercial purposes. In the Kuria region of southwestern Kenya, at the border with Tanzania, the SALIGAD project team observed during fieldwork conducted in 2000 and 2001 that a van had been dispatched from Nairobi to the village to carry orders of cattle to town—orders that had been placed by cattle raiders. This is distinctly different from the traditional intraethnic cattle stealing based on reciprocity. As such, the increasingly profitable venture of cattle rustling fuels the demand for small weapons.

Cattle rustling in Kuria also had an effect on bride-prices. Since the dowry to be paid by a young man for his bride is measured by the number of cattle he can supply, his ability to rustle cattle is thus not only a mark of his bravery, but also decides his marriage. In this case, reliable small arms enable the male and his kin to steal more cattle and, because firepower can overwhelm and intimidate the cattle owners, it minimizes the risk to the youth of getting caught, as owners prefer to let the livestock go rather than fight the armed youth. For this reason, raids have become increasingly violent because of the use of military-level weapons, such as automatic rifles, to avoid being caught.

Vendetta and warrior culture. A vendetta or a warrior culture, although in decline in the highlands of Ethiopia and the lowlands of Somalia—as well as elsewhere in the region—contributes to the internal demand for small arms. For example, in a vendetta-tolerating culture, when a person is killed, the victim's family may carry out "justice," in the form of revenge, often before the burial ceremony takes place. This naturally leads into a spiral of violence and feeds the demand for good and reliable small arms. The vendetta culture is defined by demonstrations of masculinity where a celebration of the victor and his heroism is an important part of the ritual. If, as we often witnessed and learned in the course of fieldwork, the driving force in such conflict is the assertion of a masculine identity that is demonstrated through violence, then it is difficult to make attempts at reconciliation, which could overcome the built-in preference for retribution. Although this is apparently a diminishing tradition, it is still an important cultural incentive for people to arm themselves.

Conclusion and Policy Recommendations

Weapons-related violence threatens human security and generates fear—keeping children away from school, farmers from their land, traders from markets, patients from their doctors, and voters from polling stations. When this happens, sustainable development becomes impossible. Practitioners, in their zeal to eradicate the tragedies caused by small arms supply, have learned the hard lesson that striving for complete and unconditional control and collection of small arms and light weapons is futile. Demand, driven by security concerns and sustained by embedded social practices, thwarts efforts that seek to eliminate small arms from society completely. As such, the SALIGAD project has provided a *demand-side* analysis of weapons procurement in anticipation that this approach would complement the wealth of valuable literature and research that have already been compiled on small arms *supply* and contribute to curbing the proliferation of small arms and light weapons in the Horn of Africa.

Civilians arm themselves for economic, political, and cultural reasons. Scarce employment opportunities in pastoral and farming communities encourage armed guarding of livestock and land and cattle rustling by youth. The politicization of security forces by governments—directly arming ethnic groups against others—and the inability of governments to protect their citizens also force residents to assume the responsibility of security.

Moreover, poorly compensated security officials also feed the demand for small arms through the sale or rental of officially issued weapons. In addition to economic and political factors, arms have been incorporated to facilitate cultural practices—such as paying bride-prices and retaliating in vendettas. Regional agreements, as they are currently structured, are short-sighted and narrowly focused. In addition to addressing the supply routes for weapons and accounting for their distribution in the Horn of Africa, policies to address the demand of SALWs should provide space for greater civil society participation in policymaking to create incentives to extend the government's administration, link development and security, and adequately compensate and reform security sectors. Furthermore, policymakers should work with community elders to discourage practices such as cattle rustling and vendettas.

Civil society must take the lead in identifying the demand for SALWs. Incorporating the factors that fuel the demand for SALWs can help the existing efforts to curb their supply. In this regard, for the National Focal Points to function successfully as a clearinghouse for information on violent conflicts in the region, best practices for curbing SALWs, and more important, to lobby for legislative action as envisioned,[19] it is of paramount importance that civil society be fully and equally involved. Yet, civil society can only play a constructive role if and when the NFPs acquire knowledge, information, and expertise on SALW issues—which they have been unable to do without a strong partnership with civil society. Thus, civil society must take the lead; it must undertake lobby work to reduce the demand for small arms and conduct fact-finding missions, studies, and research on the misuse and excessive accumulation of SALWs, both at the government and civilian levels.

The extension of the government's administration throughout the country is key to reducing the demand for SALWs. Failure to do so cedes the authority over security to the armed movements in the region. Particularly vulnerable are border regions. This is due not just to the porous borders, but also to the frequent movement across borders by pastoralists—many of whom are nomadic by nature. Governments must actively engage with community elders to understand the triggers for conflict in these vulnerable border areas. This will increase the credibility of government in locations that are usually outside the formal system and decrease the incentives for citizens to assume the private responsibility for security. Currently, the sporadic and biased relationship that governments have with communities in border areas, or other weakly integrated communities, results predominantly in breeding distrust. Moreover, with government taking a more active role in security, the assets of private citizens will be freed to invest in economic endeavors, education, health, and other areas that improve the standard of living and perhaps in the long run, reduce the demand for arms.

National governments, in partnership with regional and international organizations, must link development explicitly with security. Fieldwork and interviews with community elders in rural areas pointed to lack of economic opportunities as fueling the demand for SALWs in the Horn of Africa. With uncertain economic futures resulting from environmental factors, the lack of skills, or just the absence of opportunities, many—youth, in particular—turn to the use of weapons to steal cattle, which they later sell. Not only do these actions result in a spiral of insecurity as cattle herders arm themselves against the youth to protect their only sources of income, but they also decrease the economic viability of communities in general as residents find that their options to pursue traditional livelihoods are limited. Thus as national and international policymakers undertake development projects, they must consider how to protect citizens from cattle rustling, how agricultural expansion can be balanced with existing uses of land, and how youth can be trained to acquire the skills necessary to succeed outside the traditional systems. In short, development approaches must be more holistic to minimize the possibility that an improvement in one area—say large-scale farming of cash crops—will result in a deterioration of existing livelihoods.

Although many regional initiatives to curb the proliferation of SALWs seek resources to improve coordination between security agencies, seeking resources to professionalize and adequately compensate security officers is an equally important goal. Particularly in urban areas, police officers sell or rent their weapons to augment paltry salaries. This increases not only the circulation of weapons, but also the chances that police officers will be poorly armed when needed in actual emergencies—thus reinforcing the view among private citizens of the inadequacy of the state's security system and the necessity to acquire private arms. Therefore, programs to stem the proliferation of SALWs must also include incentives for the reform of the state's security sector. Notably, security-sector reform is not limited to formal security systems, but also includes informal security services. In many instances, our fieldwork revealed that governments periodically armed groups against each other to counter political dissent. Such politicization of security not only breeds distrust in government, but needless to say, impedes democratization. Regional agreements therefore must include provisions and penalties to reduce the politicization of security sectors.

Cultural practices that appear to benefit from the use of weapons will be the most difficult and delicate to approach. Traditions, such as providing a bride-price and indicating one's worth as a male, that can be facilitated by the use of weapons only reinforce their use. In closing this channel for SALWs, governments must work hand in hand with community leaders. However, it may only be after government has built trust among residents that it can provide security and development and fruitfully engage with community leaders on curbing the use of arms in traditional practices. Failing to build trust in other areas, community elders may consider government to be a hostile intruder, devoid of good intentions, and intent on further changing their way of life.

Finally, signatories to breakthrough agreements such as the Bamako Declaration and the Nairobi Declaration must maintain their commitments and continue to set up the NFP programs. The link between regional arrangements and civil society organizations must be strong in order to make agreements relevant. Only through the sustained efforts of communities, regions, nongovernmental bodies, state actors, and the international community can it be possible to curb the demand for small arms and light weapons in the Horn. Equally important, understanding both the demand and supply factors behind the proliferation of SALWs must not result in dichotomous policies; just as supply-centric policies ignore the triggers to acquire weapons, narrowly focusing on demand can overshadow other factors that do not neatly fit into the myopic demand-and-supply dualism. For example, how are factors related to ethnicity, gender, and identity served by debate that is framed by the demand of weapons? Rather, the two approaches must be used to develop a more relevant mechanism to address small arms and light weapons—one that encourages good governance, including the enforcement of rule of law and human rights, the broadening of political involvement, and balanced economic development policies.

Notes

1. Globally, approximately 639 million small arms exist. Of the estimated 30 million firearms that are in sub-Saharan Africa, nearly 80 percent are in the hands of civilians. See Graduate Institute of International Studies, Geneva, *Small Arms Survey 2003: Development Denied* (Oxford: Oxford University Press, 2003, electronic version), pp. 57, 80.

2. The SALIGAD project was jointly undertaken by BICC and the International Resource Group on Disarmament and Security in the Horn of Africa (IRG) to address the question of the proliferation of illicit SALWs in the member states of the Intergovernmental Authority on Development (IGAD)—Djibouti, Eritrea, Ethiopia, Kenya, Somalia, and Sudan. IRG is a group of disarmament and demobilization experts that explores alternative security structures and disarmament measures for the Horn of Africa. BICC is an independent nonprofit organization dedicated to promoting and facilitating the processes whereby people, skills, technology, equipment, and financial and economic resources can be shifted away from the defense sector and applied to alternative civilian uses. IRG members hold the conviction that long-term stability and prosperity in the Horn of Africa depend on the integration of security, humanitarian, political, and economic development efforts. The project is financially sponsored by Brot für die Welt (Bread for the World) and German Technical Co-operation (GTL). The SALIGAD project formally ended in 2002. Reports on the project include: Bonn International Center on Conversion (BICC), *Small Arms in*

the Horn of Africa: Challenges, Issues and Perspectives, Brief 23 (Bonn: BICC, May 2002); BICC, *Gender Perspectives on Small Arms and Light Weapons: Regional and International Concerns,* Brief 24 (Bonn: BICC, July 2002).

3. This estimate of small arms is based on the conflicts that have taken place in the region in the last four decades. IGAD member states have experienced internal armed conflicts or interstate wars since the 1960s.

4. Of the combined stockpile of arms in Africa, about 19 percent are in the hands of the armed forces (police and military) while civilians control approximately 79 percent. The remaining 2 percent are under the command of insurgents (see *Small Arms Survey 2003,* p. 80).

5. Organization of African Unity, Bamako Declaration on an African Common Position on the Illicit Proliferation, Circulation and Trafficking of Small Arms and Light Weapons, Bamako, December 2000. Reproduced by SaferAfrica (available online at http://www.saferafrica.org/DocumentsCentre/Books/Matrix/BamekoDeclaration. asp); the Nairobi Declaration on the Problem of the Proliferation of Illicit Small Arms and Light Weapons in the Great Lakes Region and the Horn of Africa, Nairobi, March 15, 2000, reproduced by SaferAfrica (available online at http://www.saferafrica.org/ DocumentsCentre/Books/Matrix/NairobiDeclaration.asp, accessed November 22, 2004). The Nairobi Declaration spawned a series of protocols—the one cited here refers to the Implementation Plan of the Co-ordinated Agenda for Action on the Problem of the Proliferation of Small Arms and Light Weapons in the Great Lakes Region and the Horn of Africa (November 2000, available online at http//www.smallarmsnet.org/doc. htm). The landmark international event on small arms and light weapons, the United Nations Conference on the Illicit Trade in Small Arms and Light Weapons in All Its Aspects, was held in New York July 9–20, 2001. The purpose of the conference was to initiate the development of national, regional, and global protocols and procedures for eradicating SALWs. United Nations General Assembly, "United Nations Conference on the Illicit Trade in Small Arms and Light Weapons in All Its Aspects, 9–20 July 2001" (A/CONF.192/SR.1). 27 July 2001).

6. The Nairobi Declaration.

7. The Group of Governmental Experts on Small Arms focuses on small arms and light weapons designed for military purposes and defines them as follows: "Broadly speaking, small arms are those weapons designed for personal use, and light weapons are those designed for use by several persons serving as a crew." United Nations General Assembly, "Report of the Group of Governmental Experts on Small Arms" (A/54/258), 19 August 1999, note 5. See also the related report, United Nations General Assembly, "Report of the Panel of Governmental Experts on Small Arms" (A/52/298, Annex), 27 August 1997.

8. Further online information regarding the classification of SALW and ammunition can be obtained from BICC, "Help Desk for Practical Disarmament," *Projects on Small Arms Control* (available online at http://www.bicc.de/helpdesk/ definition/types.html).

9. Ebla Haji Aden, "People with Arms and Grassroots Research: The Case of North-East Kenya," in *Proceedings of the Workshop on Small Arms and Light Weapons Issues in Uganda: Dynamic, Concepts and Perspectives for Action,* co-organized by the Ministry of Gender, Labour and Social Development of Uganda and the Bonn International Centre for Conversion (Bonn: BICC, April 2002), pp. 22–26. In the article, she reviews the integration of traditional and modern approaches to disarmament.

10. "Proliferation and Impact of Small Arms in Garissa, Kenya," community workshop cohosted by SALIGAD, Pastoralists' Peace and Development Initiative, and OXFAM, Garissa, Kenya, June 2000.

11. Some participants at this conference actually surrendered their weapons at the meeting hall.

12. Information obtained by the SALIGAD team from local people and church leaders. The types of weapons usually distributed are the AK-47 and, at times, the G3, which is the standard firearm of the Kenyan army.

13. Statistic on the availability of SALWs quoted from fieldwork conducted by BICC/SALIGAD during 2000 and 2001.

14. The survey was conducted by Intermediate Technology Development Group–East Africa (ITDG-EA) and United Nations Human Settlements Programme (UN HABITAT), "Crime in Nairobi," Nairobi, December 5, 2000 (available online at http://www.unchs.org/press2000/crime_in_nairobi.asp). ITDG-EA is a member of the Nairobi City Council–based Nairobi Informal Settlements Co-ordinating Committee.

15. In another example, a project by World Vision in North Shoa Zone/Ethiopia demonstrated that a sustained rural development program that ultimately improved living conditions resulted in fewer armed conflicts (personal communication between Kiflemariam and Tibebe Eshete, March 2000). See also Tibebe Eshete and Siobhan O'Reily Calthrop, "Silent Revolution: The Role of Community in Reducing the Demand for Small Arms Working," *Working Paper No. 3* (World Vision, 2003).

16. Fieldwork conducted in early 2004.

17. Fieldwork conducted in 2000.

18. The international donor agency community seems to have shifted from poverty eradication to poverty reduction and now has reached the objective of poverty alleviation, which, I argue, implies that a certain degree of poverty is acceptable.

19. The Nairobi Declaration.

3

Refugees in East Africa: Developing an Integrated Approach

Zachary Lomo

East Africa and the Horn presently host approximately 1.4 million refugees.[1] The presence of these refugees can be both a security problem *and* a resource for spurring socioeconomic development—nationally and regionally. Refugee policies and practices in the subregion, however, tend to view refugees through the lenses of the former—as potential threats to their national security and stability.[2] The perception of refugees as security threats—and not because of a genuine consideration for fostering self-reliance and development among refugees—I argue, partly explains why the governments in the region have, with the prompting of the United Nations High Commissioner for Refugees (UNHCR) in some cases, chosen to house refugees in settlements or camps. In their rhetoric, both the states in the subregion and UNHCR claim that settlements are a strategy for improving on the welfare of refugees. But settlements and camps can be dangerous to refugees.

The charter and conflict management protocol adopted by the Intergovernmental Authority on Development (IGAD)[3], the main subregional organization in East Africa and the Horn, and the East African Community (EAC)[4] claim to be concerned with ensuring security and stability as a prerequisite to social and economic progress. However, they are silent on refugee issues and lack a vision of the potential of refugees as resources for stimulating economic and social progress. In other words, the conceptual framework for dealing with refugee issues by IGAD and EAC member states is flawed. Their approaches—ad hoc and perpetuated by international actors with the wherewithal for refugee protection—only fan more insecurity and exacerbate destitution for both refugees and host communities.

Research in settlements in Uganda and Kenya demonstrates that, while in the initial stages of refugee crises, settlements and camps may appear to be the best way to maximize protection for refugees, in reality they engender dependency, helplessness, and insecurity. Sometimes in settlement and camp situations, it is not possible to separate combatants and dealers in small arms from civilians, due to the sheer numbers of refugee populations and the isolationist nature of the camp. Rebel groups can reorganize in settlements and replenish supplies. Using empirical data from fieldwork conducted predominantly in Uganda, but also in Kenya, and the 1951 UN Convention Relating to the Status of Refugees (hereinafter, the 1951 Refugee Convention), its related Protocol of 1967, and international human rights instruments, this chapter explores alternatives to placing refugees in settlements and camps as a means for dealing with security issues in the subregion. In doing so, it will specifically analyze the current policies in the subregion, drawing many examples from Uganda, because many cite its superior refugee policies in comparison with other states in the subregion.[5] However, in practice, Uganda's approaches do not differ qualitatively from the rest of the subregion.[6] The second section examines the current trends in refugee dynamics in the region. The next section reviews the consequences in the subregion of refugee policies in terms of human rights, human security, economic opportunities, and the international policymaking community. The final section offers some recommendations and concluding remarks.

Current Trends in Refugee Dynamics Within the Region

According to the latest report by UNHCR, there are approximately 1.4 million refugees in the subregion. Almost every country in East Africa and the Horn hosts refugees regardless of its own peace and security situation. Tanzania leads the region by hosting more than 600,000 refugees—nearly 400,000 of which are from Burundi. After Tanzania, Kenya hosts approximately 240,000 refugees—most from Somalia (nearly 154,000)—and almost 5,000 asylum seekers. Uganda is the third largest refugee-hosting state, with approximately 250,000 refugees within its borders, of which over 200,000 are from Sudan. In turn, Sudan hosts approximately 179,000 refugees—most of which are Eritrean refugees, and 4,200 asylum seekers. In addition, there are over 660,000 IDPs in Sudan. Ethiopia hosts almost 116,000 refugees—about 90,000 of which come from Sudan. Relatively smaller numbers of refugees are found in Djibouti (approximately 18,000— of which most are Somali) and Eritrea (approximately 4,000). While Somalia hosts approximately 18,000—most of which are returnees from Ethiopia— there are 400,000 IDPs.[7] Despite these grim statistics, the actual figures are often higher than the official ones because many refugees, for various reasons, opt to live outside settlements and camps. For example, in Uganda, UNHCR estimates that there are officially about 500 urban refugees. But the numbers could be well above 10,000.[8]

There are primary and secondary factors that force individuals and communities to leave their homes and flee to other locations—whether within their own country or crossing over an international border (see Figure 3.1). There are two sets of primary factors. The first set of primary factors is man-made—they include inequality, injustice, oppression, exploitation, greed and selfishness of those in power and positions of authority, violation of human rights and freedoms, intolerance, and poverty of ideas. Such primary factors produce secondary factors, which include deterioration in institutional systems and structures (including the state), war, conflict, insurgencies, and other forms of violent uprising. The second set of primary factors is created by natural disasters such as drought, floods, and earthquakes. It is also true to say, however, that some of these so-called natural factors—for instance, drought and famine—are, in fact, secondary factors since they result from irresponsible or even development-related human activity.[9] However, while development-induced displacement and natural disasters have had an impact, it is armed conflict that has played the greatest role in creating refugee flows in the region. The pervasive presence of such conflicts has had a profound effect on the region, rendering large areas unsafe for human habitation and generating refugees and IDPs on an unprecedented scale. Thus, any discussion on refugees within the region cannot be separated from discourses on violence and armed conflict.[10]

Consequences of Refugee Policies

To understand the relationship between security issues and refugee protection in the region, it is helpful to understand the factors that influence policy

Figure 3.1 Causes of Forced Migration

Primary Factors 1	Secondary Factors
• Inequality • Injustice • Oppression • Exploitation • Greed and selfishness of those in power and positions of authority • Violation of human rights and freedoms • Intolerance • Poverty of ideas	• Deterioration in institutional systems and structures (including the state) • War and conflict insurgencies and other forms of violent uprising • Natural disasters
	Primary Factors 2 • Natural disasters

formulation and human rights dimensions of refugee policies in the region. A typical international response to a specific refugee situation is elaborated in the UNHCR/Government of Uganda's (GoU) Self-Reliance Strategy (SRS) document as follows:

> In an emergency UNHCR usually starts by focusing on what should urgently be done for refugees. The in a (*sic*) next phase it looks at what can be done for refugees in a way that also benefits the affected nationals—this is in fact what UNHCR (*sic*) currently practicing in Uganda. The next phase is what UNHCR can do for the host communities in a way that benefit (*sic*) the refugees.[11]

This neat rendition of what happens in refugee situations is misleading because in practice, UNHCR's policies in Africa create huge obstacles for refugees to realistically reclaim their lives after experiences of loss and trauma. Above all, the description is misleading because it suggests that UNHCR cares about local ideas, systems, and structures right from the start of a refugee situation.[12] It also suggests that refugees appear to be participants in this phase of restructuring their lives in their host countries. Viewed critically, UNHCR's approach in East Africa hardly engenders any serious benefits for both refugees and hosts. As shall be demonstrated, at the epicenter of this approach is the isolation of refugees in settlements and camps. Often, it is claimed that African governments force refugees into settlements. Although in some instances that does happen, UNHCR is an accomplice in many of the moves to isolate refugees in settlements.[13]

Many official reports of refugee situations do not expose the negative ramifications of the current approaches and interventions by governments on the general security and self-reliance capacity of the refugee and host communities. In essence, official reports hide the contradiction that lies at the heart of refugee policy in the region: refugees, initially welcomed by neighboring states and placed in safe areas, are subsequently heavily restricted in the enjoyment of human rights, are exposed to increased levels of insecurity, and are less likely to develop skills for self-sufficiency. Understanding these shortcomings in the subregion's refugee policies highlights the issues of insecurity and self-reliance that are central to refugees' lives.

The Human Rights Situation of Refugees in the Subregion

African countries have been lauded for their hospitality in hosting refugees.[14] Some countries in the subregion have openly asserted that they have "the most liberal policies on refugees in the world."[15] Unlike in Europe and America, where refugees are arrested on arrival and kept in detention camps pending verification of their applications for refugee status, refugees in Africa are generally free to enter the territory of these states without restrictions. The "generosity" of African nations to refugees, in particular countries in the IGAD subregion, is often misleading because it gives the impression that refugees in these countries enjoy fundamental human rights and freedoms.

The contrast between "liberal" refugee policies in Africa and "fortress Europe," for example, can best be illustrated by the following caricature: African countries open the door for refugees to enter without serious restrictions and the deployment of police and austere-looking immigration staff hunting down "economic" migrants; however, once inside, the refugees' movements and rights are restricted. Refugees are reduced to one mass of statistics only differentiated by nationality, but sharing one common feature: peasant Africans who must live in rural settlements and camps.[16] On the other hand, Europeans barricade their gates and doors, deploying police and dogs and barbed wire, leaving a very small entrance; but once the asylum seeker has been granted refugee status, she is allowed freedom of movement and the right to choose where to reside in accordance with the 1951 UN Refugee Convention,[17] including in most cases the right to work, other forms of discrimination notwithstanding. Research in selected IGAD countries has demonstrated that there are several obstacles, mainly policy-related, that hinder refugees from enjoying social and economic rights and civil liberties that are specified in the 1951 UN Refugee Convention,[18] the framework in which all refugee policy should ground itself. Therefore, the following examines a number of the specific practices that impact the extent to which refugees are able to enjoy specific rights.

Social and Economic Rights

The 1951 UN Refugee Convention recognizes social and economic rights that refugees must enjoy in order to find solutions to their life situations. It makes provisions for the right to own property and establish businesses, the right to education and health, and the right to work.[19] For refugees to enjoy these rights requires a solid foundation of legislation and policy that secures all their rights as members of the society in which they find themselves. The findings from Uganda and Kenya indicate that the current legal framework in Uganda and the absence of a legal framework in Kenya, coupled with the policy of containing refugees in specific camps, actively impedes real enjoyment of social and economic rights by refugees in these countries.

Economic rights, such as property ownership and fair compensation, are not always extended to refugees. In some countries, refugee legislation allows for the dispossession of a refugee of his or her property. In Uganda, for example, under the Control of Alien Refugees Act of 1960, camp authorities can take a refugee's vehicle brought into Uganda, without due compensation, and use it for running programs in refugee camps.[20] Such compulsory dispossession of resources and property, like cattle or vehicles, obviously deprives refugees of the very basis for making a new economic start. Although the subregion's contracting states to the 1951 Refugee Convention would argue that they no longer confiscate the property of refugees, there is no protection against its occurrence in their refugee-specific laws.[21]

Refugees in some cases are not equitably compensated. Paradoxically, while the countries of the region have ratified a number of human rights conventions—most of which outlaw discrimination—refugees who have obtained employment within settlements are being paid less than their national counterparts, although such practice violates the right of refugees to equal pay for equal work.[22] UNHCR actively championed this discriminatory practice on the grounds that refugees receive free food and that the practice encourages the spirit of self-help.[23] Having experienced refugee life, and having been involved in building a school on a self-help basis in southern Sudan, I find such policy an affront to the intelligence, independence, and dignity of a refugee.[24] Such discriminatory practices entrench xenophobic attitudes against refugees, undermine cooperation between refugees and hosts, and, furthermore, can be a recipe for conflict and insecurity.

Social mobility, through the promise of education, also eludes refugees. Indeed, the lack of access to education, one of the highest priorities for refugees in the subregion, provides a telling example of the limitations placed on refugees' enjoyment of their rights. Although the 1951 Refugee Convention guarantees the right to primary education to refugee children[25] on the same basis as it is available to nationals, many refugee children, especially those in so-called self-settled areas, have limited access to educational facilities. In addition to the 1951 Refugee Convention, countries of the subregion have ratified the Convention on the Rights of the Child (1989), which came into force in 1990.[26] The provisions of this Convention are subordinate to state and international laws that are more favorable and emphasize the right of all children to education, specifically including refugees and asylum seekers.[27] Furthermore, it requires states to ensure that this right is provided to each child within their jurisdiction "without discrimination of any kind, irrespective of the child's national, ethnic, social origin or other status."[28]

Although the UN Convention on the Rights of the Child specifies that states should, among other things, "make primary education compulsory and available free to all . . . and make higher education available to all on the basis of capacity by every appropriate means,"[29] it is practically impossible for some countries in the region to make primary education available to all children, including refugees, given their weak economies. A few examples illustrate the inattention to education: public expenditure on education

(1999–2001) by Uganda and Eritrea, 2.5 percent and 2.7 percent of GDP, respectively, was below the median for sub-Saharan Africa (3.3 percent of GDP). In contrast, in 2002, Sudan, Ethiopia, and Eritrea spent 2.8, 5.2, and 23.5 percent of GDP on the military, respectively—above the median expenditure of 1.9 percent of GDP; Kenya and Tanzania spent 1.7 and 1.5 percent of GDP on the military.[30] Uganda's record is particularly troubling when considering that in 1997 the government introduced free universal primary education for four children in every family.

Civil Rights and Liberties

Civil rights and liberties of refugees are also restricted and violated. This stems from the fact that, at its root, the global refugee protection regime conceptualizes refugees as "passive victims."[31] Do passive victims have any rights at all, or do they have only duties? The right to freedom of movement, a case in point, has fundamental implications for a refugee's well-being. In the region, a refugee's right to freedom of movement is affected either by specific refugee legislation, as is the case in Uganda, Tanzania, and Sudan, or by policy directives. For example, under Uganda's Control of Alien Refugees Act, any refugee found in Uganda—"other than in a refugee settlement without a permit under section 8 of this Act; . . . shall be guilty of an offence and shall be liable on conviction to imprisonment for a period not exceeding three months."[32] Similarly, Tanzania's Refugee Act of 1998 penalizes refugees who, without an official permit, do not comply with the requirement to reside in a designated area, or any refugee in a designated area who makes an attempt to leave.[33] Under Sudanese refugee law, "No refugee shall exercise any political activity during his presence in the Sudan, and *he shall not depart from any place of residence specified for him.* The penalty for contravening this subsection shall be imprisonment for not more than one year [emphasis mine]."[34] As noted already, refugee policy in the region is to isolate refugees in agricultural settlements or "camps" whether or not they have the ability to support themselves through farming. This limits their right to freedom of movement. Yet the 1951 Refugee Convention provides that contracting states shall accord to refugees who are lawfully in their territories the right to choose their place of residence. It further provides that contracting states shall guarantee to refugees who are lawfully in their territories the right to move freely within their territories, subject to any regulations applicable to aliens generally in the same circumstances.[35] The right to freedom of movement is the gateway through which one can enjoy other rights.[36]

The lack of adequate means for refugees to identify themselves further curtails their civil rights through the infringement of the freedom of movement.

Although the 1951 Refugee Convention stipulates that contracting states shall provide refugees with identity papers,[37] research in Uganda and Kenya demonstrates, for example, that many refugees, especially those in settlements and self-settled areas, do not have any identity papers except food ration cards. Yet the executive committee (EXCOM) of the UNHCR also reiterated, in 1993, the necessity of the issuance of personal documentation as a device to promote the protection of the personal security of refugees.[38] Consequently, with few exceptions, people have no means of identifying themselves as bona fide refugees other than a ration card—and that is good only so long as they are still receiving food rations. Even then, in Uganda at least, field research demonstrated that the police or army does not always recognize a ration card as a proper form of identity, and such refugees have been detained on suspicion of being "rebels" or "terrorists" and even charged with treason. By contrast, self-settled refugees are safer from such threats because they pay taxes and can show a "graduated poll tax ticket." Moreover, the local authorities can verify their identity to the army or police.

Still, obtaining verification of identity from UNHCR or the camp commandant is not easy and in most cases it would involve a lengthy process. First, a refugee would have to go to see the chairperson of the Refugee Welfare Committee (RWC) of his or her area and explain his or her problem. It may take two or three weeks to get an appointment with the chairperson of the RWC. If the chairperson is satisfied that the refugee has good reason to require verification of identity or any document, then the chairperson will write an introduction letter for the refugee to take to the camp commandant. The camp commandant then reviews the reasons for a permit or document and, if satisfied that there is good reason, he will write a letter to his superiors in the district or to UNHCR field offices. According to refugee officials interviewed in one refugee settlement in northern Uganda in 1998, the letters serve to determine who has a genuine reason for leaving the settlement and also to ensure their safety. Although the intention might be good, the practice turns the requirement for letters into more of a tool for control than protection.

Refugee Policy and Its Implication for Security and Conflict Management

Thus, refugee policy in the subregion is one of containment and control—but should postcolonial African states continue to restrict resident African refugees *forever* in camps? Under the IGAD charter, for example, member states recognize that among the areas of cooperation that they will foster is the facilitation of "the free movement and right of establishment of residence by their nationals within the sub region."[39] Why, then, a containment policy? Three factors guide the prevalence of settlements as the preferred policy: first, states consider refugees as security threats; second, as a result of the first, they should be isolated; and third, states plan that refugees will soon go home. In short, states consider refugees a temporary phenomenon. By keeping refugees in settlements and camps, proponents of the policy argue that it is easy to monitor their movement and, therefore, curb activities that would compromise national security. There are four problems with the current settlements in East Africa: they are located too close to the border of the refugees' home country, they are in insecure areas, combatants and civilians are not easily distinguishable, and they are easy conduits for the illicit trade of small arms and light weapons.

Problematic Settlement Locations

In addition to isolating refugees by keeping them in camps, many camps in East Africa are located close to their countries of origin. In defending such a practice, some policymakers argue that this will ensure less costly repatriation programs in the future.[40] While this line of thought appears logical, the facts on the ground do not bear out the argument, and in fact, give cause for concern. Settling refugees close to the borders of their country of origin denies them sanctuary from the conflict from which they fled. For example, in fieldwork prior to the Comprehensive Peace Agreement in Sudan, ex-combatants from the Sudan People's Liberation Army (SPLA) expressed their fear of SPLA elements entering the camps in Uganda from Sudan and forcing them to return. Given the fact that desertion is often punishable by death, this poses a direct threat to their lives. At the same time, young boys and men feel vulnerable to forcible recruitment as the settlements present a concentrated population of potential recruits conveniently close to the war zone.[41]

In addition to a security danger, the isolationism of the settlements creates tension with the surrounding host population. For many host communities, the presence of large numbers of refugees living within their district is seen to be more of a threat than a resource, as this is the way in which they are presented. Instead of ploughing assistance into the refugee-hosting district as a whole, humanitarian assistance has tended to single out refugees at the expense of the surrounding communities. Moreover, isolating refugees has created antagonism as the national population sees refugees as competitors rather than partners. Thus the isolation of the camps and proximity to the borders not only pose several dangers to refugees, ex-combatants, and national security, but can also threaten regional security and stability.

Finally, the location of settlements not only creates problems between the host community and invites rebels to recruit, but in East Africa, refugee settlements are sometimes located in areas that are, themselves, insecure. Northern Uganda, which has experienced a relentless war against the government of Uganda carried out by the Lord's Resistance Army (LRA) since 1986, provides a telling example of this. Thousands of Ugandans have been killed, abducted, raped, or looted, and many have been displaced and are living in so-called protected villages.

By placing refugee settlements in the midst of such insecurity, refugees have become as vulnerable to attack as the Ugandan population, as demonstrated by the experience of the Achol-Pii refugee settlement in northern Uganda's Pader district. In 2002, the Achol-Pii refugee settlement hosted 24,000 refugees, as well as numerous internally displaced people (IDPs) in the surrounding area. However, this concentration of forced migrants was not reflected in the amount of protection offered and, on July 13 and 14, 1996, Achol-Pii suffered a particularly devastating rebel attack: over the course of two days, ninety-eight refugees were rounded up and systematically shot, hacked, or clubbed to death, and an additional twenty-one wounded. Subsequent calls to close down the camp and relocate the refugees to a safer location were ignored.[42] Again on August 5, 2002, LRA rebels attacked the refugee settlement, killing up to eighty refugees and abducting an unspecified number, including six aid workers. The camp was finally closed following the attack, and the entire refugee population temporarily moved further south.[43]

In September 2003, the government of Uganda declared its decision to resettle many of these same refugees back into northern Uganda, this time to Madi Okolo, in Arua district, and Ikafe in Yumbe district, which borders Sudan: not only would they once more be living within the reaches of the LRA insurgency, but they would be located within kilometers of the Sudan border. Clearly, a concentration of civilians in such an area presents a soft target for a rebel group that is desperate to exploit any available resources. Settling refugees in a conflict zone where their lives will be at risk patently breaches state responsibility in international law.

Easy Recruitment and Mobilization

Putting large refugee populations in settlements creates difficulties in distinguishing between civilians and combatants. Refugee settlements, when located in marginalized areas, can all too easily become convenient hiding places for individuals and groups who continue to promote conflict in their country of origin. At the same time, the camps can evolve as a subset of the conflict, as individuals and groups continue to be victimized by the people from whom they fled. The eastern Democratic Republic of the Congo, following the aftermath of the genocide in Rwanda, is a case in point: Members of the defeated Rwandan Armed Forces and the militia (*Interhamwe*) were able to operate with impunity within the camps and, simultaneously, benefit from the assistance they offered to them. From these camps, the defeated Rwandan forces and militia controlled the masses, recruited new militia, and manipulated international material assistance in order to sustain the struggle to regain power in Rwanda.[44] The far-reaching impact still resonates today, as perpetrators of genocide were inadvertently provided with the resources to regroup and, consequently, continue to generate their own particular brand of violence. Similarly, the refugee settlements in remote northern Uganda provided the Sudan People's Liberation Army/Movement the cover to carry out covert recruitment drives and mobilize moral and material support among the refugees for the war effort in Sudan.[45]

Finally, settlements—with their limited security and oversight—become easy places in which to hide and deal in weapons. Even though IGAD member states seem to identify the relationship between small arms and insecurity in their respective countries and the region, they ignore the relationship among insecurity, small arms, and the camps. Thus, the policy of isolating refugees from hosts does not promote security. It aggravates it. Moreover, the ease with which small arms and light weapons are traded and hidden in camps perpetuates the notion that refugees are themselves a source of insecurity. It hides the possibility that the structure and organization of the camps themselves facilitate the illicit trade in weapons. It contributes to the design of badly designed refugee policy.

Refugee Policy:
Realities of Settlements and Self-Sufficiency

In defending the settlement and camp policies, the state governments, UNHCR, and implementing nongovernmental organizations (NGOs) argue that the settlements give refugees the opportunity for a fresh start. As proof, many cite that in settlements, social services such as education and health are provided free to refugees, as are agricultural implements—tools, seeds, and pesticides—and agricultural extension workers provide supervision and advice on best practices in agriculture that improve on quality and yields. With little resources, they argue, the settlement model provides the best way to maximize protection for refugees.[46] However, as the emergency phase begins to wane, practitioners note that refugees begin to make projections for the long term, when international resources will no longer be available and host countries plan for the move from crisis management to long-term development. As argued earlier, this rendition of the refugee situation is misleading because it ignores several variables, notably the perspective of the "beneficiary."

One significant means for attaining self-sufficiency is to provide land to refugees for cultivation or other economic activities, but several fundamental factors make the settlement an incongruous model or vehicle for achieving self-reliance by refugees. Principally, settlements deny refugees autonomy—through the existing practices of land acquisition, engendering dependence on humanitarian assistance, and the absence of opportunities for self-development. Moreover, land in the settlement is limited and the quality varies from settlement to settlement. Second, in some countries, like Uganda, where land is no longer the property of the state,[47] landlords earn a higher profit by selling land to government and UNHCR to establish settlements than by selling to refugees—thus crowding out refugees who may desire to acquire land. Most significantly, empirical research bears out that a third effect of settlements is the dependency on humanitarian assistance that it sows among refugees—taking away an individual's ability to creatively map out his or her own survival in a new environment. They offer no opportunity for self-development, robbing refugees of any future prospects. In particular, settlements cannot facilitate the intention of the self-reliance strategy (SRS), which was purportedly created to provide refugees with the possibility of becoming self-sufficient.[48] This is primarily because settlements limit the freedom of movement of refugees.[49]

The SRS, while in principle a good idea, is being implemented on a fundamentally flawed premise. First, the land allocated to refugees—again, often in marginalized areas in which the host population itself struggles to survive—is often inadequate. In fact, field research in Uganda reveals that the point at which the land becomes infertile and needs to be left fallow for a year often coincides with refugees reaching the point at which they are supposed to be "self-sufficient"; they no longer receive additional external assistance with which to supplement their own yield. Second, self-sufficiency without freedom of movement is a contradiction in terms. Easy access to markets and a basic infrastructure are both prerequisites for sustainability. Initial analysis of the SRS indicates that refugees can barely survive on the piece of land allocated to them, let alone grow the excess needed to generate enough income to send their children to secondary school or buy the most basic of necessities.[50] Third and most important, as currently designed, the basic assumptions of the SRS ignore the centrality of free interaction between refugees and hosts—the integration of refugees into the normal development process cannot materialize if the purported beneficiaries are conceived as *passive victims* who can only receive the SRS, accept it, and use it without raising fundamental questions of importance to them, such as freedom to choose where to live among the host communities. In the final analysis, while the SRS claims to be a strategy for "integration of refugees into the normal development process,"[51] in practice it cannot engender integration because it is premised on control and isolation of refugees. Indeed, the SRS was simply a reaction by UNHCR and the government of Uganda to research that had exposed the lack of strategic thinking within these organizations about how refugees can become independent long after international assistance has withered out.[52]

Thus, settlements cannot provide refugees with a fresh start because their structure and policies create an ethos of dependency on the humanitarian regime and restrict the movements of refugees. By imposing fundamental limitations on their freedom of movement, settlements and accompanying requirements for humanitarian assistance disenfranchise refugees and destroy the ability of refugees to make decisions for themselves and take responsibility for their own lives. The present structure prevents creativity and, in the long run, impedes refugees from reaching a point of self-reliance because it gives refugees the false impression that as aliens they have no rights and freedoms. Rather, refugees believe that they have duties to obey the rules and orders of their host country.[53] Significantly, it ensures that refugees remain an untapped resource and, instead, become a drain on resources rather than a benefit to the host communities.

Contrasting settlement refugees with individuals who have decided to opt out of the settlement and assistance structures and have carved out their own existence highlights the negative impact of the present structure. Such "refugees" (many of whom do not even have official refugee status) are termed "self-settled." They show an alternative approach to being a refugee: they live among the national population; they often work, pay taxes, and, most important, rely on their own initiative and creativity in order to sustain themselves. Of course it is easy to overromanticize self-settled communities when, in reality, they often live with extreme hardship. However, the importance lies in the fact that they have decided to forgo external assistance in order to have a degree of autonomy over how they order their lives. Although there are some positive signs that the refugee assistance structures are beginning to recognize the need to build capacity in such a way that includes both refugees and host communities—one of the SRS goals is for refugees to share services such as water points (bore holes) and school with children in the host community[54]—it would seem that as long as the settlement structure remains, the impact would be limited.

Refugee Policy in the Eastern African Region: Regional and International Actors

Refugee policy in East Africa and the Horn is the outcome of an interplay of the structural continuities and discontinuities of international politics— the vested interests of Western countries, international agencies, and the states in the region. While external actors like the United Nations, the European Union (EU), and the United States can play a constructive role in ending the conflicts in the region, their influence, when not clearly and objectively defined with unwavering commitment, can produce interventions that only compound the problem. Why have the United States and the European Union supported refugee settlements as a model of organizing refugee protection in the region when in their own countries refugees who lawfully reside in their territories are free to choose where to live? Why has UNHCR gotten heavily involved in refugee status determination and supported settlements in Africa, yet it cannot do the same in Europe or the United States? Why have humanitarian organizations supported settlements, despite the fact that they expose women and children to sexual violence and military attacks? Why have IGAD member states housed refugees close to the borders of their countries of origin against the prohibitions of the Organization of African Unity's Refugee Convention?[55] Many of these questions lie beyond the scope of this chapter, but it suffices to say that while external actors appear to have a genuine interest in the refugees of the region because they threaten international peace, I argue that settlements are the preferred solution because they prevent refugee inflows into their own territories.

Some EU member states have taken measures to create buffer zones and help stem the inflow of refugees into northern countries. The immigration departments of some IGAD member states have been offered training and other technical support to build their capacities in order to identify forged passports being used by illegal immigrants into their countries. In addition, some EU member states have supported the policy of restricting refugees to settlements; some have offered technical support to governments in the region on how to improve on the settlement and camp policies.[56] It is in the context of the European Union's own immigration concerns that we must understand why some EU member states support refugee polices in the region that not only undermine the enjoyment of human rights by refugees, but also sustain conflict. In the final analysis, the threat to international peace is synonymous with the duty to avert refugee influxes in developed countries.

Of comparable importance, international actors, like UNHCR and its implementing partners, concern themselves with refugee policy in East Africa and the Horn not only because of genuine interest for security and stability, but because such policies ensure *visibility* of their activities, and thus evidence accountability.[57] Refugee settlements and camps provide *visibility,* and every means—including denial of food and other forms of assistance to refugees—has been used to enforce the settlement policy.[58] In addition to visibility, settlements promote fund-raising for the organizations. It is easier to fly donors to the settlements and camps and show them the sprawling tent cities and many malnourished people than to present statistics of the same people distributed all over the country.

Conclusion and Policy Recommendations

Existing refugee policies in the region promote neither security nor socioeconomic progress in host countries. The conceptual and procedural approaches to refugee assistance and protection are fundamentally flawed. External actors and the structural continuities and discontinuities of international politics exacerbate the situation. Instead of states in the region finding solutions to *the problems of refugees* and host communities, they are preoccupied with finding solutions to the *refugee problem.*

Refugees are not the main cause of instability in the region—whether or not they become agents of insecurity and agents of development is a function of policy choices by respective governments and external actors. Refugees do not have to be seen as a burden to host economies. To the contrary, they can be resources that, if intelligently deployed, can spur both economic and social progress. In the same vein, integration of refugees into the host community is the best hope of facilitating their recovery, rehabilitation, and security for host nations and the region. While the above discussion appears to be a rendition of a hopeless situation, I am optimistic and I argue with Rene Dumont[59] that Africa is not cursed. If we set our priorities correctly, we can find solutions to our problems. In that context, I propose the following recommendations to improve the refugee policies in Eastern Africa.

Effective responses to the large influx of refugees in East Africa and the Horn require policy changes at the international, subregional, national, and local levels. They require a reconceptualization of the composition of the refugee population and a strengthening of local capacities. Specifically, policymakers must reverse the prevailing perception of refugees as security threats, undertake longer-range planning, include the partnership of host communities, and, most important, honor human rights.

Policymakers in the subregional and the international arena should enact refugee policies that actively enable social and economic progress. Crucially, national governments and international actors should recognize that refugees are a resource. Attitudes and perceptions of refugees as being entirely a threat to national security and a burden on fragile economies must change. Policy and legislative frameworks that allow refugees to exploit their own creative ability must be put in place. This will help spur socioeconomic progress for both refugees and host communities. In this regard, the charters governing the EAC and IGAD must be revised to incorporate a progressive conceptual and policy framework that conceives refugees as a resource that must be factored into national and regional development matrices. As it stands, the constitutive charters for EAC and IGAD consider refugees entirely from a negative perspective: security risks. Yet refugees are human beings; there is no resource better than human beings.

Refugee policies must plan for the long term. Given that settlements and camps effectively perpetuate both the physical insecurity and economic dependency of refugees, such arrangements should be transitional—for periods ranging from six to twelve months, depending on each situation. At best, settlements and camps can suitably address an emergency situation, sort out armed elements among the civilian population, and obtain an accurate count of those displaced. But as the crisis that forced the migration in the first place continues, host communities should be provided with incentives to integrate refugees and refugees should be evenly integrated throughout the country.

A key element to the long-term stability of refugees is the cooperation of host communities. Hence, national and regional policies should involve local communities and citizens of the whole country in refugee protection from the onset of a humanitarian crisis. Indeed, properly integrating refugees into host communities can also dispel many of the stereotypes that perpetuate ineffective policies. In particular, well-integrated refugees and strong partnerships between local organizations—like Uganda's Local Councils that tend to have nearly universal information on people in their villages—may weaken the presumed relationship between refugees and insecurity and also demystify refugee camps.

Finally, refugee policies must be grounded in the promotion of human rights and freedom, because they are the basic building blocks for progress and conflict prevention mechanisms. Presently, the charters of the EAC and IGAD, as well as international policy incentives, place more emphasis on states and economic development than on the people of the subregion. In particular, refugees should be given greater rights to freedom of movement and choice of residence in order to build a strong foundation upon which refugees can become independent sooner. In this regard, it will be useful for EAC and IGAD to review the protocol of the freedom of movement by the Economic Community of West African States.[60] Equally important to long-term viability, refugees should be represented in tripartite voluntary repatriation agreements[61] so that they can have direct input to the determination of the conditions under which repatriation—often a time fraught with uncertainty and instability—can occur.

Notes

1. United Nations High Commission for Refugees (UNHCR) *Global Report 2004* (Bucharest: RA Monitorul Oficial, 2004, electronic version), pp. 165–171, 179–237.

2. See Richard Mutumba, "Congo Refugees a Threat—MP," *The New Vision* (Uganda) (September 27, 2002): 4. Similarly, Tanzanian president Benjamin Mkapa stated that refugees are a security threat. See *Annual National Congress of Chama cha Mapinduzi (CCM)*, Dodoma, October 28, 2002.

3. IGAD members include Djibouti, Eritrea, Ethiopia, Kenya, Somalia, Sudan, Tanzania, and Uganda.

4. EAC members include Kenya, Tanzania, and Uganda.

5. Of the subregion's countries that host refugees, Uganda is touted as a model with liberal refugee policies. Yet, in practice, Uganda does not have any policy (as

a strategic thinking or blueprint) on refugees. What passes for policy, namely the requirement that refugees must live in settlements and assistance must be provided only for those who agree to live in settlements, are the rules and control measures put in place by the colonial regime before its independence in 1962.

6. I contend that many of the credits attributed to Uganda's refugee policy are undeserved. First, the current settlement policies were started by the British colonial regime. Second, donor countries, desperate for a success story in Africa, have exaggerated Uganda's achievements in refugee protection, just as they have done so with respect to its economy and politics.

7. UNHCR, *Global Report 2004*, pp. 165–171, 179–237.

8. As per senior protection officer, Directorate of Refugees, Ministry of Disaster Preparedness and Refugees, Office of the Prime Minister (OPM), in a discussion with the author (Kampala, October 2002).

9. Some scholars have demonstrated that droughts and famines are products of politics: Amartya Sen, *Poverty and Famines: An Essay on Entitlement and Deprivation* (Oxford: Oxford University Press, 1981); Jean Dreze and Amartya Sen, *Hunger and Public Action* (Oxford: Oxford University Press, 1989).

10. However, I argue that a discussion of root causes of refugees is an exercise in futility because refugee protection involves issues affecting refugee rights in host countries and not in their home countries. In other words, refugees are an after-the-fact phenomenon.

11. OPM/UNHCR, "Strategy Paper, Self Reliance for Refugee Host Areas in Moyo, Arua, and Adjumani Districts, 1999/2003" (1999), p. 10.

12. In practice, UNHCR usually ignores local ideas. It only comes to consider these when it is planning to phase out its involvement with refugee protection. In Uganda for example, the handover of the Kiryandongo Refugee Settlement to Masindi district authorities collapsed because the local administration believed that UNHCR and its implementing partners were "offloading" refugees on them at a time when it was running short of funds. Moreover, UNHCR and the partners did not involve the local district authorities right from the establishment of the settlement.

13. In Uganda a former branch office representative of UNHCR, Hans Thoolen, believed that refugee settlements presented the best policy for protecting refugees and was angry with this author for making statements that undermined the policy (letter on file with author).

14. See Sadako Ogata, United Nations High Commissioner for Refugees, Speech at Makerere University Main Hall, August 1998.

15. Per Carlos Twesigomwe, then deputy director, Directorate of Refugees in the Office of the Prime Minister, in an interview with Uganda Human Rights Commission's magazine *Your Rights* (interviewed by Rose Mary Kemigisha, *Your Rights* 3, no. 1 (January 2000): 10). Carlos Twesigomwe is now commissioner for disaster management and refugees, Office of the Prime Minister, Uganda.

16. While a majority of the refugees in Africa are of peasant background and therefore can cope well with rural subsistence agricultural activities, a good percentage of refugees are from urban areas; some are professionals and can only cope well in urban environments. Sadly, the international assistance paradigm apparently deliberately collapses these differences in the name of nondiscrimination but often with adverse implications for the refugees.

17. UNHCR, Convention and Protocol Relating to the Status of Refugees (published as UNHCR/PI/CONV-UK1.PM5/AUGUST 1996), Article 26. Save where a state that is party to the convention has entered reservations, a refugee lawfully in the territory of any state that is party to the convention should be free to choose where to reside.

18. For example, the recent study "The Enjoyment of Human Rights: A Socio-Legal Study" is part of a larger study sponsored by the European Union, titled "Refugee Health and Welfare in and Outside Refugee Settlements and Camps," that covered Uganda and Kenya from April 1997 to February 2000. See Barbara E. Harrell-Bond and Guglielmo Verdirame, "The Enjoyment of Human Rights by Refugees in Uganda: A Socio-Legal Study" (Refugee Studies Centre, University of Oxford, 1998). The results of this research are published in Barbara E. Harrell-Bond, Guglielmo Verdirame, Zachary Lomo, and Hannah Garry, *Rights in Exile: A Janus-Faced Humanitarianism* (Oxford: Berghahn Books, 2005). The author was involved in this research from September 1997 to August 1999 as a legal research officer.

19. UNHCR, Convention and Protocol Relating to the Status of Refugees, Articles 13 (ownership of physical and legal property), 14 (ownership of intellectual property), 18 (engaging in commercial activities), 22 (education), and 24 (labor rights and social security).

20. Government of Uganda, Control of Alien Refugees Act, 1960, 1964 edition, volume 2, section 16.

21. For example, the government of Uganda's Directorate of Refugees has argued with the author in a number of meetings, especially in 1999, 2001, and 2002, that it does not enforce the provisions of the Control of Alien Refugees Act that give settlement commandants the power to take property of refugees and use it for the benefit of the refugee population without due compensation.

22. United Nations General Assembly (UNGA), Universal Declaration of Human Rights (Res/217A [III], December 10, 1948, Article 23(2); UNHCR, *International Covenant on Economic, Social, and Cultural Rights,* 1966 (entered into force January 1976), Article 7; African (Banjul) Charter on Human and Peoples Rights, June 27, 1981 (OAU Doc. CAB/LEG/67/3 rev. 5, 21 I.L.M. 58 [1982], entered into force October 21, 1986), Article 15.

23. Per Mr. William Sakataka, head of the UNHCR Field Office in Adjumani, in a follow-up field trip interview with author in August 1998 in his offices in Adjumani.

24. When the idea of building a senior secondary school on a self-help basis was broached by refugees who were on Barbara Harrell-Bond's research team in early 1983, it was not as a result of our "helpers" (UNHCR et al.) denying equal pay to some Ugandan refugees working with them in order to make them self-reliant. Rather, it was refugees who actually realized that the international assistance paradigm was designed to make them dependent and not independent, which is why the idea of refugee youth building a school for themselves was scoffed at and met with lots of resistance. However, thanks to Barbara Harrell-Bond's action-oriented research we realized our dream of building a school as refugees. I owe my future to that school; I spent fourteen months as a volunteer and was not paid a penny or dime—nor was I threatened by an organization. Refugees are human beings. They dream, philosophize, and are creative.

25. UNHCR, Convention and Protocol, Article 22(1).

26. The Convention on the Rights of the Child came into force on September 2, 1990. Save for Somalia, all the other IGAD member states have ratified the Convention on the Rights of the Child. See United Nations General Assembly (UNGA), Convention on the Rights of the Child (A/RES/44/25), November 20, 1989 (entered into force September 2, 1990).

27. Ibid., Articles 22, 28, and 41.

28. Ibid., Article 2.

29. Ibid., Article 28.

30. United Nations Development Programme, *Human Development Report 2004: Cultural Liberty in Today's Diverse World* (New York: United Nations Development Programme, 2004, electronic version). The figures represent the most recent data. Figures on education for Sudan, Somalia, Djibouti, and Tanzania are not available for 1999 through 2001. Similarly, the figures on military expenditure for Somali and Djibouti for 2002 are not available.

31. InDRA, University of Amsterdam Conference Concept Paper, "Refugees and the Transformation of Society: Loss and Recovery," April 1999.

32. Government of Uganda, Control of Alien Refugees Act, 1960, section 11(a).

33. Government of Tanzania, The Refugees Act, 1998, November 1998, section 17(3)(a)(b)(c).

34. Government of the Sudan, Regulation of Asylum Act 1974, *Democratic Republic of the Sudan Gazette* 1162 (June 15, 1974): 183–186 (available online at http://www.unhcr.ch/cgi-bin/texis/vtx/rsd, accessed March 15, 2005), section 10(2).

35. UNHCR, Convention and Protocol Relating to the Status of Refugees, Article 26.

36. Zachary Lomo, "The Role of Legislation in Promoting 'Recovery': A Critical Analysis of Refugee Law and Policy in Uganda," 1998 (unpublished paper).

37. UNHCR, Convention and Protocol, Article 27.

38. UNHCR, *Personal Protection of Refugees,* Executive Committee Conclusions, no. 72(44)(b), 1993.

39. Assembly of the Heads of State and Government, Agreement Establishing the Inter-Governmental Authority on Development (IGAD/SUM-96/AGRE-Doc), Nairobi, March 21, 1996, Article 13A(o).

40. For example, in an interview in April 2002 with the author in Kampala, Uganda, the UNHCR representative in Uganda, Saidy Saihou, argued that settlements were not only the best way of organizing protection for refugees, but also a cheaper way of organizing repatriation than when refugees were scattered all over the country.

41. See Lucy Hovil, "Refugees and the Security Situation in Adjumani District," Refugee Law Project, Makerere University, Working Paper No. 2. Kampala, Uganda, 2001, p. 10ff.

42. Between April 17 and May 1, 2002, the Refugee Law Project undertook research in the Achol-Pii refugee settlement. The findings made it clear that the camp was still vulnerable to attack and that, given the recent resurgence of the war in northern Uganda, the lives of the refugees and those in the surrounding area were in grave danger; Lucy Hovil and Alex Moorehead, "War as Normal, the Impact of Violence on the Lives of Displaced Communities in Pader District, Northern Uganda," Refugee Law Project, Makerere University, Working Paper No. 5. Kampala, Uganda, June 2002.

43. To say that the refugees were moved is a misrepresentation of what really happened. When the rebels attached in August 2002, refugees simply scattered and thousands walked and found safe haven in the Kiryandongo refugee settlement more than 200 km south of the refugee settlement.

44. For a fair account of what happened in the refugee camps in eastern DRC after the genocide, see, for example, Lawyers Committee for Human Rights, *Refugees, Rebels and the Quest for Justice,* 2002; "The Rwanda Emergency: Causes, Responses, Solutions?" *Journal of Refugees Studies* 9, no. 3 (1996), special edition.

45. For example, Lucy Hovil, "Refugees and the Security Situation."

46. For reasons why humanitarian organizations support policies of camps and settlements, see Barbara Harrell-Bond, "Pitch the Tents," *The New Republic*

(September 19 & 26, 1994): 15–19; Wim Van Damme, "Do Refugees Belong in Camps? Experiences from Goma and Guinea," *The Lancet* 346 (August 5, 1995): 360–363; Médecins Sans Frontières (*MSF*), "Learn More About Shelter," MSF-USA: Refugee Camp Project (available online at http://www.refugeecamp.org/leanmore/shelter/index.htm, accessed March 18, 2005).

47. Article 237 of the Constitution of Uganda vests landownership in the people; however, it allows that state and districts hold some lands in trust for the people. The state and districts can also acquire land for public use. But all these have to be done in accordance with the Land Acquisition Act, which lays down the procedure that government must follow in order to acquire legal interest in any land for public interest (Government of Uganda, The Constitution of the Republic of Uganda, September 22, 1995; "The Land Act," 1998, *Laws of the Republic of Uganda* [revised edition], December 2000, vol. IX, p. 4779).

48. OPM/UNHCR, "Strategy Paper: Self-Reliance for Refugee Hosting Areas in Moyo, Arua, and Adjumani Districts," p. 8.

49. Eric Werker, "Refugees in Kyangwali Settlement: Constraints on Economic Freedom," Refugee Law Project, Makerere University, Working Paper No. 7, Kampala, Uganda, December 2002.

50. Lucy Hovil, "Free to Stay, Free to Go? Movement, Seclusion and Integration of Refugees in Moyo District," Refugee Law Project, Makerere University, Working Paper No. 4, Kampala, Uganda, May 2002.

51. Hans Thoolen, "Report of the Roundtable Conference on the Self-Reliance Strategy for Refugee Hosting Areas in Arua, Moyo, and Adjumani Districts," June 11, 1999, p. 5. Thoolen was the representative of the UNHCR branch office in Kampala, Uganda.

52. Barbara Harrell-Bond's research, which started in April 1997, began to address the question of the long-term strategy of making refugees independent. The attitude of policymakers then was that refugees are a temporary phenomenon and will soon go home. In my own research on refugee rights, carried out in 1995 and 1996, the only strategy known in both UNHCR and the Directorate of Refugees was that settlements are the best way of organizing refugees because they provide refugees with the opportunity to make a new start in life, there are social services like schools and dispensaries, and refugees are protected from clashes with local communities. In addition, the deputy director of the Directorate of Refugees in the Office of the Prime Minister argued that refugees are a threat to national interests and security. No one in UNHCR agreed to talk to me despite several attempts to secure an appointment.

53. These were some of the views expressed by refugees in settlements in northern Uganda during fieldwork in 1998, 2001, and 2002.

54. OPM/UNHCR, "Strategy Paper." It is not surprising that the SRS policy document includes sharing services between refugees and hosts. This was one of the criticisms by Barbara Harrell-Bond of the existing refugee policy in 1997. The main question concerned the establishment of parallel services for refugees in settlements and host communities. Why not develop policies that allow refugees and hosts to share services?

55. Organization of African Unity, Convention Governing the Specific Aspects of Refugee Problems in Africa, September 10, 1969 (electronic version).

56. In Uganda, Deutsche Gesellschaft für Technische Zusammenarbeit (GTZ), a development enterprise of the German government (http://www.gtz.de/en/index.htm), provides technical support to the Directorate of Refugees in the Office of the

Prime Minister (OPM). In one instance, the technical advisor of GTZ at the OPM was angry with the author in a meeting following a demonstration by refugees against what they believed were mismanagement and mistreatment by UNHCR and its implementing partner, Interaid. He accused the project for which the author was working of inciting refugees and creating problems for the government officials dealing with refugees. He stated that the government of Uganda had the best refugee policies he had ever known, far better than those in Europe, including his country, Germany. Despite the fact that Uganda does not have any refugee policy to talk of, this author went ahead and described to him the difference between Uganda's "wonderful" refugee policies and those of Western Europe as follows: Uganda and Africa open their gates, with their chains hidden behind. Once the refugees are in, they are immediately chained forever to live in isolated settlements. They have to depend on the international community for all their basic needs. While Western Europeans close the doors to their countries; they put in dogs and electronic fences. They rigorously vet who gets in and sometimes many refugees are locked up in detention camps. But once they are cleared to be genuinely in need of international protection, then their chains are removed. They walk free, they choose where to live, they are free to go, think, and create. Of course there are those who fall through the system. But I argue that the latter policy is superior.

57. See Van Damme, "Do Refugees Belong in Camps?" p. 360; and Harrell-Bond, "Pitch the Tents," pp. 15–19.

58. In Uganda, in a workshop hastily organized by UNHCR to "beat in line" organizations that provide support to refugees in Kampala, thereby "undermining" the settlement policy, the then-UNHCR representative bluntly retorted that food was being used as a tool to enforce the settlement policy. This was in response to a question I posed to him about cases of refugees who were denied assistance because they refused to go to the settlements, as required by UNHCR and the government.

59. Rene Dumont, *False Start in Africa* (London: Earthscan Publication, 1988).

60. Economic Community of African States, Protocol on the Free Movement of Persons, Right of Residence and Establishment (A/P.1/5/79), May 29, 1979.

61. Usually the parties to the tripartite agreement are the host country, the country of origin, and UNHCR. Presently, refugees are not represented at the meetings of the three official actors and their insights and sensibilities on what a successful repatriation entails are not factored into the resulting tripartite agreement.

4

Kenya's Internally Displaced: Managing Civil Conflict in Democratic Transitions

Jacqueline M. Klopp

After decades of often severe repression, in December 2002, Kenya witnessed the beginning of a historic peaceful change of power through elections. Civil society, street protestors, and reformist politicians, including those within the ruling party, and some donors played a crucial role in this transformation, which constitutes one of the major governance successes in the region. This triumph was all the more striking given that throughout the 1990s, Kenyan president Daniel arap Moi and a hardline faction of his party carried out violent internal displacement (the clashes), threatening to tear Kenya apart.[1] Many Kenyans bore the consequences of this violent strategy to manage political change; approximately 500,000 people were displaced and many thousands killed and maimed.[2]

The legacies of this violence create profound governance challenges for Kenya and draw attention to the need for ongoing advocacy for the internally displaced even after a democratic transition has taken place. Two years after the change in government, more than 350,000 internally displaced people (IDPs) in the country continue to live in poverty and distress.[3] Further, the government has taken only halting steps to address the problems of IDPs, even though a failure in this regard lays the ground for further conflict. Given the even greater challenges faced by the internally displaced in other countries in the region, Kenya's failure to address the plight of its IDPs—even with more democratic rule, a strong international (including UN) presence, and one of the most vibrant civil societies in East Africa—is sobering. If "better governance" (i.e., more transparent and accountable government) promoted through democratization is the long-term solution to the desperate problem of internal displacement, Kenya's failure to improve the conditions of its IDPs or to find long-term solutions to their plight becomes of clear policy concern.

This chapter critically scrutinizes the Kenyan case, aiming to obtain a deeper understanding of potential obstacles to redress for displaced populations in a postconflict, posttransition context and further to explore the implications of these obstacles for the prevention of future violent displacements. After a brief look at the dynamics of displacement in Kenya and the internal resistance and humanitarian response to this violence, this chapter next focuses on the potential and limitations of civil society when confronted with violence and then when faced with IDP resettlement and compensation as a long-term policy issue. Finally, it suggests how international actors can strengthen local advocacy networks of and for the internally displaced. Such advocacy has the potential to deepen Kenya's governance reform in a way that will work to prevent future violence.

Some Theoretical Considerations:
Civil Society, Governance, and Internally Displaced People

Defined broadly as people forced to leave their homes by coercion but who remain within their national borders, IDPs continue to increase across the globe. In the 1970s, an estimated 5 million people were internally displaced; in 2002, the number grew to 25 million.[4] Reflecting serious governance problems on the continent, Africa produces more displaced people than the rest of the world combined—approximately 13.5 million as of 2001.[5] East Africa and the Horn are currently home to approximately 7 million IDPs.[6] As the Kenyan case will highlight, bad government is most often the root cause of this large-scale human tragedy, "with the most repressive governments producing the largest numbers of IDPs."[7] Dismantling despotism through democratization is thus a long-term means to addressing the problem of internal displacement.

Ensuring human security through better governance is one of the stated rationales behind democracy promotion in foreign policy circles in the United States and elsewhere. One cornerstone of this broad democracy promotion agenda over the past decade has been support for civil society, which has largely come to mean associations existing between family and the state that serve to protect society from repression—particularly from the state.[8] This repression stems from what the state does, such as the violence it uses against its own citizens. It also stems from what the state does not do, such as the failure to protect and to provide policies and resources to allow people to, at minimum, subsist. Hence, civil society is most often juxtaposed against a notion of state violence, both direct and structural.

The view of civil society actors as bulwarks against violence, as democracy promoters, and as peace-builders is bolstered by more recent work suggesting that certain forms of local civil society or associational life generate interethnic trust and hence can "constrain the polarizing strategies of political elites" that very often generate ethnicized violence.[9] Trust-generating forms of associational life are currently encouraged, although not always adequately funded, as part of conflict-prevention and peace-building activities. However, as the Kenyan case illustrates, local civil society actors face major limitations when confronted with the organized violence that tends to generate internal displacement. Support for civil society, while important, is not a substitute for international advocacy, which is necessary for protecting both the displaced and those working on their behalf, particularly in the context of state-organized violence.[10]

This may be particularly necessary in transitional moments when the struggle over democratization ensues.[11] Violence may arise in these moments when opposition forces create challenges to the power of authoritarian governments; key government actors may then take advantage of the state's monopoly on the use of force to ensure their survival.[12] In the process, the deliberate use of violence by state actors to derail or manage democratization can fragment and destroy even very closely knit and intermarried communities.[13] Although donors who promote democratization are clearly not directly responsible for such violence, many are hesitant to fully explore the contradictory impacts of their uneven and often incoherent democracy promotion pressures; this also allows avoidance of their responsibilities to those who suffer the consequences of any "backlash."[14]

Violence and Democratization in Kenya: The Background to the Creation of the Internally Displaced Person

The Kenyan case illuminates many of the problems with seeing civil society as an answer to a violence-prone democratization process. Kenya's civil society was very vibrant, but this was not enough to stop the violent displacements that began with the campaign for multiparty politics in the early 1990s and coincided to a large extent with two multiparty elections in 1992 and 1997. However, this does not mean that key civil society actors were not important in resisting the violence, preventing greater polarization in society, and providing relief to the displaced. Further, the networks created at this time formed a template for a local advocacy network in the post-transition period. Before we examine this Kenyan resistance to the clashes, we should take a brief look at the dynamic of displacement.

Like other parts of Africa, by early 1990, Kenya's highly repressive form of single-party rule was experiencing pressure for change. Crowds filled Nairobi's streets and demanded multi-partyism and relief from the stifling repression that had deepened dramatically over the 1980s. Many of the major donors grew increasingly disenchanted with the scale of corruption and were more inclined to support some limited reforms. In November

1991, a group of major donors, including the World Bank, took the unusual step of coordinating their actions, forming the group of like-minded donors. Pending reforms, they suspended US$350 million in nonhumanitarian balance-of-payment support to the Moi government.[15]

To both the external and internal pressures, President Moi acted quickly. By early December 1991, Moi signaled to donors his willingness to introduce *formal* reform; he legalized multi-partyism. When given a choice between formal reforms and an aid reduction, without hesitation the highest levels of the Kenya African National Union (KANU) government chose to introduce competition from other parties. No doubt, this choice stemmed from the calculation that KANU could still win elections as long as the president and his closest ministers had adequate resources to maintain key patronage networks and retain control of state institutions including the monopoly on violence.

The most powerful political opponents of KANU at the time were from among the Kikuyu, Kenya's largest ethnic community. Accounting for roughly 30 percent of the electorate, this potential voting block constituted a serious threat to KANU's hold on power—even with the use of fraud. As a way to counter this threat, KANU hawks argued publicly that under a multiparty system, minority groups needed protection from a feared Kikuyu domination of the state. Part of the "threat" lay in the fact that Kikuyu are found in the Rift Valley, where KANU had its support base. Besides being vectors for opposition ideas, Kikuyu residents represented key swing votes in many "KANU" constituencies.

Beginning in 1991, as a counteroffensive against such "threats," a constellation of members of parliament (MPs) representing KANU, ministers, and local officials associated with the Rift Valley parliamentary representative to the KANU governing council, Nicholas Biwott, launched a new counteroffensive against multiparty advocates. In a series of 1991 rallies in the Rift Valley, KANU stalwarts overtly threatened multiparty proponents with violence. For example, on September 21, 1991, at the Kapkatet rally, MP Paul Chepkok encouraged the audience to "take up arms and destroy dissidents on sight."[16] Cabinet Minister Biwott appealed to Kalenjin pride (the president's and Biwott's ethnic identification) by arguing, "The Kalenjin are not cowards and are not afraid to fight any attempts to relegate them from leadership."[17] Biwott meant, of course, attempts to change the presidency and his own position of influence and power. The rally participants also countered the idea of multi-partyism by painting it as an exclusionary and ethnic project of domination to control land. Ethnicizing the multi-ethnic opposition as Kikuyu and playing on fears of Kikuyu domination in particular, the speakers asserted that all those Kikuyu settled in the Rift Valley would have to pack up and go.[18]

Kenya's first wave of violence came very quickly on the heels of the September rallies. At the end of October 1991, "Kalenjin warriors" began attacks on multiethnic "migrant" families on Meteitei farm in Rift Valley province.[19] These clashes spread to Western and Nyanza provinces, peaking before and after the elections in December 1992 and 1997, and were linked to electoral politics.[20] Indeed, by creating an atmosphere of profound intimidation, displacing and hence disenfranchising voters, and creating "emergency zones," which prevented campaigning, this violence assisted President Moi and KANU's win in 1992 and 1997. For example, in December 1992 the Commonwealth observer group monitoring the election suggested that KANU won sixteen Rift Valley parliamentary seats unopposed, as a result of the violence.[21]

Those who experienced these initial attacks pointed to the rallies as the start of the trouble. Before the parliamentary committee on the clashes, witnesses implicated prominent figures in the government. The witnesses suggested that these government ministers and MPs had incited local people to fight through "utterances urging the Kalenjin to remove *madoadoa* (spots) from the area."[22] Furthermore, they claimed that these politicians transported warriors to the area and paid them for each person killed. These accounts would be repeated and corroborated throughout the decade in human rights reports, parliamentary debates, another government commission, and an independent study by the Law Society of Kenya.[23]

The violent attack on multiethnic communities, first in the Rift Valley, Western, and Nyanza provinces and later on the coast, constituted one of the most decisive and dangerous breaks in Kenya's independence politics. In particular, this violence created a great deal of fragmentation among Kenya's communities[24] and in some cases triggered local civil war dynamics. Despite the fact that the violence was organized from above and carried out by militias and small groups of collaborators at a local level,[25] those communities "represented" by the KANU ministers later would live in fear of collective retribution. An informal survey carried out around Nakuru, one of the epicenters of violence, showed that many clash victims identify their Kalenjin neighbors with the KANU government and thus blame the Kalenjin as a whole for the violence. Interestingly, even while propounding this logic, some clash victims felt that the provincial administration was the one that needed punishment.[26]

Whereas this violence targeted "outsiders" as part of an electoral strategy, it also aimed at policing community boundaries through fear and, in this way, undermining potentially threatening transethnic organizing. There is the tendency to assume that transethnic organizing is rare in Africa. In fact, wheeling and dealing across fuzzy ethnic boundaries has been an essential part of politics on the continent. In a multiparty context, different local factions find alternative parties as national allies in their local struggles. In the process, this draws migrants into national politics, often as important swing voters who need to be courted or, in the multiparty period, "cleansed." Kenya's perpetrators of the ethnic clashes as much wished to minimize dissent within their strongholds by "cleansing" migrant swing voters and potential allies of dissenters "from within" their ethnic fold as they wished to merely get rid of recalcitrant voters.

The victims of Kenya's violence were then expected to "disappear"— if they had resources, they would get absorbed into farming communities where they have relatives; if not, they were to become part of the anonymous poor. By 2004 roughly 350,000 to 600,000 people, approximately one in every sixty Kenyans, continued to suffer from lack of redress for the violent displacement, loss of property and livelihood, but also murder or mutilation of loved ones they experienced during the clashes. The most recent international report on Kenya's IDPs by the Norwegian Refugee Council describes their living conditions as follows:

> The majority of IDPs in Kenya continue to live in urban areas in dire conditions such as streets and informal settlements. Displaced who live in camp-like conditions in schools or church compounds and abandoned buildings lack access to clean water, food and sanitation. Over 70 percent of the heads of households interviewed in the cited UN commissioned report of 2002 were single mothers with up to eight children by different men. These women, in addition to the tremendous burden of putting food on the table for so many children, are often exposed to physical and sexual violence. Coping mechanisms include petty trade, charcoal burning and commercial sex work.[27]

Kenya's IDPs now live on the margins of Kenyan society, in urban slums or tucked away in forests.[28] In essence, they live in deliberately constructed poverty and marginalization.

The Role of Civil Society: The Ethnic Clashes and the Aftermath

Why is the IDP issue not being adequately addressed as part of ongoing democratization efforts in Kenya? To answer this question, we must look at the role of civil society during the clashes and then at what happened in the posttransition period. This section briefly examines the resistance that emerged to the clashes, locates which actors played key roles, and then examines their limitations as a way to understand how the IDP issue would languish as part of the reform agenda.

During the struggle over democratization, as Kenyans were being killed and violently displaced, resistance occurred at the local level, as well as from key civil society organizations, reformers in government, opposition politicians, and the media at the national level.[29] Churches, media, and parliamentarians—those actors which had access to institutionalized rural linkages and "umbrella" organizations in the center—played a particularly significant role. MPs, as political representatives of key constituencies, had a rural base and the platform of parliament to agitate at the national level. Indeed, pushed by reformers in parliament and civil society, the KANU government set up two commissions of inquiry. Both commissions pointed fingers at the perpetrators within the government. At key moments, parliamentarians protested, virtually shutting down the house. Similarly, the press, especially *The Nation* and the *East African Standard,* had representatives throughout the country and the resources to send reporters to cover the violence. These newspapers with national circulation also became a key arena for dissent. The media, in particular *The Nation,* courageously revealed the state's hand in the violence and the plight of the victims. Finally, some church organizations, such as the Catholic Church and the National Council of Churches of Kenya (NCCK), had an extensive rural reach as well as central organization with international linkages. Under dangerous conditions, the Kenya Human Rights Commission, the NCCK, and the Catholic Church documented the nature, dynamics, and human consequences of the violence and—in the case of the church organizations—tried to provide relief. Consequently, it is perhaps not surprising that in Kenya these three groups of actors were some of the first to raise the alarm about the clashes, with the Catholic Church and NCCK initially doing the most to document its dynamics and impact, cater to the displaced, and attempt reconciliation.

The impact of most urban-based civil society organizations favored by donors, however, was much more restricted. Many of the newer Nairobi-based NGOs seen as most emblematic of civil society played a role in this resistance, but not always the key role. Under the auspices of the National Council of NGOs, 120 organizations formed the "Ethnic Clashes Network" in August 1993, helping to document the clashes and assist with creating local capacity for peace-building.[30] One prominent member, the Kenya Human Rights Commission, also played a fundamental role in documenting, analyzing, and publicizing the violence and its cause. However, the older institutions of the Catholic Church and the National Council of Churches of Kenya played more central roles in directly assisting the victims and using their networks to counter government propaganda about the clashes and promote reconciliation.

This suggests the limits of NGOs as civil society actors. Besides the persistent problem of donor dependency, many NGOs lack interethnic rural extension. Despite rapid urbanization, the continent is still primarily rural. Yet NGOs concentrate in urban centers, especially Nairobi. Nevertheless, this "urban bias," a common basis of critique of African civil society, does not preclude numerous interlinkages between urban-based organizations and rural areas.[31] Indeed, a recent survey by Stephen Orvis showed that NGOs in Nairobi were reaching out to rural areas. However, they were doing so "by what many critics and donors would consider 'uncivil' means;

they have used personal, political, ethnic and community networks that almost always involve flows of patronage in rural Africa."[32] One consequence of such narrow network-based activity was that, with the exception of the Kenya Human Rights Commission, during the ethnic clashes it was hard for NGOs to get adequate information about the clashes in regions where they had no personal linkages. Further, some areas like the Kalenjin heartland faced particular repression and were not "covered" by many NGOs. As a result, urban-based NGOs' responses to the clashes were often sporadic and fragmented.

The actual immediate task for taking care of hundreds of thousands of people fell to civil society in the form of local communities and, very critically, key church organizations that had their roots in welfare work in the colonial period. Particularly prominent in these efforts were the NCCK—an umbrella organization of Protestant churches, with a membership of about 6 million—and the Catholic Church. When ethnic clashes started at the end of 1991, victims often fled to church compounds in neighboring parishes or towns as sanctuaries. Marshalling resources and assistance from local communities, many churches took up the responsibility of feeding and sheltering people in their compounds, ferrying people to hospitals in their vehicles, and serving as firsthand witnesses to the violence. Without the role of these churches, no doubt the number of IDP deaths from wounds, malnutrition, and disease in the makeshift camps would have been far greater.[33]

The leadership of these churches also came out as influential critics of the government's role in the violence. For example, in response to the clashes, the NCCK held a special executive committee meeting on January 31, 1992, where they decided to draw national attention to the violence through a countrywide day of prayer for the victims. The organization also set up a mechanism for an investigation of the violence. By March 1992, the NCCK roundly criticized the government, demanding in a press release that "the Government stops forthwith the unnecessary spilling of innocent blood and the wanton destruction of property."[34] Similarly, immediately after the clashes started, the Catholic bishops, Zacheus Okoth, Ndingi Mwana a Nzeki, and Cornelius Korir (respectively from the towns of Kisumu, Nakuru, and Eldoret), demanded government assistance for IDPs, insinuating that the government was complicit in the violence. In a March 1992 pastoral letter of the Catholic bishops they urged reconciliation and assistance for the victims, and they noted that the government had failed in its responsibilities to protect its citizens: "So far only the churches and nongovernmental organizations have taken care of the victims of the clashes."[35]

At the time, few involved in relief thought the violence would persist past the December 1992 election. When the violence continued and even escalated in some areas, and the government by and large obstructed efforts at reconciliation and possible resettlement, the situation became desperate.

For example, in 1993 the NCCK was spending 16 million Kenyan shillings ($200,000) each month just to feed the displaced. One higher-level NCCK official involved in these efforts speculated that the government was in fact eager to keep the churches bogged down in relief efforts draining their resources and keeping them from fighting for political change.[36] As the IDP situation became a chronic condition in Kenya, church activists took an ever more vocal role in promoting the rights of the displaced, including their right to vote. For example, the Catholic church in Mombasa encouraged the displaced to vote, going so far as to rent 600 houses for them to avoid the government harassment at the church compound.[37]

Such work made the government deem relief activities "subversive." Gatherings of IDPs were disrupted and assistance confiscated or blocked. For example, the government took checks for over 200,000 Kenyan shillings ($4,000) collected by the Catholic diocese of Ngong and earmarked for school fees for displaced children, and, in February 1995, food aid from the Naivasha Catholic parish and three opposition MPs was also blocked. One of the most blatant acts, however, stands out: the demolition of the Maela IDP camp by the government on January 1, 1995, and the relocation of IDPs at different sites depending on the place of birth noted on their ID cards. To the consternation of the United Nations Development Programme (UNDP), the government put the costs of the fuel to relocate the displaced on the UNDP account.[38]

From 1993 to 1995, efforts by Kenya's local civil society were supplemented by a UNDP project that sought to facilitate the reintegration and reconciliation of IDPs with the local community and reduce the chance of a resurgence of conflict. However, UNDP is mandated to work through governments, in this case a government responsible for the violence and unwilling to promote reintegration and reconciliation. This unfortunately creates strong disincentives for the UNDP resident coordinator to push for the kind of protection necessary for IDPs and further results in a tendency to downplay state responsibility for violence, giving the government confidence in its own impunity.[39] According to Human Rights Watch, in the Kenyan case, the government in fact "consistently used the UNDP program as a basis for asserting to the international community that the violence had ended and that the situation had been normalized, while continuing to pursue its policy of ethnic persecution."[40]

Initially, the NGO response to UNDP involvement was extremely positive. Kenya's local humanitarian action, while impressive, often suffered from the common problems of NGOs anywhere: lack of coordination, inefficiency, and emphasis on short-term relief without sufficiently strategizing about long-term approaches to the problem.[41] Indeed, the UNDP program did succeed in settling and assisting many IDPs. However, UNDP's "neutrality," in light of government harassment of the displaced and the local civil society actors assisting them, meant that the relationship between UNDP and these actors grew strained. Rather than building on impressive local relief networks, the UNDP program tended to move away from partnerships with local organizations. Worse, according to multiple Kenyan accounts, local structures were "hijacked" and donor funding was funneled through UNDP, undermining local relief efforts.[42]

Under criticism by local and international human rights groups, UNDP eventually pulled out in 1995. Indeed, by this time, most foreign actors left the scene and remaining donors put pressures on the churches and their partner NGOs to move toward resettlement and development activities and away from relief.[43] However, without support from the government to provide security in former clash areas, which clearly was not forthcoming, resettlement became problematic. The activist churches thus moved toward peacebuilding, which was necessary to create enough reconciliation for eventual return of some of the victims or at least to allow some of the victims to use their farms during the day. The NCCK subsequently set up a "Peace and Rehabilitation Programme" in 1992, intensifying this effort throughout the 1990s. From 1996 to 1999, hundreds of "Good Neighbourliness Workshops" were held in an attempt to promote reconciliation. These workshops incorporated local government officials and involved "silent diplomacy" aimed at getting their support for reconciliation and assistance for clash victims.[44] This new focus did not mean that the basic needs of the displaced—food, shelter, schooling, and health care—were being met, and the displaced continue to live in state-constructed poverty.

In brief, the relief to Kenya's hundreds of thousands of displaced that was provided by the NCCK, Catholic diocese, and local NGOs assisted by international organizations—such as ActionAid and the International Committee for the Red Cross—as well as by the UNDP, prevented even greater suffering and death. However, key limitations of civil society emerged when faced with the actual violence, its root causes, and the chronic nature of the displacement. Clearly, without greater international sanction, local civil society could not itself prevent violence that was coordinated and financed by a small clique in power. Indeed, it was only the choice of President Daniel arap Moi to name a Kikuyu and Jomo Kenyatta's son to be his successor that made further largely anti-Kikuyu and antimigrant violence politically unproductive, leading to remarkably peaceful elections in 2002.

Despite these limitations, the courageous resistance by NGOs, especially the churches, at times supported by the press and parliament, not only mitigated the dire circumstances of the displaced but also worked to reveal the perpetrators of the violence. By targeting specific individuals for crimes and not whole communities, this action served to minimize potentially greater polarization within society. It also drew some international attention to the Kenyan government's responsibility for the violence, although the response, particularly by donors, was disappointingly weak.[45] Finally, as we shall see, civil society action generated the template for an internal advocacy campaign for IDPs in the posttransition period, which continues to be their best hope for change. This is especially true in light of the fact that Kenya's IDPs have largely been forgotten within the international community.

Toward a New Advocacy Network: Challenges and Opportunities

Many IDPs and their advocates placed their hopes on a new government, and energies went into the oppositional politics that brought victory to the National Rainbow Coalition (NaRC) in December 2002. However, the IDP issue has languished under the new NaRC government for a number of reasons. First, the National Rainbow Coalition that united numerous parties against Moi decided that to win the election, it was necessary to bring in former KANU players, many of whom were responsible for the clashes. This means that any attempt to bring to justice these players would undermine the fragile coalition holding the government together. This helps explain why the government task force report advocating a Truth, Justice, and Reconciliation Commission has largely been shelved, with the president seeing it as too polarizing.[46] The elevation last year of key perpetrators of the clashes, such as William ole Ntimama, Kipkalia Kones, and Noah arap Too, to cabinet posts reinforces the notion that the government is likely to sacrifice transitional justice for reasons of political expediency. The campaign of Nicholas Biwott for the chair of KANU, the main opposition party, suggests how quickly the ethnic clashes and the IDPs have been rendered invisible among the political class.

A second reason why the government has moved slowly on redress for the internally displaced is that large numbers of IDPs do not wish to return to the former sites of trauma, especially as the lower levels of the administration and neighbors complicit in the violence still live there.[47] This means that redress would involve resettlement, and this in turn means land would have to be found for these landless, something the government, which consists overwhelmingly of landowners, wishes to avoid as an issue. Indeed, it would be very hard to start settling clash victims without addressing the needs of local landless as well. This helps explain how IDPs are not mentioned by name in the National Land Policy Formulation Process Paper guiding how land policy will be transformed[48] and why the minister of lands argued recently that the number of IDPs in Kenya "could not be more than 10,000."[49]

Third, in the posttransition context, the NGOs that were involved in the IDP issue saw their staff, donor funding, and support move out of civil society and into the new government, weakening them just at a time when they needed to rethink their role as they move away from organizing resistance toward more policy and advocacy work. This dynamic was compounded by donor fatigue and forgetting issues relating to the internally displaced. For example, the latest UNDP Country Programme Action Plan, which emphasizes support for "good governance and realization of rights," mentions IDPs only once in the context of an HIV/AIDS program.[50] This forgetting is reinforced by rotations of international staff so that linkages among the UN, donors, and civil society are weakened and institutional memory lost. Finally, the predominantly urban orientation of many NGOs means that clash victims have become invisible—in Nairobi they blend into the wider urban poor whose needs are also urgent or they are tucked away in forests or small towns. As IDPs become backdrops on the political landscape, the press loses interest also, and IDP issues fade from the public dialogue on governance and reform.[51]

Despite these obstacles, Kenya's new political space, won through much struggle, is beginning to be exploited by an incipient IDP advocacy network. At the core of this network are the IDPs themselves assisted by some of the same organizations and actors that resisted the clashes. On June 21, 2003, at St. Mary Pastoral Center in Nakuru, survivors of ethnic violence in Kenya officially launched their network with representatives from eleven different zones in the country and support from the Kenya Human Rights Commission, the NCCK, and the Catholic Peace and Justice Commission. In a statement on September 28, 2003, a representative of the new clash survivor network stated his vision:

> [W]e as survivors of ethnic clashes have resolved to channel our efforts to establish a formidable national network of survivors of ethnic clashes. The network will represent our key organ for articulating matters concerning us. We anticipate that all related government agencies, intergovernmental organizations, religious organizations, development organizations, human rights organizations and other stakeholders, will co-operate with us in our struggle.[52]

In the long run, most IDPs would like to see some form of truth and justice commission as recommended by the government task force. Out of this, they would like to get compensation. Some would like resettlement in their homes; most wish for a piece of land elsewhere. However, in the short term, they are pragmatic as their immediate needs continue to be pressing and basic: "food, clothing, education, health, water and livelihoods."[53]

Besides the usual allies within civil society, Kenya's IDPs have new advocates in government, including parliament, although they currently operate in an ad hoc fashion. This is the silver lining to the brain drain out of civil society. Thus, whereas many in the NaRC government, particularly those implicated in the clashes, would like to suppress or manage the IDP issue, reformers within the government serve as key supporters and sources of information for the incipient IDP advocacy network. One such ally is MP Koigi wa Wamwere, who proposed a motion on "assistance to the ethnic clash victims," sparking debate. On July 23, 2003, the motion narrowly passed.[54] At the time, the minister of state, Office of the Vice-President and Ministry of National Reconstruction, Lina Kilimo, responded in support of the motion and suggested that

> the government is committed to resettle the displaced persons as soon as practicable. However, to do so requires the Government to identify the genuinely displaced persons, to establish the status of the land from where they were evicted and to put the necessary security measures in place to guarantee their personal safety and property.
>
> In cases where the ownership of the land from which they were displaced is in dispute, my Ministry is in liaison with the Ministry of Lands and Settlement. We will identify land for resettlement. Meanwhile, my Ministry is in the process of setting up a committee whose objective will be, one, to study all reports by the Government, Non-Governmental organizations (NGOs) and individuals touching on the tribal land clashes.[55]

However, it is only recently that prodding from MPs from constituencies with large numbers of IDPs, an exposé of the government's inaction in the *East African Standard,* and lobbying by the IDP network and its supporters have pushed the government to react. The president appointed a National Resettlement Committee with some civil society input. Some officials in the Ministry of Lands have also opened their doors to dialogue with IDP representatives, an unprecedented openness.

The problems of resettlement, restitution, and reconciliation for IDPs are complex. In the case of Kenya, the IDP issue intersects in complicated ways with interrelated areas of land and forestry policy. For example, the presence of many IDPs in forests means that new forestry policy that threatens to evict these people, as well as take away their livelihoods as reforesters, has created much suffering and hardship.[56] Further, without a clear and comprehensive approach to the IDP issue nationally, certain evictions may serve to deepen ethnic tensions. For example, on August 28, 2004, Kalenjin clash victims were evicted from Sururu forest by forestry officials. These victims were rendered homeless through revenge attacks by Kikuyu victims of the ethnic clashes in the 1990s and settled by KANU in the forest. Other Kalenjin farmers were settled in nearby Likia and Mauche settlement schemes on land that was formerly owned by Kikuyu farmers vacated by the clashes. After the clash, victims from Sururu forest were evicted; this time around, they stayed on the edge of the forest, next to Kikuyu clash victims and the settlement schemes. The brutal way that the IDPs were evicted with no time to collect their meager property meant that livestock escaped, and accusations of theft by local Kikuyu created tensions in the area. Before the government reacted, four people were killed and more than twenty were injured, several houses were burned, and a hundred women and children took shelter at the local church.[57]

As this case also suggests, it also becomes difficult to address the broader issues of land policy without grappling directly with the victims of displacement. Many of the displaced possessed title deeds—as do some of the beneficiaries and even perpetrators of the violence. As the Kenya Land Alliance notes:

> The failure to resettle the displaced will send a dangerous message to the people regarding the sanctity of title in the country. It could also serve as a precedent for politically instigated ethnic evictions in other parts of the country. The potential for civil war cannot be ruled out if such phenomena were to spread countrywide.[58]

Given the present circumstances, it may be difficult to push for the punishment of the perpetrators of the clashes. However, official forgetting only deepens the sense of impunity and leaves many long-standing tensions to fester, providing fertile ground for a recurrence of clashes especially as elections approach.

The Sururu case also suggests that one of the key areas of contention will be the issue of who is a "genuinely displaced person." Initially, even high-ranking Kikuyu political figures suggested that the Sururu victims could not be IDPs based simply on the fact that they were Kalenjin. To further cloud the picture, the beneficiaries of the largest pieces of land in Sururu forest were allocated not to IDPs, but rather to the politically connected, including clash perpetrators. This reflects the general problem that settlement schemes throughout Kenya's history have been sources of patronage, and often the poorest of the poor have fallen through the cracks. Thus, should the NaRC government decide to resettle IDPs, given the land pressures, the government may also wish to reduce the numbers to be settled by creating difficult criteria (e.g., complete documentation, title deeds) that many victims—some displaced multiple times—will be unable to provide. Indeed, in the past, in places where clash victims were given temporary allocations, many victims were left out. Here are the very relevant observations by the late Father Kaiser of the vetting process of Enoosupukia clash victims in Maela:

> None of the members of the committee was chosen by the refugees and I did not think any of them would have been able to stand up to [the District Officer] Mr. Hassan, if ever that became necessary. The committee had no representation from the churches, NGOs or even UNDP.
> It took Mr. Hassan and his team about three weeks to finish their first registration, and because no systematic order of interviewing was followed,

the registration exercise was seriously flawed and caused great suffering. I know of many Enoosupukia displaced people, including some old women, who walked from Ngondi to Maela (a ten-kilometre distance) daily for three weeks in the hope of being registered. Many of them were never interviewed.

I knew many of the displaced people from Enoosupukia who possessed legal documents as proof of land ownership but were not registered during this exercise. I also knew of some wealthy people from Kongoni and Naivasha who had never lived in Enoosupukia but were nonetheless interviewed.[59]

This means that should the NaRC government go ahead with a resettlement process, the clash victim network and its civil society allies will have to maintain steady pressure and vigilance.

Dealing with the IDP issue in a fair and comprehensive manner will thus require ongoing support from the many stakeholders. This is because of the tremendous political and policy complexity of the issue. Contributing substantially to this complexity is not only the presence of clash perpetrators in high-level positions in government, but also the many categories of victims:

1. Some victims had land to flee to or had savings accounts that allowed them to resettle elsewhere in Kenya. They are still victims and deserve consideration.
2. Other victims were landowners in possession of title deeds for their land.
3. Still other victims were in settlement schemes and had paid for their land but had never received title deeds because of problems in the administration or had not quite finished payments.
4. Many victims were tenants, engaged in informal leasehold agreements. They hold no paper evidence of these agreements. Nevertheless, they lost people, property, and livelihood and still deserve to be settled.
5. Some of the poorest victims were in fact planting trees in forests in return for access to land for cultivation and were evicted through the clashes.
6. Many are pastoralists who did not own land but lost cattle.
7. Most are children, including orphans; many lost educational opportunities, which means that their future opportunities for a decent life were destroyed.
8. Some families had loved ones killed and deserve compensation.

Whether these many and diverse victims, as part of an inclusive advocacy network, will be able to push for an amelioration of their plight and some form of compensation and reconciliation within Kenyan society remains to be seen. Nevertheless, to a large extent whether they succeed or fail will determine the extent to which "good governance" will be entrenched, creating strong disincentives for the use of displacement as political strategy in the future. What is clear is that much will hinge on the strength and strategies of civil society—with allies in the government, the press, and the international community.

Conclusion and Policy Recommendations

The former Special Representative of the United Nations Secretary-General for IDPs, Francis Deng, suggests, and the Kenyan case confirms, "Displacement is only a symptom of deeper causes, reflected in conflicts, communal violence, human rights violations and human-made disasters."[60] This means the problem of preventing displacement and caring for existing IDPs is a profoundly challenging governance problem. Deng has worked hard to push for more international recognition of this problem, including adoption of the Guiding Principles on Internal Displacement. However, the key dilemma for advocates for the displaced is that according to international law, national governments have the ultimate responsibility over the dislocated. Yet, as we have seen in the Kenyan case, the government often has a hand in the violence that caused the displacement in the first place. In light of this policy conundrum, too often what occurs is official forgetting, and as in Kenya, the displaced "disappear" and are reimagined as the poor without history.

Tragically, this chapter has shown, a shift to more democratic government is often when international and local attention to the IDP problem fades. This is in part because it is often wrongly expected that the new government will take responsibility for the plight of its dislocated citizens. Yet the Kenyan case shows that IDPs require continuing protection instead of neglect.[61] The policy challenge is to sustain and adapt IDP advocacy under these new and potentially hopeful conditions.

IDP advocates need to develop creative strategies to combat forgetting and prevent the loss of opportunities opened by democratic change. Some of these strategies might be:

- Support IDPs' efforts at self-organization by helping them to build the capacity to create and monitor registries and lobby interested parties in parliament and the press. As part of this initiative the Guiding Principles on Internal Displacement should be more widely disseminated. More donor resources need to go to those key civil society organizations that participate in these efforts, and these organizations should be involved in genuine partnerships with UNDP, UNHCR, and OCHA.

- Develop institutionalized networks for information flow to assist in documentation of ongoing IDP conditions and actions. This can also serve as an early-warning mechanism for further problems such as in the Sururu forest case, where the IDP coordinator for the region warned of potential violence, but was largely ignored until after people were killed.[62]
- Make IDPs an explicit category for development planning, particularly in the eastern African and Horn countries that have large numbers of IDPs. This would be a nonconfrontational way to keep the concerns of IDPs on the agenda over time and to push for integration of peacebuilding and development efforts.
- Treat government policy and action toward IDPs, including adoption of the guiding principles, as a key indicator of better governance, at both national and regional levels, rather than ignore it in most governance assistance programs, as is currently the case.[63]
- Given the complexity of the IDP issue and its intersection with forestry and land policy, provide support for policy capacity-building at both the civil society and government levels, starting with those who have distinguished themselves as advocates for IDPs. One aim of these efforts would be to build better links between government and the policy and advocacy communities on IDP issues.

After some disorientation following the transition, signs are that Kenya's civil society, with key new allies in government, is using hard-won political space and rising to the challenge of creating an advocacy campaign. This organizing deserves far more international support, for if Kenya, with a new more reform-oriented government, freedom of expression, relatively strong civil society, and a large international presence, cannot adequately address the legacy of internal displacement and prevent its future occurrence, which country in the region can?

Notes

1. Ahmednasir Abdullahi, "Ethnic Clashes, Displaced Persons and the Potential for Refugee Creation in Kenya: A Forbidding Forecast," *International Journal of Refugee Law* 9, no. 2 (1997): 196–206.

2. These figures are estimates and most likely are lower bounds. Numbers of displaced are derived from the following sources: Human Rights Watch (HRW), *Divide and Rule: State Sponsored Ethnic Violence in Kenya* (New York: HRW, 1993), p. 1; African Rights, "Violence at the Coast: The Human Consequences of Kenya's Crumbling Political Institutions," *Witness* 2 (October/November 1997); and press reports on the 1998 violence. According to the Kenya Human Rights Commission (KHRC), approximately 15,000 people died in the clashes through direct

violence: *Killing the Vote: State Sponsored Violence and Flawed Elections in Kenya* (Nairobi: KHRC, 1998).

3. The figures on IDPs vary, but a recent report cites 350,000: United Nations Office for the Coordination of Humanitarian Affairs (OCHA), *Affected Populations in the Horn of Africa* (Nairobi: OCHA Regional Support Office for Central and East Africa, December 2004), p. 2. There are probably many more IDPs—clash victims from pastoral areas and urban violence are often not counted. A recent survey found that at least 164,457 people have been displaced in northern Kenya, 70 percent of these being women and children below fourteen years of age: Intermediate Technology Development Group (ITDG), *Conflict in Northern Kenya: A Focus on Internally Displaced* (Nairobi: ITDG, 2003).

4. Norwegian Refugee Council, *Internally Displaced People: A Global Survey* (London: Earthscan Publications, 2002), p. 4.

5. Ibid., p. 4.

6. Current figures are: Ethiopia 150,000, Eritrea 62,000, Kenya 350,000, Somalia 377,000, Sudan 6,000,000. See OCHA, *Affected Populations,* p. 2. Uganda numbers nearly 1.7 million (OCHA, Uganda: 2005 Mid-Year Review, June 29, 2005, electronic version), p. 1. Tanzania is the only country in the region without IDPs.

7. Makau wa Mutua, "The Interaction Between Human Rights, Democracy and Governance and the Displacement of Populations," *International Journal of Refugee Law* (July 1995/Special Issue), p. 42. Of course, displacement can be caused by natural disasters and development projects, but the vast majority of IDPs are linked to internal violence: Roberta Cohen and Francis Deng, *Masses in Flight: The Global Crisis of Displacement* (Washington: Brookings Institute, 1998), p. 3.

8. Lively debates exist about how to define civil society: David Lewis, "Civil Society in African Contexts: Reflections on the Usefulness of a Concept," *Development and Change* 33, no. 4 (2002): 569–586; Thomas Carothers and Marina Ottaway, eds., *Funding Virtue: Civil Society and Democracy Promotion* (Washington, DC: Carnegie Endowment for International Peace, 2000).

9. Ashutosh Varshney, *Ethnic Conflict and Civil Life* (New Haven and London: Yale University Press, 2002), p. 4. Varshney's work should be compared to Lauren Morris MacLean, "Mediating Ethnic Conflict at the Grassroots: The Role of Local Associational Life in Shaping Political Values in Côte d'Ivoire and Ghana," *Journal of Modern African Studies* 42, no. 2 (2004): 589–617.

10. Simon Bagshaw and Diane Paul, "Protect or Neglect? Toward a More Effective United Nations Approach to the Protection of Internally Displaced Persons," Brookings—SAIS Project on Internal Displacement and United Nations Office for the Coordination of Humanitarian Affairs (OCHA), November 2004.

11. Some of the recent works arguing this include Amy Chua, *World on Fire: How Exporting Free Market Democracy Breeds Ethnic Hatred and Global Instability* (New York: Random House, 2003); Demet Yalcin Mousseau, "Democratizing with Ethnic Divisions: A Source of Conflict?" *Journal of Peace Research* 38, no. 5 (2001): 547–567; Jack Snyder, *From Voting to Violence: Democratization and Nationalist Conflict* (New York and London: W.W. Norton, 2000); Fareed Zakaria, *The Future of Freedom* (New York and London: W.W. Norton, 2003); Michael Mann, *The Dark Side of Democracy: Explaining Ethnic Cleansing* (Cambridge: Cambridge University Press, 2005).

12. On political liberalization, democratization, and violence: Jacqueline M. Klopp and Elke Zuern, "The Politics of Violence in Democratization," paper presented to the seminar on contentious politics, Columbia University, 2003; Peter Uvin, "Ethnicity and Power in Burundi and Rwanda: Different Paths to Mass Violence," *Comparative Politics* 31, no. 3 (1999): 253–272.

13. V. P. Gagnon, *The Myth of Ethnic War* (Ithaca, NY: Cornell University Press, 2004).

14. The most trenchant critique in this regard is Peter Uvin, *Aiding Violence: The Development Enterprise in Rwanda* (West Hartford, CT: Kumarian Press, 1998).

15. On the donor interventions: Stephen Brown, "Authoritarian Leaders and Multiparty Elections in Africa: How Foreign Donors Help to Keep Kenya's Daniel arap Moi in Power," *Third World Quarterly* 22 (October 2001): 725–739; Samantha Gibson, "Aid and Politics in Malawi and Kenya: Political Conditionality and Donor Support to the 'Human Rights, Democracy and Governance' Sector," in *Common Security and Civil Society in Africa,* eds. Lennart Wohlgemuth, Samantha Gibson, Stephan Klasen, and Emma Rothchild (Uppsala: Nordiska Afrikainstitutet, 1999).

16. "Klenjin Solidarity," *Weekly Review,* 27 September 1991, p. 6.

17. Ibid.

18. On the historical roots of the idea of "Kikuyu domination": E. S. Atieno-Odhiambo, "Hegemonic Enterprises and Instrumentalities of Survival: Ethnicity and Democracy in Kenya," in *Ethnicity and Democracy in Africa,* eds. Bruce Berman, Dickson Eyoh, and Will Kymlicka (Oxford: James Currey, 2004).

19. The key instigator of the Meteitei violence was Henry Kosgey, minister of tourism and wildlife at the time, along with other KANU officials. See Government of Kenya, *Report of the Parliamentary Select Committee to Investigate the Ethnic Clashes in Western and Other Parts of Kenya* (Nairobi: Government Printer, 1992).

20. For more details: Claire Médard, "Les Conflits 'Ethniques' au Kenya: Une Question de Votes ou de Terres?" *Afrique Contemporaine* no. 180 (October/December 1996): 62–74; Claire Médard, "Dispositifs Electoraux et Violences Ethniques: Réflexions sur Quelques Strategies Territoriales de Régime Kényan," *Politique Africaine* 70 (June 1998): 32–39; Jacqueline M. Klopp, "Ethnic Clashes and Winning Elections: The Kenyan Case of Electoral Despotism," *Canadian Journal of African Studies* 35, no. 2 (2001): 473–517.

21. Commonwealth Observer Group, "The Presidential Parliamentary and Civic Elections in Kenya" (London: Commonwealth Secretariat, 1993), p. 18.

22. Government of Kenya, *Report of the Parliamentary Select Committee,* p. 51.

23. Human Rights Watch, *Divide and Rule: State Sponsored Ethnic Violence in Kenya* (New York: HRW, 1993); Kenya Human Rights Commission, *Ours by Right, Theirs by Might* (Nairobi: KHRC, 1996) and *Killing the Vote* (Nairobi: KHRC, 1998); Law Society of Kenya (LSK), *Impunity Report of the Law Society of Kenya on the Judicial Commission of Inquiry into Ethnic Clashes in Kenya* (Nairobi: LSK, 2000).

24. John Rogge, *The Internally Displaced Population in Kenya, Western and Rift Valley Provinces: A Need Assessment and a Program Proposal for Rehabilitation,* report prepared for UNDP, Nairobi (October 1993).

25. Francis Gitaari of the Nakuru Catholic Diocese collected affidavits from military personnel who were recruited to participate in the clashes as part of the evidence prepared by the Nakuru Diocese for the Akiwumi Commission of Ethnic Clashes, but was not allowed to present them.

26. I am grateful to Romulus Okoth and Keffa Magenyi Karuoya for their assistance with this. Interviews were also carried out by the author in Nakuru in October 2000.

27. Global IDP Project, "Kenya: Tensions Rise as Government Fails to Address Internal Displacement," Norwegian Refugee Council (November 30, 2004). Other documents describing the conditions of IDPs include Norwegian Refugee Council, *Profile of Internal Displacement: Kenya* (October 6, 2003), pp. 7–8; Prisca Kamungi, "The Current Situation of Internally Displaced Persons in Kenya" (Jesuit Refugee Service, March 2001); UN Development Fund for Women (UNIFEM), *The Lives and*

Life-Choices of Dispossessed Women in Kenya, African Women in Crisis Programme (January 2002); and OCHA, *Kenya's Internally Displaced Persons: Numbers and Challenges,* Department of Disaster Prevention, Management and Coordination Unit (December 2002).

28. For example, a group of 867 IDPs have been living in Kyeni forest outside of Thika, where the author visited them in July 2004. They have survived until now on relief food; since 2000 they have no longer been allowed to plant trees in exchange for access to land for cultivating ("the shamba system") and are living in deplorable conditions. Forests have traditionally been places of last resort for the poor, including in recent times for the IDPs in Kenya. Unfortunately, new laws to protect forests may in fact deepen the plight of IDPs in Kenya.

29. See cases highlighted in Jacqueline Klopp, *Electoral Despotism in Kenya: Land, Patronage and Resistance in the Multi-Party Context,* Ph.D. thesis for the Department of Political Science, McGill University (January 2001).

30. National Council of Churches of Kenya (NCCK), *Cursed Arrow: A Report of Organized Violence Against Democratic Kenya* (Nairobi: NCCK, 1992) and *Deception, Dispersal and Abandonment* (Nairobi: NCCK, 1995). The NCCK also put out a monthly newsletter called *Clashes Updates,* which provided important information on what was happening in different parts of the country.

31. Celestin Monga, *The Anthropology of Anger* (Boulder: Lynne Rienner, 1996), pp. 27–29.

32. Stephen Orvis, "Kenyan Civil Society: Bridging the Urban-Rural Divide," *Journal of Modern African Studies* 41, no. 2 (2003): 266.

33. Many children and elderly did die as a result of worsened health conditions linked to displacement. See the excellent study by Francis Lelo, *A Report on the Health/Medical Needs Assessment of Olenguruone Parish* (The Catholic Diocese of Nakuru, 1996).

34. NCCK Press Release, February 12, 1992. For the results of the investigation: NCCK, *Cursed Arrow.*

35. Pastoral Letter of the Catholic Bishops of Kenya, *A Call to Justice, Love and Reconciliation* (Nairobi: St. Paul Publications, 1992), p. 5.

36. Author interview with Rev. Murimi, Catholic Diocese of Nakuru (Nakuru, October 26, 2000). The Catholic Church and NCCK were heavily involved in the constitutional reform movement.

37. Peter Mwangi Kagwanja, "Strengthening Local Relief Capacity in Kenya: Challenges and Prospects," in *Eroding Local Capacity: International Humanitarian Action in Africa,* eds. Monica Kathina Juma and Astri Suhrke (Uppsala: Nordiska Afrikain Institutet, 2002), p. 108.

38. Akiwumi Commission evidence prepared by Francis Gitari, Nakuru Catholic Diocese. On the Maela incident: Klopp, "Ethnic Clashes." For firsthand accounts of the Maela incident: John Anthony Kaiser, *If I Die* (Nairobi: Cana Publishing, 2003). Father Kaiser was an American advocate for the internally displaced who was found dead with a bullet in his head August 24, 2000. Most believe he was killed for confronting powerful perpetrators of the clashes.

39. Cohen and Deng, *Masses in Flight,* p. 134.

40. Human Rights Watch, *Kenya: Old Habits Die Hard* (New York: HRW, 1995), p. 5. For additional critiques of the UNDP project see Human Rights Watch, *Failing the Internally Displaced: The UNDP Displaced Persons Program in Kenya* (New York: HRW, 1997) and Binafer Nowrojee, "UN and African Regional Responsibility to Provide Human Rights Protection to the Internally Displaced: Learning Lessons from the Experience of UNDP in Kenya," *Refugee Survey Quarterly* 18, no. 1 (1999).

41. Kagwanja, "Strengthening Local Relief Capacity in Kenya," p. 109; Robert Shaw and Wamuyu Gatheru, eds., *Our Problems, Our Solutions: An Economic and Public Policy Agenda for Kenya* (Nairobi: Institute of Economic Affairs, 1998), p. 291; Monica Kathina Juma, *Unveiling Women as Pillars of Peace: Peace-Building in Communities Fractured by Conflict in Kenya,* An Interim Report for the Management Development and Governance Division, Bureau for Development Policy, UNDP (2000).

42. Kagwanja, "Strengthening Local Relief Capacity in Kenya," p. 118; Juma, *Unveiling Women as Pillars of Peace.*

43. Juma, *Unveiling Women as Pillars of Peace,* p. 38.

44. Interview with NCCK Peace and Reconciliation Coordinator for Nakuru, Labon Korellach, Nakuru, October 25, 2000.

45. Donor response was disappointing—aid was cut off only for financial improprieties. It was rarely used as a leverage to protect the hundreds of thousands of victims of Kenya's state-organized violence. Stephen Brown, "Quiet Diplomacy and Recurring 'Ethnic Clashes' in Kenya," in *From Promise to Practice: Strengthening UN Capacities for Prevention of Violent Conflict,* eds. Chandra Lekha Sriram and Karin Wermester (Boulder: Lynne Rienner, 2003), pp. 69–100.

46. Government of Kenya, *The Task Force on Truth, Justice and Reconciliation* (Nairobi: Government Printers, 2003). The president's position was communicated to me through an unattributable interview with a cabinet minister, who had discussed the issue directly with him, Nairobi (July 2004).

47. Discussions with IDPs at NCCK in Nakuru, July 9, 2004. Similar findings came out of Kenya Human Rights Commission consultations with IDPs in different parts of the country.

48. Government of Kenya, Ministry of Lands, *National Land Policy Formulation Process* (Nairobi: Ministry of Lands, March 2004). Vague reference is made to redress of historical injustices more generally.

49. Dauti Kahura, "Kimunya: Internally Displaced Opportunists," *East African Standard* (Nairobi: September 11, 2004).

50. United Nations Development Programme and Government of Kenya, *Country Programme Action Plan 2004–2008* (Nairobi: UNDP), p. 32. The brief mention of IDPs is on page 35.

51. For an exception: *East African Standard,* Special Reports on IDPs (Nairobi, September 12, 2004). This was the result of active lobbying on the part of IDP advocates. These reports include "Revenge Mission Fanned the Flames of Ethnic War: Displaced Six Times in 30 Years"; "Huruma Residents Are the Picture of Disillusionment"; "Fourteen Years Later, It's a Hard Life in the Cold"; "Rift Valley MPs Seek Justice for Clashes Victims"; "Reprieve for Squatters as Forest Ban Lifted"; "Kimunya: Internally Displaced Opportunists; It's a Tough Life for the Displaced."

52. Cyrus Oyugi, Samuel King'ori, Mohamed Tabia, Keffa Magenyi, Irene Wambui, and Ndung'u Wainaina, "A Joint Statement by Survivors of Ethnic Clashes," A Preparatory Conference to Precede the Launch of a National Survivors Network for the Internally Displaced Persons (IDPs) in Kenya (Kasarani, Kenya, September 26–28, 2003) (available online at http://www.db.idpproject.org/Sites/idpSurvey.nsf/16F3E57093335B82c1256F4E0053A0EB/$file/IDPs+National++Conference+Report++Sept++2003.doc), p. 22.

53. Oyugi et al., "A Joint Statement by Survivors of Ethnic Clashes."

54. *Hansard,* Parliamentary Debates, July 30, 2003, p. 2496.

55. Ibid., pp. 2499–2500.

56. In Kenya, the colonial "shamba system" has worked quite well as a cost-effective way to do reforestation. Poor people are given access to forest land to

cultivate in exchange for planting trees. According to environmental organizations, such as the Forest Action Network and the Kenya Forests Working Group, this is a good system. The problem was violation of rules as a result of corruption in the Forestry Department. As a stopgap measure, reinstatement of the shamba system is one way to provide support for some of the poorest clash victims. See "Another Blow to Land Clash Victims," *The Nation* (Nairobi), May 31, 2004, and Government of Kenya, Ministry of Lands, *National Land Policy Formulation Process*.

57. Keffa Koruoya Magenyi, "Situational Likia Mau Narok Clashes," IDP Coordinator, Subukia Zone, October 5, 2004 (unpublished memorandum).

58. Kenya Land Alliance, *The National Land Policy in Kenya* (Nairobi: KLA, 2004), p. 9.

59. Kaiser, *If I Die,* pp. 50–51.

60. Francis Deng, Opening Statement by the Representative of the UN Secretary-General on Internally Displaced Persons (UNSG/IDP), International Symposium on the Mandate of the UNSG/IDP Vienna (December 12–13, 2002).

61. See Bagshaw and Paul, *Protect or Neglect?* This chapter reinforces the broad recommendations in this report.

62. This is also recommended in *Protect or Neglect* (2002), p. 60.

63. This recommendation came out of civil society consultations facilitated by the International Peace Academy in Nairobi, June 21–22, 2004. Jacqueline M. Klopp, "Civil Society and the State: Partnerships for Peace in the Great Lakes Region" (New York: International Peace Academy, June 2004).

5

Nationalism and Identity in Ethiopia and Eritrea: Building Multiethnic States

Dominique Jacquin-Berdal and Aida Mengistu

Ever since the early 1960s, nationalism has figured critically in the politics and international relations of the Horn of Africa; regimes have toppled under its impact, boundaries have been challenged on its behalf, and states have emerged in its name. Consider the fall of Mengistu in 1991 at the hands of an ethnically defined coalition, or Somalia's former irredentist campaigns that culminated in the 1977–1978 Ogaden war against Ethiopia, or Eritrea's thirty-year-long struggle for independence, all carried out under the banner of nationalism. Even during the events that preceded and followed the 1974 revolution, nationalism, or the "nationalities question" as it was then known, figured prominently. And, while it may not have directly contributed to the outbreak of the 1998–2000 war between Ethiopia and Eritrea, nationalism undoubtedly played a significant role as the conflict unfolded.

Yet, however conspicuous nationalism may be, as the aforementioned examples illustrate, its meaning and consequences for the Horn of Africa are far from unambiguous. This should come as no great surprise to students of nationalism, accustomed as they are to the unending debates that have marked this field of inquiry. Defined by Ernest Gellner as "primarily a political principle, which holds that the political and the national unit should be congruent,"[1] nationalism must also be understood as a cultural phenomenon capable of inducing a powerful sense of belonging.[2] But while the majority of scholars on nationalism would accept nationalism as a modern phenomenon whose origins can be traced back to eighteenth-century Europe, disagreement arises as to how the nation ought to be defined and how it has come about. A number of scholars, frequently grouped under the modernist-instrumentalist label, argue that nations are creations or inventions, the result of relatively recent historical forces that are ideological, socioeconomic, or political and whose origins are intrinsically bound to the modern state. John Markakis follows this line of thought and argues that in the context of the Horn of Africa, contestations in the language of national- ism and ethnicity were driven by the desire to obtain and use state power.[3] Although for some, education and literacy may be powerful ingredients in shaping the nation, war is for others the main catalyst toward nation forma- tion, thereby characterizing the relation between nationalism and war as not merely one of cause and effect. Whichever factors they may privilege, most modernists would no doubt agree with Gellner when he writes that "nation- alism sometimes takes pre-existing cultures and turns them into nations, sometimes invents them, and often obliterates pre-existing cultures."[4] Less certain is the extent to which they would endorse his claim that "it is nation- alism which engenders nations, and not the other way round."[5]

For another group of scholars, only nations rooted in premodern ethnic identities and traditions will have any long-term prospects and can thus be considered "true nations." This position is best defended by Walker Connor and Anthony Smith for whom the ethnic community's main attributes include a collective proper name, a myth about common origin, common historical memories, a level of common culture, an attachment to a specific territory, and a feeling of solidarity among a significant part of the population.[6] Though nations and nationalism are, they agree, modern, they cannot explain the loyalty and sense of belonging they inspire—modernity is deemed to have constructed them ex nihilo. They must, if they are to have any emotional resonance, be grounded or founded upon an *ethnic substratum* that will pro- vide them with the prerequisite myths, memories, values, and symbols.

Informed by the literature on nationalism and identity formation, this chapter analyzes the ways nationalism and identity have played out in Ethiopia and Eritrea, where struggles over economic and political factors often take the form of ethnic conflict.[7] It examines specifically how Ethiopia and Eritrea have sought to foster a sense of national identity that centers on the state and the challenges they still face in this process. Clearly, national- ism and conflict are intrinsically bound. Yet, however disruptive a force it may have been in the recent history of the Horn, it seems indisputable today that any long-lasting solutions to the region's ongoing conflicts must incor- porate the issue of nationalism and national identities within a democratic framework, rather than avoid or suppress them as in the past. Elucidating the meaning and consequences of nationalism would therefore seem like a log- ical first step toward any attempt to achieve peace in the region.

Ethiopia

The "nationalities question" has been at the center of the Ethiopian conflict for many years. And as illustrated by the publication of Walleligne Makon- nen's article in November 1969 and the reactions it prompted, the issue is closely linked to controversies regarding the legitimacy of those in power and their policies.[8] In the history of modern Ethiopia, there have been three major attempts at creating national identity to forge unity and maintain the power of the state. Emperor Haile Selassie and the military government of Mengistu Haile Mariam used the central power of the state to forge nationalism. Haile Selassie used it to equate the Ethiopian nation to the Amhara identity, whereas Mengistu used it to advance the communist ideology. Although Mengistu's regime initially conceded to grant, at least nominally, a right of self-determination to all nationalities, it eventually reverted to a policy not all that dissimilar from that of its predecessor. The failure of these regimes to deal with the "nationalities question" eventually led to their demise. Seeking to avoid a similar fate, but informed also by the particular experience of the Tigray People's Liberation Front (TPLF), the current government of Ethiopia introduced ethnic federalism based on increased regional autonomy.

Under the present regime, although government intended to address the "nationalities question" through a federal system based on ethnicity, this system has introduced a set of problems whose resolution could become the focal point for cooperation between the ethnic political parties. The effects of the policy of ethnic rationalization have been profound. Administrative structures have been left to the regions, including the judicial system, as have all powers of government outside those national prerogatives of defense and foreign relations. To have a better understanding of the challenges faced by the current government to stabilize the country, one must go back in time and analyze nationalism in modern Ethiopia.

Ethiopia comprises numerous ethnicities encompassing more than eighty language groups. The Oromo constitute the largest language group and span more than half the country's territory. The Amhara, traditionally the cultural and political elite, are the second largest, and the Tigrigna the third. Ethnic Somalis, also found in Djibouti and Somalia, and Afars, who also live in Djibouti and Eritrea, command strategic, if not numerical, importance because they live in border areas that have been a source of international conflict. Amharic and Tigrigna, both of which are derived from the ancient Ge'ez, as well as Oromo and Somali are the four main languages of Ethiopia and are spoken by two-thirds of the population. Approximately 40 percent of the people identify themselves as either Ethiopian Orthodox Christian or Muslim whereas 60 percent are Protestant, Roman Catholic, or followers of traditional religions.

Within the context of this complex composition of nationalities, three events stand out as particularly significant in terms of providing the building blocks for Ethiopia's national identity based on one common cultural identity, prior to the current government's attempt to accommodate the different ethnic nationalities, while maintaining stability:

- Haile Selassie's rule consolidated the power of the centralized state initiated by Menelik II. He fostered unity through the development of a national army, a pan-Ethiopian economy, modern education and communications, and an official culture whose main features were the promotion of the Coptic Orthodox Church as a national church and Amharic as the official language in government and education.
- Mengistu's military dictatorship continued to maintain the compulsory ethnic harmony under a powerful centralized state and adopted a socialist ideology that disregarded the reality of the country's ethnic diversity to foster a national identity. This diversity was to be subsumed through the mobilization of the proletariat across ethnic nationalities to form one communist state.
- To contrast sharply with the centrist policies of Haile Selassie's and Mengistu's eras, Meles Zenawi's current government attempted to address the "nationalities question" and devised an ethnic federation that gave relative autonomy (at least on paper) to ethnic-based regions. In the absence of a clear unifying ideology, economic growth, and internal stability, the war with Eritrea from May 1998 to December 2000 created a common sense of nationality, helping the government to keep the country together and to retain its power.

The Creation of the Modern State

Ethiopia was constructed as a nation-state between the mid-nineteenth and early twentieth centuries by succeeding emperors. Some of the well-known kings include Emperor Tewodros II of Gondar, who governed from 1855 to 1868 and consolidated control over the Highland area; Yohannes IV, who governed from 1872 to 1889; and Menelik II (1889–1913), who established the main territorial features of present-day Ethiopia by expanding his empire to the south and east through conquest and diplomacy. His successful defense of this territory against an Italian invasion and his victory at Adowa in 1896[9] further consolidated the national and international status of the Ethiopian nation-state. Menelik II later cooperated with the British in a series of military engagements that allowed him to gain and strengthen his control of the Ogaden region, inhabited primarily by ethnic Somalis. However, it was under the imperial rule of Haile Selassie that Ethiopia became a modern nation-state.

The beginning of the twentieth century introduced vital institutions for economic and political development that were completely lacking in the nineteenth century.[10] Emperor Haile Selassie ruled Ethiopia from 1930 until 1974, a period during which most modern economic and some political institutions had arrived in Ethiopia. The emperor's government was highly centered on the emperor himself. Land distribution was highly skewed—the royal family, for instance, owned between 50 percent and 60 percent of all land, and less than 1 percent of the population controlled 70 percent of the land. In addition to the royal family, the main wealth holders included the Ethiopian Orthodox Church as well as senior military officers and civil servants.[11]

Historically, the Semitic Amhara and Tigre people of the northern highlands of Ethiopia have dominated political life in the region. Between 1941 and 1974, Emperor Haile Selassie attempted to promote an Ethiopian entity and discouraged aspirations of the different nationalities within the empire. To use Ernest Gellner's analogy, Haile Selassie attempted to create a standardized culture with the use of the press, education, and the support of the Orthodox Church. Amharic and Amhara culture became the essential attributes of being Ethiopian. As a result, peoples of the south, in particular, suffered comprehensive domination—economically, politically and culturally.[12] However, although Haile Selassie did reestablish Ethiopian authority in Eritrea, he never managed to consolidate factions within the kingdom. Factors that undermined Selassie's authority included Eritrean, Oromo, and Tigre separatist movements, as well as growing dissatisfaction among young modernists and the military.

The Communist Rule

In the midst of general discontent with the emperor's rule, a nationalist group of military officers (the "Derg") deposed the emperor in 1974. Later on, the Derg adopted a Marxist-Leninist agenda. Political ties to the United States were subsequently cut and instead the Soviet Union became the new major donor and arms supplier. State ownership of lands, industries, and trading activities was enforced. In 1977, Lieutenant Colonel Mengistu Haile Mariam became the leader of the Derg, instituting a Marxist-Leninist one-party state. The budgetary expenditure of the central government increased fourfold and 40 percent of this money went to the military, which became among the strongest on the African continent. Violence erupted again in 1977–1978, when during the so-called red terror an estimated 100,000 people were killed in a move to eradicate all political opposition.[13]

Between 1974 and 1991, the military dictatorship attempted to maintain the territorial integrity of the state while modernizing and secularizing the country, primarily by breaking down the social and economic power of the church and aristocracy. The Christian church lost its lands and the financial support of the state while the official recognition of three Muslim holidays raised the status of Islam.[14] Accusing Haile Selassie's regime of cultural repression, the Derg encouraged, if somewhat ambiguously, the cultural self-assertion and expression of various ethnic groups. While secession was not considered, the Programme of the National Democratic Revolution (PNDR) of April 1976 nonetheless stated that the right of self-determination of all nationalities would be recognized and fully respected. The PNDR appeared to signal a decisive shift in the Derg's position toward the nationalities question. Indeed, and as expressed in the first of its 1974 ten-point program, the Derg had previously clearly signaled its intent to maintain a united Ethiopia, "without ethnic, religious, linguistic and cultural differences."[15] The promotion of ethnic diversity was carried out through various policies. At the same time, the military dictatorship, using communism as its ideological mandate, centralized authority and imposed land tenure and supposedly "progressive" social policies, undermining the peasants' historic connection to the state and the land. Resettlement, villagization, mass political organizations, and the command economy conspired to alienate the people from their natural allegiances. Even though the new regime repeatedly proclaimed the equality of all nationalities and cultures in Ethiopia and promised them regional autonomy and local self-government, it insisted on the unity of the state, just as the feudal regime had done before it. "Ethiopia First" and "Unity or Death" were the slogans of the state.

The Somali invasion in 1977 put an end to the tendency of allowing regional autonomy. The Derg introduced a number of measures that seemed to promote the country's ethnic diversity, such as authorizing printing and broadcasting in other languages, the staging of ethnic cultural shows, the launch of a wide-ranging literacy campaign in 1979, the teaching of local languages using the Amharic script, and the creation of an Institute of Nationalities in 1983 to study the "nationalities question" and recommended reforms.[16] But these were merely symbolic. After the Ogaden war in 1978, Mengistu exploited clan differences between the two largest dissident pastoral communities, the Afars and Somalis. A third, smaller group, the Boran in Sidamo who opposed Somalia's expansion plans under Siad Barre, was driven into the arms of the Derg. Despite a history of ethnic-based rebellion and the existence of the Oromo Liberation Front (OLF), the Oromo ethnic group failed to create an effective nationalist movement. Other local peoples in the south, such as the Gurage and the Sidamo, also wanted to create separate states, but complicated residence patterns would make drawing boundaries impossible.[17]

Under Mengistu's seventeen-year reign, ruthless suppression of ideological adversaries fostered growth of nationalistic movements and ongoing civil wars,[18] and the Derg tried to purge all citizens suspected of harboring ethnic or any other identity-based loyalties, especially Eritreans. The Derg wanted to maintain its power over the bureaucracy and the military because it feared loss of control over the central power of the state. The regime felt threatened by the ambition of the radicals to construct a popular foundation for political power through the parastatal and mass organizations created by the revolution.[19] Eventually, the state's inability to compromise politically led to its demise and further encouraged the breakup of the larger nation.[20]

Ethnic Federalism

In May 1991, the Ethiopian People's Revolutionary Democratic Front (EPRDF), a coalition of movements dominated by the initially Marxist-Leninist Tigray People's Liberation Front, marched into Addis Ababa.[21] The transitional government that resulted and overthrew Mengistu's regime had to find ways of dealing with the vacuum left by the fall of Mengistu's autocratic and centralized regime. It chose the approach of a federation based on ethnicity.

A federalist approach, based on ethnicity, could acknowledge the realistic landscape of the country and ensure representation of most needs and attitudes among the country's population. Although this seems to be a noble idea in its concept, some problems exist in the context of the realities in Ethiopia. There is, most saliently, the issue of setting up boundaries to acknowledge these ethnic-based regions, since there has been considerable intermingling among the different communities. Furthermore, the lack of experience with this kind of system by most of the population, including the government, has been an important obstacle to its effectiveness.

Currently, Ethiopia is organized into 9 states or regions, 64 zones, 550 districts, and thousands of *kebeles* or neighborhood/rural organizations.[22] Although in the long run, this decentralization could theoretically stream down policies to affect individuals in each community, in the short run, federalism is very expensive and requires large numbers of qualified staff to carry out programs at the different levels of government. Some critics argue that one of the many drawbacks of the Ethiopian federal system is that it has been imposed from the top, with no real consultation with the rest of the population.[23] In doing so, these critics argue that the EPRDF has managed to maintain a central grip on power without giving the different regions adequate autonomy. In addition, the centralization of resources and capable personnel in the capital makes it difficult for the different regions to administer their areas without relying on the central government.[24] Although the process of establishing regional and local self-governments along ethnic lines differs fundamentally from the previous regimes' centralized and hierarchical structure of the Ethiopian state, the newly established self-governments still depend on the central government and are equally accountable to it as to the people that elect them at the regional level. The central government has a long way to go to effectively implement the federal system. It has to demonstrate political will and encourage the genuine autonomy of the regional entities.

Unfortunately, some people in Ethiopia already doubt the government has the will to make this system work for everyone. Although ethnic federalism empowers ethnic groups to self-governance and even secession, Meles Zenawi's government has cracked down on opposition and separatists on several occasions in the past. For instance, in March 2001, long-standing tensions within Zenawi's own political party, the TPLF, exploded into a full-fledged power struggle between moderates loyal to Zenawi and hardliners who apparently opposed Ethiopia's December 2000 peace treaty with Eritrea. Zenawi's government launched a major crackdown, which lasted for months, arresting many dissidents that included state officials, opposition and human rights activists, university lecturers, and businessmen on charges of corruption. In late April, Addis Ababa University students rioted to protest the presence of armed police on their campus. Government officials dismissed the riots and local police moved aggressively to restore order. More than thirty people died in the unrest, and police detained thousands of students.[25]

These contradictory actions from the government lead critics in the country to argue that Zenawi's government wants to disintegrate the country by dividing it into small regional pieces and to serve his own minority TPLF party, and that the regime ultimately depends on the use of ethnic politics and the federal formula to ensure the political hegemony of the TPLF. These critics believe that the overemphasis on ethnicity in the government's policy could be used by ethnically based political parties as a means to obtain political power and to pursue an agenda of self-determination, hence diverting government, as well as opposition parties, from more fundamental priorities such as economic development.[26] They support this argument by pointing to the example of Eritrea. Unfortunately, however, opposition leaders have not offered alternative approaches.

Eritrea

After a long and protracted conflict whose origins generally trace back to 1961, Eritrea achieved its independence from Ethiopia in 1991, when the troops of the Eritrean People's Liberation Front (EPLF) entered Asmara. Following a UN-monitored referendum on independence in 1993, its status as Africa's newest member state was internationally sanctioned. Whether Eritrea constitutes an exceptional example of a successful secession or represents instead the outcome of a long-deferred decolonization remains hotly debated and is perhaps best addressed by international lawyers. Nevertheless, it is difficult to ascribe Eritrea's quest for national self-determination to ethnonational motives.

Like Ethiopia, Eritrea is a multiethnic state and includes at least nine officially recognized nationalities: the Afar, the Bilen, the Hadareb, the Kunama, the Nara, the Rashaida, the Saho, the Tigre, and the Tigrigna; it is estimated that the Tigrigna represent 50 percent of the total population. Although the EPLF may now seem predominantly Tigrigna, it would be inaccurate to depict Eritrea's nationalist struggle as having been launched by this group. Indeed, many Tigrigna, at least initially, supported Eritrea's unification with Ethiopia. This is perhaps not all that surprising since Eritrea's Tigrigna are ethnically related to Ethiopia's Tigrigna: they speak the same language, which like Amharic derives from the ancient Ge'ez; they practice the same religion; and they share other cultural traits. Until recently, the Tigrigna were referred to as Eritrea's Tigrigna, a designation that several commentators and analysts still use. Except for the demands made by some Tigrigna separatists in 1947—and this is rather counterintuitive, given what the ethnonationalist logic would predict—Eritrea's Tigrigna did not seek reunification with their fellow Tigrigna stranded across the border in Ethiopia.[27] Instead, as described below, Eritrea's Tigrigna have increasingly distanced themselves from their Ethiopian counterparts to the extent that the two communities now seem to regard themselves as distinct.

Thus, rather than being rooted in an underlying ethnic substratum, Eritrea's national identity appears to have resulted from historical circumstances. Three events have proven particularly significant in this process, each providing the building blocks for Eritrea's emerging national identity:

- First, the creation in 1890 of Eritrea as a colonial state provided Eritrea not only with its name and geographical identity, but also with a history distinct from that of Ethiopia. The colonial period also introduced many important transformations that were deemed necessary for the emergence of nationalism: industrialization, urbanization, and education.
- During the second period, federation, which spanned from 1952 to 1962, Eritrea acquired the institutions and symbols of autonomy. The gradual erosion of Eritrea's autonomous status triggered civilian unrest and launched the armed liberation struggle.
- The third period was the liberation war itself. During this period, the nationalist struggle gradually spread from a small elite to encompass the Eritrean masses. The war also cemented Eritrea's identity and its characteristics—exemplified by the dominant movement, the EPLF.

The Colonial Legacies

By giving the country its name and territorial contours, Italian colonization, which lasted from 1890 to 1941, provided Eritrean nationalism with, to paraphrase Gellner, its navel. In addition to this, Italian colonization altered, albeit partially, Eritrea's socioeconomic bases. Many of these changes, which could be subsumed under the label of modernization, were introduced in the latter stages of the colonial period as Italy prepared to expand its empire into Ethiopia. Italian investment in the industrial sector, notably from the 1920s onward, "transformed Eritrea's society from one that was overwhelmingly rural and traditionally based to one with a significant urban and industrial component."[28] Attendant developments in the realm of communication further facilitated the country's political and economic integration. And although the British and Ethiopian armies subsequently destroyed many of the railway lines and motor roads, the remaining networks represent one of this period's more impressive legacies. Frequently identified as a prerequisite for the growth of nationalism, mass education remained rather modest throughout Italian occupation. Nonetheless, the publication by Catholic missionaries of textbooks in which Eritrea is depicted as a distinct geographical entity with its own history and cultural attributes proves particularly significant. As spelled out in the introduction of one such "instruction manual," the primary purpose of these textbooks was to instill a deep affection for Eritrea into the hearts of its "indigenous" population.[29]

This is not to suggest that a strong sense of Eritrean national identity was established when the British took over from the Italians in 1941. Of those polled by the British administration in 1947 to ascertain the future of Eritrea, 48 percent expressed their support for the Unionist Party, which advocated Eritrea's unification with Ethiopia.[30] Nonetheless, the colonial experience clearly provided the basis for the identity that was subsequently articulated and propounded by the EPLF, as illustrated by the fact that more than the flag (a combination of the EPLF and the federal flag) and more than the camel (the country's official symbol since 1991), the new state's favorite emblem is the country's geographical map.[31] And, while the motivational dynamic behind Eritrea's march toward self-determination may have been triggered by fears of dissolution brought about by the British proposal to dismantle Eritrea under the Bevin-Sforza Plan and then, more evidently, by Ethiopia's incorporation of Eritrea, Italian colonization implanted the necessary foundations upon which Eritrean identity could be "imagined" and crystallized.

The First Nationalist Stirrings

Ethiopia's progressive abrogation of Eritrea's status as a federated yet autonomous region throughout the 1950s, a status established in 1952 by UN Resolution 390 A(V), fanned the flames of what was to become Eritrea's nationalist movement.[32] This initially manifested itself through acts of civil disobedience carried out by urban intellectuals, as well as students and worker groups. Although protestors did not always explicitly couch their claims in nationalist terms, they were to play an important "symbolic" role in future mobilization.[33] In 1958, Eritrea's first nonsecular anti-Ethiopian organization, the Eritrean Liberation Movement (ELM), was established by Muslim Eritrean exiles and students in Port Sudan. Although ELM's aim was to preserve Eritrea's autonomy, its efforts were in vain. Step by step, Eritrea lost its various symbols of autonomy, and in December of that year, Eritrea's flag was abolished. In 1961, the first shots of what is now rightly or wrongly remembered as the beginning of the armed struggle rang out.

That Muslim expatriate students established the ELM, and the first armed liberation movement, the Eritrean Liberation Front (ELF), should not lead observers to the conclusion that the Eritrean struggle for independence originated as a religious affair, one that opposed Eritrean Muslim lowlanders to their Christian counterparts. Although, as mentioned above, many Tigrigna-speaking Eritreans initially endorsed unification with Ethiopia, calls for Eritrean independence were also voiced from the earliest moments by Christian highlanders, the former editor of the *Eritrean Weekly News,* Woldeab Woldemariam, being perhaps one of its better known advocates.[34] Moreover, and to its founding members' surprise, the support provided from the onset by Christian students and workers to the ELM was such that it could only highlight the extent to which a deep sense of alienation had started to emerge—even among those Eritreans who should have been more sympathetic to union with Ethiopia.[35] It is difficult at the best of times to assess the breadth and depth of nationalism. In the case of Eritrea, although its first movements might have recruited across religious and ethnic divides, it is unlikely that a distinct sense of Eritreanness permeated all strata of society at this stage. Confined mostly to Eritrea's educated elites, nationalism percolated down a stage further in the following period.

The Liberation Struggle and the Consolidation of National Identity

If any factor enabled Eritrean nationalism to gain broad-based support, it would no doubt have to be the ferocity with which Ethiopia responded to Eritrea's calls for self-determination. As the Ethiopian army began to bomb civilians indiscriminately in the lowlands and highlands, popular support for the nationalist movement started to swell. The harder Ethiopia tried to stifle Eritrea, the more it kindled Eritrean feelings of identity. The intensity and protractedness of the liberation war not only strengthened Eritrean cohesion, but also endowed it with its distinctive features.

The EPLF's military defeat of the ELF in the early 1980s enabled it to impose—unchallenged—its own conception of Eritrean identity and promulgate a series of sociopolitical reforms. These were destined to transform Eritrean identity from one characterized only by its opposition to Ethiopia to one defined positively from within. First propounded by the ELM in the late 1950s and early 1960s, pan-Eritrean secular identity was hailed as the cornerstone of the EPLF's program. Representatives of all Eritrea's society were included: Christians and Muslims participated equally in the decision-making process, peasant and pastoralist concerns were addressed, and women were fully integrated in all levels of the fighting. Operating in the newly liberated territories, the EPLF set out to educate, politicize, and train the population, providing both food and health services.

> In large areas of the territory, particularly around Keren, the guerrillas established an efficient administration to govern a mostly sympathetic population: hospitals and factories functioned underground, plantations and farms once owned by the Italian expatriates and later nationalized by the government in Addis Ababa were taken over by guerrilla co-operatives. Rural bus services run by the rebels linked towns in the "liberated areas."[36]

In short, the EPLF was beginning the process of nation-building. And, with the introduction of "compulsory military service," the war continued to further provide Eritrea with the emotional attachment essential to nation formation. Yet, these favorable depictions should not obscure the fact that the EPLF was a highly centralized organization: because the EPLF is primarily a military organization, it has been relatively ruthless in dealing with dissidents. Control over members of the organization is effected through allowing very little time for individual reflection and separate thought. Most fighters eat together, sleep together, attend meetings together, and rarely are left alone to reflect about their life and family.[37]

When Eritrea achieved its independence, nationalism became the new government's guiding ideology. Secularism, the rejection of ethnic or religious political parties, national service, the redrawing of Eritrea's internal administrative borders so that they do not coincide with or reflect any particular ethnic division, and the lack of any official language—all indicated the government's eagerness to consolidate Eritrea's national unity and gloss over, if not stifle, the expression of any potentially divisive sub-Eritrean identities. No event was more fully exploited for this purpose than the liberation war itself.

The ultimate expression of Eritreanness, the war, has provided the new Eritrean state with its defining symbols of identity. The 65,000 Eritrean Liberation Army fighters that died during the struggle are now commemorated on June 20, Martyrs' Day. Following Eritrea's constitution, the members of the National Assembly, the president, and the judges shall pledge their oath in the name of the Eritrean martyrs. In downtown Asmara stands a monument—a giant pair of sandals representing those worn by the fighters during the struggle. Another indication of the war's central role in Eritrea's national identity is the name given to the country's new currency. The *Nacfa*, introduced in November 1997, is the name of the mountain redoubt from where Eritrean resistance was organized—one of the few towns the Ethiopian army could not recapture after the Eritrean forces had taken control of it in March 1977.

The importance of the liberation war in Eritrea's national identity should come as no surprise. After all, the war lasted thirty years, and although no official figures exist, estimates of civilian casualties range between 150,000 and 250,000—this in a country with a population of about 3.3 million. The war has affected every section of the Eritrean population, and anyone who traveled to Eritrea in its aftermath was struck by the apparently indelible scar it had left on the country and its people. Several years after the end of the liberation war, the road from the capital city of Asmara to the port of Massawa was still strewn with the defunct carcasses of rusting Soviet tanks, while unexploded ordnance and landmines continued to litter the countryside, maiming men, women, and children.

That the leadership of the EPLF decided to pursue some of the policies that had served it so well in the field is perhaps somewhat understandable, yet governing under conditions of peace differs from that operating in the midst of war. By defining citizenship in its broadest terms, to include Eritreans living abroad, the government of Eritrea may have ensured the initial support of the Eritrean diaspora and furthered the foundations of a truly pan-Eritrean identity. But, however powerful a sense of cohesion the liberation struggle may have inspired, this in itself may not suffice in the longer term, and particularly so if the government pursues the repressive measures with which it has now come to be associated since the end of 2001.[38] As the government continues to indefinitely postpone elections and curtail freedom of speech, it weakens the meaning and attractiveness not only of Eritrean citizenship but also of Eritrean national identity.

The Ethiopia-Eritrea War

The war that erupted between Ethiopia and Eritrea in May 1998[39] caught almost everyone by surprise, including even the protagonists themselves. Triggered by local confrontation in the border area of Badme, the conflict degenerated into a full-blown war that lasted more than two years, killed between 70,000 and 100,000 people, and displaced an estimated 1.2 million. Before the outbreak of the conflict, the two new governments and their leaders, Meles Zenawi and Isaias Afwerki, enjoyed what appeared to be good bilateral relations, based on the alliance they had forged in their seventeen-year struggle against Mengistu Haile Mariam's rule. Rumored to be distant cousins and longtime friends, Zenawi and Afwerki were hailed by the Clinton administration as part of a new breed of strong African leaders capable of achieving political stability and economic prosperity. That they did not consider an immediate, formal demarcation of the common border a priority seems, retrospectively, a tragic mistake. Border skirmishes had after all brought the two countries' armies face-to-face before. In the years that preceded the war, clashes had occurred, among other places, in Adi Murug and Bure. From 1993 to 1998, representatives of the two governments held numerous meetings to resolve what perhaps they still perceived as minor local disturbances, but should have clearly given more pressing consideration. It is of course also possible that territorial demarcation seemed too potentially explosive an issue to be addressed head-on and in the open.[40]

As relations soured, informed in part by their diametrically opposed visions of how to achieve national cohesion in multiethnic states, but also by the domestic pressures they then faced, both leaders realized the close economic and political interdependence of their countries. But rather than working together for their mutual benefit, Zenawi and Afwerki increasingly became suspicious and distrustful of each other. Real trouble started after Eritrea introduced its own currency, the *Nacfa,* and Ethiopia insisted on using hard currency for all future trading. As the boundary acquired new saliency, this had a devastating impact on Eritrea, which saw prices of its goods rise and its economy slow down. In response, Eritrea raised all port-related charges on Ethiopian-bound goods through the port of Assab. In retaliation, Ethiopia announced that it would use Djibouti, rather than Assab, as its main port and started negotiations with Kenya and Sudan as well.

Eritrea's independence from Ethiopia in 1993 left Ethiopia landlocked, and many voices within Ethiopia still felt that Eritrea should never have been allowed to follow this course. Many Ethiopians believed that Afwerki had moved his troops across the border in reaction to these developments, calculating that a war would be devastating to Zenawi whose political support within Ethiopia was thought to be low. Waging a war against Eritrea was thus perceived as the only means to safeguard Ethiopia's national sovereignty. In contrast, many Eritreans feared that Ethiopia wanted either to reclaim Eritrea or to replace its current government with one friendlier to Ethiopia. For Afwerki this was also a war for survival, because Eritrea depended almost entirely on Ethiopia's economy and agriculture.[41]

National Identity and the War

The Ethiopia-Eritrea war could hardly be defined as an ethnically motivated conflict. After all, the leadership of these two states, as indicated above, is both of Tigrigna origin. Nonetheless, the significance of nationalism should not be underestimated. In the mid-1980s, the tactical alliance struck by the EPLF and the TPLF to overthrow Mengistu came under severe strain because of the two fronts' differing positions about the right of nationalities to secede. Though the TPLF argued that all nationalities in Ethiopia ought to be granted the right of self-determination up to secession, the EPLF insisted that while greater autonomy should be given to the nationalities, independence could only be granted to nations (as distinct from nationalities) or former colonies. The EPLF was thereby not only insisting on the particularity of its own case but also seeking, given its own multiethnic composition, to fend off any potential threats to its vision of a united Eritrea.

Although the TPLF eventually dropped from its program any reference to Tigrigna independence, non-Tigrigna Ethiopians frequently believe it to be pursuing its own agenda and interests through its privileged position within the government. Some Ethiopians thus regarded the war as a way of serving the parochial interests of Zenawi's Tigrigna constituency, whose members were left to enjoy political and economic privileges over other ethnic groups. Eritreans have also had suspicions of what they perceive as Tigrigna irredentist ambitions. These suspicions were fanned in late 1997, when the Tigrigna administration in Mekele, Ethiopia, issued and distributed a map that pushed the region's administrative boundaries into what Eritrea deemed to be its territory. As the "map incident" and subsequent events suggest, there is within the TPLF a more radical nationalist faction with which Meles Zenawi has had to contend. The war, while perhaps not initiated for this reason, nevertheless arguably provided him with a welcome relief whereby he could reconcile the pressures that came from within his own party and those voiced by those Ethiopians who felt that he had sold out their country to Eritreans. And, in the midst of all the confusion and general skepticism about the ethnic federalism, the war against Eritrea seemed to have fostered a sense of common Ethiopian identity.

Also noteworthy is the way in which identities are being remolded and redefined, to the point that Eritreans now constitute an ethnic category. Indeed, following the wave of deportations that have accompanied the war, Eritreans are frequently referred to as "ethnic Eritreans."[42] Ethiopia's policy toward its citizens of Eritrean descent has thus been described as a case of "mild ethnic cleansing."[43] Even the history of Eritrea's Tigrigna-speaking population has been "rewritten" so as to emphasize its distinctiveness from that of Ethiopia's Tigrigna speakers. According to Asmarom Legesse:

> The Tigrayans and the highland Eritreans are next-door neighbors; they speak the same language and have a common history. However, they diverge sharply from each other in culture and character. The divergent developments are not merely a function of the colonial experience of Eritrea: the divergence goes back to the fourteenth century when Eritrea began writing her own customary laws and developing her own grass roots democratic institutions. The deep antipathy that some Tigrayans have now developed toward ethnic Eritreans is, however, a new phenomenon and will probably subside once the hate campaign runs out of steam.[44]

Notwithstanding this claim's dubious historical foundations, it is nevertheless quite revealing of the way the ongoing war between Ethiopia and Eritrea appears to have further sharpened the identity of Eritrea's Tigrigna as distinct from that of Ethiopia's Tigrigna.

Conclusion and Policy Recommendations

In their attempts to foster national unity amidst ethnic diversity, the cases of Ethiopia and Eritrea could not provide more contrasting strategies. While Ethiopia has apparently adopted what on paper seems an extreme blueprint for ethnoregional federalism, this arrangement, insofar as it represents a projection of the particular concerns and history of Ethiopia's Tigrigna onto the whole of country, is, according to some commentators, misguided. Eritrea for its part has instead opted for a more overtly centralized process of nation-building that seeks to paper over subnational identities. Isaias Afwerki thus recently condemned the current Ethiopian government's policies: "Ethiopia," he says, "could fragment, because it is controlled by minority Tigreans who have created a Balkanized arrangement of ethnic groups rather than trying to forge an imperial melting pot, in the way of Haile Selassie."[45] If the jury is still out on the relative success of the so-called melting-pot strategy, it nonetheless appears that its success depends on a measure of assimilation. Whether or not Eritrean national unity withstands the test of time is impossible to assess. Though most commentators agree that the great majority of Eritreans are animated by a deep sense of national identity, internal divisions should not be underplayed. And although Eritrea's national identity may have initially been reinforced by the latest Ethiopia-Eritrea war, the regime's increasingly unpopular measures could lay the preconditions that are propitious for a heightening of ethnic or other subnational identities.

National unity and political stability do not only exist in ethnically homogeneous societies. The Horn of Africa, after all, provides a good example of how even such societies will fracture if authoritarian measures prevail. Once hailed as one of the rare African examples of a "true" nation-state, Somalia is now better known as the prototypical example of state collapse, thereby demonstrating that ethnic homogeneity is no guarantee against instability and fragmentation. Despite what Eritrea's president may believe, the history of Ethiopia may provide some salutary warnings. Specifically, good governance in Eritrea must consider the balance between ethnic autonomy and addressing issues that cut across ethnic lines.

Both Emperor Haile Selassie's regime and Mengistu Haile Mariam's dictatorship failed because of their tendency of centralizing the state, repressing any opposition, and ignoring the identity and nationality questions.

Just as Zenawi's government in Ethiopia needs to find the balance between regional autonomy and national unity (in giving autonomy to the regions and fostering stability), Isaias Afwerki's government needs to assess the situation in the country and respond positively to voices of discontent or opposition based on ethnicity-related as well as other social, political, and economic concerns.

Ethiopia for its part may still have a lot to do before it achieves any semblance of internal cohesion. But in either case, a solution seems to lie in the adoption of more open and democratic government. As Paul B. Henze noted:

> If the common denominator in Marxist authoritarian regimes has been maintenance of compulsory ethnic harmony by a powerful centralized state, is there a common denominator in the experience of countries as varied as Switzerland, India, and the United States? There is, indeed, and it is a crucial one. It is adherence to the practice of democracy with firm recognition of the rights of the individual citizen taking precedence over all other rights within the framework of the absolute rule of law. This is the essential difference between political systems that accommodate ethnicity with relative success and those where ethnicity becomes a disruptive factor in national life.[46]

According to Henze, ethnic federalism should thus be complemented with more determined attempts to mobilize support for pressing issues that cut across ethnic groups, such as addressing poverty, land tenure issues, the rights of individuals, and famine. Other actions that would ensure the stability of the country, without jeopardizing the regional autonomy of the regions, are to review the system periodically and concentrate on individual rights rather than on an ethnic group.[47]

Notes

1. Ernest Gellner, *Nations and Nationalism* (Ithaca, NY: Cornell University Press, 1983), p. 1.

2. Anthony D. Smith, *National Identity* (London: Penguin Books, 1991), p. vii.

3. John Markakis, "Nationalism and Ethnicity in the Horn of Africa," in *Ethnicity and Nationalism in Africa: Constructivist Reflections and Contemporary Politics,* ed. Paris Yeros (New York: St. Martin's Press, 1999).

4. Gellner, *Nations and Nationalism,* p. 49.

5. Ibid., p. 55.

6. Smith, *National Identity,* p. 21; Walker Connor, *Ethnonationalism: The Quest for Understanding* (Princeton, NJ: Princeton University Press, 1994).

7. Julia Maxted and Abebe Zegeye, "Human Stability and Conflict in the Horn of Africa: Part One," *African Security Review* 10, no. 4 (2001): 95–110.

8. Entitled "On the Question of Nationalities in Ethiopia," this article, first published in the November 1969 issue of *Struggle,* signaled a peak in student defiance

toward the government of Emperor Haile Selassie. For a discussion of this see Randi Balsvik Rønning, *Haile Selassie's Students: The Intellectual and Social Background to Revolution: 1952–1977* (East Lansing: Michigan State University, 1985), p. 277.

9. While the Italians retained control of the Eritrean coast, the victory assured Ethiopia of its continued independence from European powers.

10. Bahru Zewde, *A History of Modern Ethiopia 1855–1991,* 2nd edition (Oxford: James Currey; Athens: Ohio University Press; Addis Ababa: Addis Ababa University Press, 2001).

11. Ghelawdewos Araia, *Ethiopia: The Political Economy of Transition* (Lanham, MD: University Press of America, 1995), p. 44; Girma Kebbede, *The State and Development in Ethiopia* (Atlantic Highlands, NJ: Humanities Press, 1992), p. 11.

12. Daniel Teferra, *Social History and Theoretical Analyses of the Economy of Ethiopia* (Lewiston, NY: Edwin Mellen Press, 1990), pp. 39–40, 45–46.

13. Economist Intelligence Unit, *Country Profile—Ethiopia* (London: Economist Intelligence Unit, 1998), p. 5; Teferra, *Social History,* pp. 54–55.

14. John Markakis, *National and Class Conflict in the Horn of Africa* (Cambridge: Cambridge University Press, 1987), p. 239.

15. Christopher Clapham, *Transformation and Continuity in Revolutionary Ethiopia* (Cambridge: Cambridge University Press, 1988), p. 45 and chapter 8.

16. Ibid., pp. 240–242.

17. Maxted and Zegeye, "Human Stability," pp. 95–110.

18. Kinfe Abraham, *Ethiopia: From Bullets to the Ballot Box: The Bumpy Road to Democracy and the Political Economy of Transition* (Lawrenceville, NJ: The Red Sea Press, Inc., 1994), pp. 6–7, chapter 2, chapter 9, pp. 153–172.

19. See Markakis, *National and Class Conflict,* pp. 237–271.

20. Harold G. Marcus, *A History of Ethiopia* (Berkeley: University of California Press, 2002).

21. After the fall of communism, other parts of the world suffered similar fates to Ethiopia. In Yugoslavia, for instance, the losses of communism and Tito as unifying factors and economic crisis brought ethnic identities to the fore, leading to the declaration of independence of Slovenia, Croatia, and Bosnia.

22. Government of Ethiopia, Constitution of the Federal Democratic Republic of Ethiopia (December 1994).

23. In fact, it is not very clear to what extent the regional institutions are truly autonomous from the central structure of the government.

24. Lovise Aalen, "Ethnic Federalism in a Dominant Party State: The Ethiopian Experience: 1991–2000," Report R (Bergen, Norway: Chr Michelsen Institute, February 2002); Edmond Keller and Lahra Smith, "Obstacles to Implementing Territorial Decentralization: The First Decade of Ethiopian Federalism," in *Sustainable Peace: Democracy and Power-Dividing Institutions After Civil Wars,* eds. Philip Roeder and Donald Rothchild (Ithaca, NY: Cornell University Press, September 2005).

25. Nita Bhalla, "Protests Radicalise Ethiopia's Youths," *BBC News,* May 4, 2001 (available online at http://news.bbc.co.uk/2/hi/africa/1312348.stm); Martin Plaut, "Political Turmoil in Ethiopia and Eritrea," *BBC News,* June 5, 2001 (available online at http://news.bbc.co.uk/2/hi/africa/1371175.stm).

26. Sandra Fullerton Joireman, "Opposition Politics and Ethnicity in Ethiopia: We Will All Go Down Together," *Journal of Modern African Studies* 35, no. 3 (1997): 387–408.

27. Tekeste Negash, *No Medecine for the Bite of a White Snake: Notes on Nationalism and Resistance in Eritrea, 1890–1941* (Uppsala: Uppsala University

Press, 1986). This may seem all the more surprising given that blueprints for a Greater Tigray were historically available. First, during the fascist occupation from 1936 to 1941, under the Italian East African Empire, the Tigrigna-speaking people were grouped under a single province, which roughly encompasses today's Eritrea and Tigray. Then, although it was never implemented, the British administration advocated a plan for a Greater Tigray.

28. Tom Killion, "The Eritrean Economy in Historical Perspective," *Eritrean Studies Review* 1 (Spring 1996): 101.

29. *La Colonia Eritrea. Manuale d'Instruzione Italiano-Tigrai. Ad uso delle Scuole Indigene per cura Della Missione Cattolica,* Tipografia Francescana, Asmara (1917), p. 8.

30. Lloyd Ellingson, "The Emergence of Political Parties in Eritrea, 1941– 1950," *Journal of African History* 18, no. 2 (1977): 263.

31. Jean-Louis Péninou, "Guerre Absurde Entre l'Ethiopie et l'Erythrée," *Le Monde Diplomatique* (July 1998): 15.

32. UN General Assembly, "Eritrea: Report of the United Nations Commission for Eritrea; Report of the Interim Committee of the General Assembly on the Report of the United Nations Commission for Eritrea" (A/Res/5/390A, December 2, 1950).

33. The workers' organization is frequently quoted in Eritrea's nationalist "mythology" as one of the first nationalist uprisings. Although this is not exactly the case, it constitutes nevertheless an important moment in the process. For a thorough and balanced account of Eritrea's workers' organizations, see Tom Killion, "Eritrean Workers' Organization and Early Nationalist Mobilization: 1948–1958," *Eritrean Studies Review* 2 (Spring 1997): 1–58.

34. Jeremy Harding, "A Death in Eritrea," *London Review of Books* (July 6, 1995): 10.

35. Markakis, *National and Class Conflict,* p. 106.

36. *Strategic Survey 1977,* International Institute for Strategic Studies, London (1977), p. 22.

37. Tekle Mariam Woldemikael, "Political Mobilization and Nationalist Movements: The Case of the Eritrean People's Liberation Front," *Africa Today,* 2nd quarter (1991): 35. See also Clapham, *Transformation and Continuity,* p. 212.

38. Although the Eritrean government's authoritarian tendencies may be traced back before the 1998–2000 war, notably with the establishment in 1996 of a Special Court, its crackdown on dissenting voices intensified in 2001. Among the measures it took at the time were the deportation of about 2,000 students of the University of Asmara to a camp in Massawa, the arrest without charge of eleven members of the so-called G-15, the closure of the country's eight independent newspapers, the expulsion of Italian ambassador Antonio Bandini, and the arrest without charge, of two local employees at the US embassy.

39. On the 1998–2000 war: Patrick Gilkes and Martin Plaut, *War in the Horn: The Conflict Between Eritrea and Ethiopia,* Discussion Paper 82 (London: The Royal Institute of International Affairs, 1999); Tekeste Negash and Kjetil Tronvoll, *Brothers at War: Making Sense of the Eritrean-Ethiopian War* (Oxford: James Currey, 2000).

40. According to Ghidey Zeratsion, "The border issue was raised for the first time at the meeting between the TPLF and EPLF in November 1984 . . . both agreed to postpone the demarcation and maintain the existing administrative regions." See Ghidey Zeratsion, "The Ideological and Political Causes of the Ethio-Eritrean War: An Insiders View," paper for the International Conference on the Ethio-Eritrean Crises, Amsterdam (July 24, 1999).

41. Aida Mengistu, "Eritrea and Ethiopia: Uneasy Peace," *The World Today* 57 (May 2001): 9–10.

42. For example: Asmarom Legesse, *The Uprooted: Case Material on Ethnic Eritrean Deportees from Ethiopia Concerning Human Rights Violations,* report written on behalf of Citizens for Peace in Eritrea, Asmara, Eritrea (July 26, 1998); and Ruth Iyob, "The Ethiopian-Eritrean Conflict: Diasporic vs. Hegemonic States in the Horn of Africa 1991–2000," *The Journal of Modern African Studies* 38, no. 4 (2000): 669.

43. Craig Calhoun, "Ethiopia's Ethnic Cleansing," *Dissent* 46 (Winter 1999): 47.

44. Asmarom Legesse, *The Uprooted—Part Two: A Scientific Survey of Ethnic Eritrean Deportees from Ethiopia Conducted with Regard to Human Rights Violations,* report written on behalf of Citizens for Peace in Eritrea, Asmara, Eritrea (February 22, 1999).

45. Robert Kaplan, "A Tale of Two Colonies," *The Atlantic Monthly* (April 2003): 54.

46. Paul B. Henze, *Ethiopia and Eritrea in Transition: The Impact of Ethnicity on Politics and Development Opportunities and Pitfalls* (Santa Monica, CA: Rand Corporation, 1995), p. 122.

47. Ibid., p. 122.

6

US Policy in the Horn: Grappling with a Difficult Legacy

Ruth Iyob and Edmond J. Keller

Africa has never been central to US foreign policy. As Peter Schraeder comments, "US policies from the founding of the American Republic in 1789 to the end of the Cold War have been marked by indifference, at worst, and neglect, at best. Africa has been treated as a *backwater* in official policymaking circles, compared to the time and resources allocated to other regions considered to be of greater importance."[1] Others have argued that the United States has consistently followed a "hands off" policy toward Africa, only becoming engaged with African countries when it was perceived by US policymakers that the country's vital national interests were at stake.[2] Accordingly, a consistent axiom of US foreign policy has been that the United States has no permanent friends or enemies, but only permanent interests—a line of argument that is supported by the evolution of US policy toward the countries of the Horn of Africa.[3] In this case, when the United States could benefit geostrategically by "engaging" or "disengaging" with one or another country of the Horn, it took the necessary steps to do so.[4] Moreover, US engagement in the Horn has depended largely on its foreign policy needs with countries outside of Africa.

Prior to the onset of the Cold War, the only significant American presence in the Horn was in Ethiopia. But, at the height of the Cold War, as US interests shifted toward countering the Soviet Union's efforts to secure a physical presence in the region, its key alliances shifted to the countries surrounding pro-Soviet Ethiopia, such as Sudan and Somalia. With the end of the Cold War, alliances have once again shifted, and, after a brief period of disengagement, the United States appears now to be reengaging with the countries of the Horn in the new war on international terrorism. As in the past, the reengagement by the United States in the Horn is selective, as demonstrated by the different levels of engagement with Djibouti, Ethiopia, Eritrea, and the former Republic of Somalia. Moreover, the type of engagement by the United States has also changed and been refined. In its recent engagement, rather than direct support to government, the United States focuses on providing logistical support and military training to ostensibly enhance peacekeeping capacity, direct and indirect mediation of interstate and intrastate disputes, and support for democratic forces in civil society and democratic institution-building. The reason for this shift, as in the past, has more to do with perceived US vital national interests—*outside Africa*—than with a desire to help African states to help themselves.

This chapter traces the involvement of the United States in the Horn—from engagement, to disengagement, to reengagement. It begins with outlining the rationale behind the US engagement with Ethiopia at the start of the twentieth century—highlighting the domestic consequences of such engagement. The chapter continues by documenting the effect of changes in US foreign policy guidelines on its relationship with Ethiopia and the other countries in the region and the relationships among the countries of the Horn. As this chapter shows, the policies of US involvement in Ethiopia, Eritrea, Sudan, and Somalia—despite conflicting strategies and objectives—have slowed the development of democracy, worsened the political and military insecurity in the region, exacerbated the proliferation of arms, and contributed to the silencing of civil society.

Ethiopian-US Relations:
From Strategic Ally to Strategic Enemy

Ethiopia has always been the cornerstone of US policy toward the Horn of Africa. Although the United States and Ethiopia have had diplomatic relations since 1903 and concluded treaties of arbitration and conciliation as far back as 1929, a close relationship did not emerge until after World War II.[5] In the aftermath of the Italian fascist occupation of Ethiopia, which lasted from 1936 to 1941, the British reinstated Emperor Haile Selassie and until 1952 assisted him in administering part of modern-day Ethiopia. The Ethiopian emperor determined that events like the Italian occupation should not be repeated and felt that his best means for ensuring this was to secure the close support of the United States, the rising superpower. For its part, the United States had, since the early 1940s, coveted a base at Asmara in Eritrea, the Kagnew Station,[6] along the Red Sea, where it could establish a link in a worldwide radio communications network.

The establishment of the Kagnew Station and securing access to the Red Sea led to significant involvement by the United States in the foreign and domestic policies of the Horn. In particular, US engagement led to its embroilment in the guerrilla wars waged by Eritrean nationalists that were supported by radical Arab regimes. This involvement led to a much longer and sustained involvement in domestic and regional affairs than US strategic planners had ever expected. At its peak, US policy centered on keeping Haile Selassie in power and keeping the region relatively stable and free from communism. Thus, the strategic interests of the United States came to intersect historically with Haile Selassie's domestic and regional interests. The United States, with only occasional reluctance, committed arms and other military assistance to help the emperor put down internal upheavals and fend off the irredentist designs of ethnic Somalis in the Haud and Ogaden.

The partnership with the United States began in the early 1950s with two agreements signed in May 1953 that formalized the new relationship between the United States and Ethiopia: the Mutual Defense Assistance Agreement and the Agreement for the Utilization of Defense Installations Within the Empire of Ethiopia. Following these agreements, the United States, in effect, guaranteed Ethiopia's security. In fact, by 1975, the total US military assistance to Ethiopia amounted to almost $280 million. Besides receiving military assistance from the United States after 1953, the Ethiopian military benefited from the presence and activity of a US Military Assistance Advisory Group (MAAG), which was established in 1954 to work with the Ethiopian military down to the battalion level. By 1970, the total number of MAAG personnel exceeded 100. American personnel were also involved in officer training at two Ethiopian military academies.[7] In addition, over the same period, Ethiopia received $350 million in economic aid in the form of technical assistance, capital goods, and food. This assistance contributed significantly to the military capacity of the Ethiopian state, as well as to its efforts at economic development.[8] With these economic and military arrangements, the United States and Ethiopia started as mutually dependent partners, advancing each other's foreign and domestic goals in the subregion. US aid guaranteed that the emperor could step up the modernization of his military and use it as a more effective instrument of domestic control, while the United States had use of the Kagnew Station.

US assistance also helped Ethiopia advance its military and political influence in the subregion. Significantly, a series of secret agreements between the two governments from 1960 until 1964 resulted in the modernization and dramatic expansion of the Ethiopian military. The stated purpose was to prepare Ethiopia's defenses for the assumed Somali threat.[9] In addition, between 1953 and 1976 some 3,978 Ethiopian military personnel—more than half of all African soldiers in the same category—were sent to study in the United States, at a cost of almost $23 million.[10] The United States also supplied Ethiopia with counterinsurgency training and advisers to help suppress the Eritrean movement for national independence after 1962. It is difficult to form an accurate estimate of the extent of that help since the US government tried to conceal its role by referring to the advisers as members of "Civic Action Teams."[11] The scale and character of US military involvement in Ethiopia served as the catalyst for the development of a low-intensity arms race in the Horn involving Eritrean liberation movements, Somali irredentists, the government of Somalia, and Ethiopia. However, in this era prior to the Brezhnev Doctrine, which established the Kremlin's commitment to support fledgling socialist states, these insurgency movements could not gain ground, as Ethiopia held the balance of power in the Horn.[12] Later, this chapter shows that with the advent of the Cold War and the proxy wars fought between the two superpowers, instability in the region began to escalate.

Still, despite the close Ethiopian-US relationship, its permanence was always in doubt. In order for it to continue, each side had to perceive that the benefits outweighed the costs. By 1970, with only eight years left on the lease of the Kagnew Station, the United States was beginning to reconsider the necessity of its presence in Ethiopia. The Eritrean region had become extremely unstable and the strategic need for maintaining the Kagnew Station seemed less compelling. The Soviet Union was now building an Indian Ocean fleet, and the Western powers felt that it was necessary to counter that challenge on equal terms. With this in mind, the United States leased the Indian Ocean island of Diego Garcia from the British government in 1966 and made plans for the construction of a large naval facility to be completed on the island by 1973. Accordingly, from 1971 to 1976, the number of US personnel based at the Kagnew Station was trimmed from over 3,000 to less than 40.[13] Indeed, by 1976 it was obvious that the United States perceived that its interests had ceased to mesh with Ethiopia's, adding to the vulnerability of the faltering imperial state.

Haile Selassie was deposed on September 12, 1974, and succeeded by what was to become a Marxist-Leninist military junta. The social revolution that followed Selassie's fall created widespread unrest both at the center of the country and in the periphery. The new regime resorted to whatever means it felt necessary to maintain itself in power and to pursue its "scientific socialist" development strategy, while at the same time trying to maintain good relations with the United States. Even as the need for the Kagnew Station diminished, a US presence in Ethiopia remained valuable to the administration of President Gerald Ford. Because of its proximity to the Middle East, Ethiopia continued to be regarded as a key to blocking the full implementation of the Soviets' Brezhnev Doctrine in the region.[14]

As the social revolution unfolded in Ethiopia, the international community began to decry what appeared to be gross violations of human rights on the part of the new regime. This issue became an electoral campaign issue in the 1976 US presidential campaign. The ultimate victor in that election, Jimmy Carter, declared that his administration would not provide military assistance to countries like Uruguay, Argentina, and Ethiopia because of their human rights records. Even though the previous administration of President Gerald Ford had not acted firmly toward Ethiopia because of its poor human rights record, beginning in 1975 it did delay the delivery of badly needed military aid. With Carter about to take office in January 1977, the complete cutoff of US military aid to Ethiopia became a real possibility. The junta was desperate, and it turned to Turkey, Yugoslavia, China, Vietnam, Libya, and Czechoslovakia for its arms needs. In December 1976, the Soviet Union signed an agreement with Ethiopia for the delivery of $100 million in military supplies.[15] At the time, however, Ethiopia appeared to have no intention of completely turning away from the United States, but merely sought to supplement US military aid.[16]

Realignment and US Policy
Toward the Horn of Africa: 1977–1989

On assuming the US presidency, Jimmy Carter moved swiftly to establish human rights as the centerpiece of his foreign policy, with serious consequences for Ethiopia and the region. On February 25, 1977, the United States announced that because of continued gross violations of human rights by Ethiopia and other governments, US military aid to those countries would be reduced over the following six months. Simultaneously, the United States and other Western countries began to apply economic pressure on Ethiopia.[17] Sensing that the Ethiopian military regime was vulnerable because it was waging internal wars on multiple fronts, the army of the Republic of Somalia invaded the Ogaden in support of the irredentists' claims of Somalis living there. In six months, Somali forces came to occupy a large portion of southeastern Ethiopia. However, with the help of Soviet, Cuban, and Yemeni forces, the Ethiopians were able to recapture their lost territory by early 1978.

US-Ethiopian relations broke down entirely in April 1977, when the government of Ethiopia demanded that the United States completely pull out of the Kagnew Station, end all of its MAAG activities, and cease any other official activities except for maintaining its embassy. The embassy staff was to be reduced to only essential personnel. This move seems to have been a direct reaction to Carter's announcement that the United States would move closer to Somalia—it was the beginning of Carter's "encirclement strategy," designed to entice Ethiopia's neighbors with military and economic development aid. Separate agreements were reached with Kenya, Egypt, Sudan, Somalia, and Oman[18] to allow their territories to be used as staging grounds for the US Rapid Deployment Force (RDF), which could be used to project US military power into the Middle East and Persian Gulf.[19] In late 1981, Operation Bright Star, a mock RDF exercise, was staged in the region, causing Ethiopia, South Yemen, and Libya to enter into an alliance and declare their intent to jointly resolve to repulse any efforts by the United States or its proxies to intervene in their affairs.

Inadvertently, Carter had provided an opening for the Soviets to adopt Ethiopia as a client state in the Horn in addition to their involvement in Somalia—fueling instability in the subregion. Initially, the Soviets continued to supply arms to both Somalia and Ethiopia, while attempting to negotiate peace between the two sides. The United States responded by intensifying its own efforts to woo Somalia away from the Soviets. The strategy was twofold: (1) to consider direct military assistance to Somalia and (2) to encourage indirect aid to that country from third-party countries in the region friendly to the United States (such as Egypt, Saudi Arabia, and Sudan). The result of Carter's policy shift, and its continuation by the Reagan administration, resulted in increasing the instability in the region by sparking an arms race that would facilitate interstate wars and encourage insurgency movements in the region. In the end, this policy proved to be fatally flawed and contributed to escalation of an arms race from which the Horn has never recovered.

After Carter lost his bid for a second term, his successor, Ronald Reagan, expanded the encirclement strategy in the Horn, and throughout the 1980s, the two superpowers postured against one another through their respective clients. From 1977 to 1987, the armies of the countries in the Horn grew tremendously. The size of the Ethiopian armed forces grew from 54,000 in 1977 to more than 300,000 a decade later. Somalia's army swelled from about 32,000 in 1977 to 65,000 in 1987. The growth of the military of Sudan was less dramatic (numbering 52,100 in 1977 and 58,500 in 1987, with fluctuations reaching as high as 71,000 in 1981 and 1982),[20] but in the 1980s, internal military activities grew significantly as the Ethiopian-supported Sudan People's Liberation Army (SPLA) was able to capture and control large areas of southern Sudan. In the same period (1977–1987), the Ethiopian defense budget grew from $103 million to almost $472 million. From 1977 to 1985, Somalia's defense expenditures rose from $36 million to $134 million and Sudan's from $237 million to $478 million. This level and pattern of growth in military expenditures could not have taken place if the countries of the Horn had not been able to rely upon superpower patrons for increasing levels of military assistance. It is estimated that throughout the entire greater Horn region—Ethiopia, Somalia, Sudan, and Kenya, excepting Djibouti and Eritrea—from 1981 to 1987 a total of $7.5 billion in weapons were delivered.[21]

While the Soviet Union and the United States jockeyed to check each other, the countries of the Horn—in particular Somalia, Ethiopia/Eritrea, and Sudan—seem to have been inspired primarily by internal conflicts rather than by the need to protect the border zones of each country. In

Somalia, the devastating defeat of the Somali army and the irredentist Western Somali Liberation Front in the Ogaden War (1977–1978) caused internal opposition to surface against Somali president Siad Barre. Over the next decade, the internal crisis escalated until the entire country was in turmoil; Somalia has remained without a central government since 1991, after the defeat of Barre. The 1980s also witnessed an increase in the capacity and efficiency of the Eritrean liberation movements and internal conflicts in Sudan.

After being routed by the Ethiopian army in the late 1970s, the Eritrean People's Liberation Front (EPLF) was able to regroup and by 1987 begin to make serious inroads toward liberating Eritrea from Ethiopian control. The success of the EPLF was enhanced by the fact that the Tigray People's Liberation Front (TPLF) and the Ethiopian People's Democratic Movement combined to form the Ethiopian People's Revolutionary Democratic Front (EPRDF). (The TPLF remains the most influential party in the EPRDF.) In May 1991, Ethiopian president Mengistu Haile Mariam fled into exile, and his army of 600,000 collapsed. On May 24, 1991, EPLF guerrillas entered Asmara, extending their control from their rural strongholds to the capital. Four days later, on May 28, the EPRDF was able to seize control of the capital, Addis Ababa, without significant resistance. Many of the weapons used by the Ethiopian army at this time found their way into the black market in Somalia and Djibouti, as fleeing soldiers sold their arms to anyone willing to buy them and in the process, fueled and expanded the military activities of Afar rebels fighting the government of Djibouti.[22]

External forces fueled Sudan's internal conflict. Sudan had been a client of the Soviets until the failed communist coup in 1971 by General Jaafar al-Nimeri prompted the government to develop closer ties to the United States and to present Sudan as its trusted ally. Nimeri made regular trips to Washington, pledging to help the United States build a "high wall against communism" in the Horn. For its part, the United States not only provided Sudan with substantial military and economic aid, but also supported Sudan in its dealings with the International Monetary Fund and the World Bank. Concurrently, Nimeri moved quickly to make peace with the SPLA, which had been waging war against the government of Sudan since the 1970s, and to moderate his policies.

Despite Nimeri's efforts to reach out to the SPLA and acquiesce to internal demands, he began to lose support on the domestic front. Hardline Islamists began in 1977 to demand that the Addis Ababa Agreement, which had ended Sudan's civil war in 1972, be reviewed, and also that the government be reorganized on the principles of *sharia,* or strict Islamic law.[23] By the early 1980s, Nimeri had begun to capitulate to the demands of the fundamentalists, even as his regime and his military were seen by the general population as weak and dependent on the United States. Nimeri was overthrown in a popular uprising in the spring of 1985. The new civilian regime of Sadiq al Mahdi expanded the policies designed to make Sudan an Islamic state. However, it too was overthrown by the Sudanese military in June 1989 with the support of the Muslim Brotherhood, and Sudan moved closer to radical Islamists in the Middle East. That move caused the United States to condemn Sudan for harboring terrorists.

Selective Reengagement in US Policy on the Horn of Africa

President George H. W. Bush's Africa policy in the late 1980s and early 1990s established the parameters for the shift in US policy from disengagement at the time of the ending of the Cold War to one of limited and selective engagement. The shift was partly a response to the humanitarian crisis in the Horn after the collapse of the Republic of Somalia, and partly based on the United States' perceived need to establish a broader strategic presence in the region. The United States thereafter increased its role as a long-standing mediator in the region. In fact, the disengagement of the Soviet Union from Ethiopia that had begun in 1989 was facilitated by the United States' role as the most visible arbiter of conflict in the Horn of Africa.[24] This signaled a shift from the fifteen-year-old policy of engaging with the countries surrounding Marxist Ethiopia for the purpose of containing the Soviet Union in the region.

However, the terms of reference for the United States' reengagement changed; in the post–Cold War period, the United States linked development aid to the recipient's record on human rights, political reform, and economic growth. By 1991, US assistant secretary of the Bureau of African Affairs, Herman Cohen, could announce the new US ultimatum of "no democracy, no aid."[25] Such statements celebrated the "triumph" of liberalism over communism; however, the ultimatum was only applied selectively in Africa; subsequent actions by the United States—which followed the earlier patterns—did not effectively adhere to the tenet that only "democratic" regimes would get aid. As such, the United States was perceived as only supporting a limited version of democracy, raising suspicions of its motives in the region and limiting the progress of political reform.

In the end, US reengagement did not produce the democratic transformations hoped for by the US government or the civil society groups in the Horn. In Eritrea and Ethiopia, wholesale acceptance by the United States of Isaias Afwerki and Meles Zenawi as "new leaders" obscured the human rights abuses and political marginalization taking place. In Somalia, the absence of a cohesive leadership over the territory led to the fragmentation of the nation into fiefdoms under rival warlords and thwarted US efforts to identify any acceptable "new" leader. Meanwhile, in Sudan, the Bashir-Turabi regime was avowedly anti-American, thus necessitating the severance of diplomatic ties and the imposition of sanctions on the country. Viewed from a regional perspective, US reengagement yielded mixed results owing to a misreading of the realities on the ground. Notably, the factors that the United States hailed as harbingers of reform—namely, new leaders in Ethiopia and Eritrea and changes in Sudan—were not as significant as initially hoped. The lessons learned from that experience have yet to be translated into coherent guidelines by Washington.

The first stumbling block to US reengagement with its traditional ally, Ethiopia, emerged with the growing dissension of numerous Ethiopian political groups who felt marginalized by the EPRDF and challenged the authenticity of US claims to uphold democracy. Ethiopian opposition groups demanded a guaranteed forum to enable them to participate openly in the politics of post-1991 Ethiopia.[26] The EPRDF's refusal to accommodate dissent from groups other than those within its constellation of liberation groups signaled difficulties on the road to democracy and undermined the assertion by the United States that democratic reform would be rewarded with development assistance. The second difficulty in the reengagement phase occurred when the new Eritrean government refused to adopt US-supported democratic ideals and suppressed civil society's voice.

US Engagement with the New Ethiopia

In 1991, the reengagement of the United States with transitional Ethiopia was premised on the commitment of the new leadership, spearheaded by the EPRDF, to political reform, sustainable economic development, and multi-partyism. During their first two years, Ethiopia's new rulers made a smooth transition from rough-edged guerrillas declaiming Marxist principles to statesmen conversant in the lexicon of democracy. The United States provided aid for postwar economic reconstruction as well as constitution-making, civic education, and establishment of civil society groups. The Inter-Africa Group, staffed by cosmopolitan Ethiopian returnees with close ties to Ethiopia's political groups, was regarded as an ideal interlocutor between the new regime and a population unwilling to trust the "nationalist" credentials of what had been considered a ragtag army bent on dismembering "historic" Ethiopia.

Ethiopia's new regime, however, did not provide evidence of democratic reform. The Ethiopian elite were especially suspicious of the cooperation between the two major guerrilla armies—the EPRDF and EPLF; the Ethiopian intelligentsia viewed it as an ominous sign that the democratization process would, once again, become hostage to the interests of ruling African elites and their US supporters. Notably, the TPLF/EPRDF and EPLF also considered their alliance a short-term tactical strategy, rather than the platform for regional cooperation that it was made out to be by Afro-optimist scholars and members of the US policymaking circles.[27]

In particular, ordinary Ethiopians viewed the "two cousins"—EPRDF's Meles Zenawi and EPLF's Isaias Afwerki (also from the Tigrigna ethnic group)—as imposing their vision on the majority of non-Tigrigna-speaking Ethiopians. This rearticulating of old communal hostilities and dynastic rivalries between Amhara and Tigrigna peoples provided an undercurrent of uneasiness about the new leaders.[28] To Ethiopian communities without any affiliation to either the Amhara or Tigrigna ethnic group, their exclusion from the top decision-making strata of the EPRDF led to both a festering mistrust of the claims to pluralism in Ethiopia and a questioning of American support for Ethiopia's "democracy."[29] Finally, the United States' embrace of the EPRDF—which excluded other political movements—led to a sense of betrayal by a majority of Ethiopian nationalists who regarded the United States to be not a guarantor of democracy but a "patron" of military victors. When the EPRDF-led coalition government announced a proposal to establish a federal system based on ethnicity and to acquiesce to the EPLF's demand for an international referendum to enable Eritreans to determine their political destiny, the majority of Ethiopian nationalists—who opposed secession and disapproved of ethnicity as a basis for federalism—reacted with hostility. Both proposals were regarded as a sellout of the nation's patrimony: a unified Ethiopian legacy consolidated by nineteenth- and twentieth-century emperors (the chronology of which has been elaborated in Chapter 5 by Dominique Jacquin-Berdal and Aida Mengistu). The Ethiopian elite argued that it too should be allowed to have a voice in the decision on Eritrean secession, even though Eritrean independence was a de facto reality by late 1991. The US and UN backing for the referendum, scheduled for April 1993, added to the bitterness of Ethiopian nationalists who had lost countless lives in defense of what they perceived as their country's territorial integrity.[30]

Despite the continued pressure of Ethiopian opposition groups, the government of Meles Zenawi reiterated that war did not necessarily result in unity. The resentment of much of the Ethiopian public did not deter the Transitional Government of Ethiopia (TGE) from pursuing its vision of a viable "ethnic" federal system minus Eritrea.[31] With yesterday's "enemies of the nation" at the helm of government, citizens swallowed their bitterness and anxiously sought assurances that the United States would guarantee the emergence of a democratic system. Their fears were well grounded since both the TGE/EPRDF in Ethiopia and the new government in Eritrea continued abductions of political opponents as well as incarcerations of new dissenters and former officials of the Mengistu government. As the EPRDF held its first, albeit flawed, national elections in 1992, there was no follow-up by the United States on the threat to use aid as a deterrent to incipient dictatorship. Ethiopian opposition groups, inside and outside the country, brought this omission to the attention of the architect of the US ultimatum, Herman Cohen. His response was that "while Ethiopia has a long way to go before it has true democracy, the Ethiopian political system has become far more open and liberalized than under Mengistu."[32] A high level of sympathy for the "new leaders" hid any anxieties that policymakers may have had of Washington's commitment to the new policy of engagement and political reform.[33] The ultimatum of "no democracy, no aid," enunciated so confidently in early 1991, was quickly deflated as the United States came to accept new regimes that emphasized the virtues of development over true democracy and human rights. The view of political stability as the sine qua non for development—a key concern of realpolitik-centered policymaking of the Cold War era—reemerged as the new regimes formulated the basis for reestablishing alliances in the post–Cold War period.

US Engagement with Eritrea

Eritrea took pride of place in both Bush's and Clinton's African policy. The Provisional Government of Eritrea (PGE)/EPLF got things done efficiently and enjoyed a high level of legitimacy from the majority of the populace. Unlike the TGE in Ethiopia, the PGE/EPLF regime was unencumbered by any pretense of setting up a coalition government. The victorious EPLF leadership had no plans to include the Eritrean Liberation Front (ELF)— which it had defeated with the help of the TPLF—in the governance of the new country.[34] The marginalization of the ELF, previously associated with Pan-Arabism and some Islamist movements, was accepted by both American and longtime Eritrean supporters of the EPLF. In fact, the forthright rejection by Eritrea of "alien" modes of governance and confidence in establishing a "self-reliant" Eritrea was considered a positive factor, which endeared them to policymakers who had been exhausted by other African leaders' patrimonial demands. The liberated populace of Eritrea, too, embraced the victors. Indeed, no one questioned (at least in public) why the EPLF delayed immediately declaring independence until 1993.

Although the EPLF was a beneficiary of US aid from the outset, its official rhetoric reflected a brash contempt for US visions of democratic development, regarded as "imperialist." In Eritrea, the US ultimatum of "no democracy, no aid" was blunted by the PGE's refusal to accept $26 million from USAID claiming that any conditionalities, even establishing democratic institutions, were "crude enticements" camouflaging an imposition of American power.[35] The general public was more welcoming of the US presence—after eliciting some form of apology that the United States was wrong to side with the Ethiopian Empire in the 1950s—and continued to be hopeful that the brash new leaders would bring about a dynamic economy and an accommodating political framework for its citizens. The majority of urban dwellers perceived the reengagement with the United States in a positive light, due to nostalgia for the "good old Kagnew days"—which they associated with a busy port and steady revenues generated by activities from the US base, rather than with a realignment with the United States' ideological values.

Despite the United States' contribution to the democratization project,[36] Eritrea's rulers continued to be discomfited by the liberal democratic rhetoric of US policymakers, and "capacity-building"—a term which Eritrean policymakers interpreted to mainly mean "infrastructural development/ economic employment"—remained a term they preferred over "democratization" in Eritrea. This unwillingness to buy into even the language of the new policy continued to lead to tension in US-Eritrean relations. Then, in February 1994, the EPLF recast itself as a new political organization and announced to its civilian citizens that it no longer operated through its clandestine (Maoist/Marxist) party and renamed itself the People's Front for Democracy and Justice (PFDJ). Voting for the new leadership was conducted using electronic methods—which enhanced the PFDJ's image, but did nothing to allay grassroots fears that behind the carefully orchestrated transformation was a realignment of EPLF hardliners that pushed out more moderate nationalists.

However, the Eritrean government continued to move away from any semblance of a Western-style democratic system. Nonetheless, US officials who were aware of these developments remained blinded by the persuasiveness of the rhetoric of the regime, which now called—privately—for a developmental model of state-building borrowed from Singapore, South Korea, and the People's Republic of China (PRC). Political reform was also slow; the PFDJ drew out the constitution-making process over three years, from 1994 to 1997, but failed to implement it as the supreme law of the land despite its ratification by the Constituent Assembly in May 1997.[37] Indeed, even a decade after its liberation from Ethiopia, the PFDJ government had yet to deliver even the minimal concessions to democratic institutions that would enable its citizens to participate in national affairs, other than to rubber-stamp the National Assembly's resolutions.

Nonetheless, US officials who were aware of these developments appeared to be persuaded by the government's rhetoric. Indeed, despite the Afwerki regime's close ties with the PRC, the muzzling of democratic institutions, and nagging questions about PFDJ officials' tours to Iraq and Iran, US policymakers believed in the American ideological victory over those of their communist rivals, choosing to ignore these issues. The silence of the United States on these developments in Eritrea also discouraged grassroots organizations and civil society groups from overtly criticizing the regime's policies of monopoly over *all* aspects of citizens' lives; the PGE/EPLF was rarely criticized openly for the micromanagement of all national and civil society projects. As a result, citizens and the budding civil society groups became emblematic symbols of a transitional Eritrea while in reality they were shut out from meaningful participation in national reconstruction projects. Fear of governmental reprisal as well as the culture of conformity that was deeply entrenched in postwar Eritrea discouraged civil society groups from becoming dynamic actors contributing to the nation's democratization. Notwithstanding audible voices of reason cautioning US officials against neglecting the aspiration of citizens—such as that of Stephen Morrison, who sought balance between the new "hands-on" policy and linkage to leaders and fulfilling the US promise of "no democracy, no aid,"[38] the two representatives of a "new generation of African leaders" emerged as the heroes of their nations and were portrayed in the United States as hardworking and self-reliant personalities—a far cry from unsavory dictators like Mengistu, Siad Barre, and Idi Amin.

Thus, even though US observers were aware that the elected Ethiopian regime was adept at orchestrating public support for its policies,[39] there were many other developments that were seen as concrete results of US investment in democratization of the country. For instance, the government of Ethiopia ratified and implemented its constitution (with numerous lapses and arbitrary arrests) and could boast of two (flawed but nevertheless well-executed) elections.[40] In Eritrea, criticism was staved off by reminding the United States and other Western donors of their "collective guilt" in colluding with Ethiopia to derail Eritrean aspirations for self-determination.[41] Ultimately, however, US credibility as a supporter of democratizing governments was eroded due to the undemocratic policies enacted by the new governments of Afwerki and Zenawi.

Things Fall Apart: A New War and Old Hostilities

The eruption of the border war between Ethiopia and Eritrea in 1998 finally shook US policymakers and scholars of the Horn of their optimism and also brought out the degree of anti-American sentiment in the region.[42] The US government realized that given the opportunity to select their pace, the Eritrean guerrillas-turned-statesmen would not gradually embrace an appropriate democratic framework.[43] In particular, the Eritrean team accused the United States of being a power which believes in "easy fixes and in ramming solutions down our throats."[44] It appeared that earlier insistence by the United States to delay Eritrea's declaration of independence in May 1991 had fueled an already existing reservoir of anti-Americanism.[45] Only when, in September 2001, Isaias Afwerki imprisoned hundreds of dissidents, including a group of parliamentarians asking for the implementation of the 1997 Constitution and two national employees of the US Embassy in Asmara did the United States finally rebuke the slow pace of democratization. The Eritrean government angrily dismissed the US protests—leading to a souring of relations.

A shift in Eritrean attitude and a moderation of its anti-American rhetoric only emerged in 2002 when the PFDJ leadership, facing internal outrage and diminishing aid, sought to maintain its hold on power by inviting the United States to use its ports as military bases for the war on terrorism.[46] Yet, despite the Eritrean government's attempts to regain US bases (and thereby strengthen its hold on power to counter grassroots opposition to the constant state of mobilization and rise of organized opponents to its hegemony), Gen. Tommy Franks, commander of the US Central Command at the time, laid to rest rumors that Eritrea had been "chosen" by the United States as the optimal host for US counterterrorist campaigns. General Franks stressed that US troops are "based in Djibouti. They are not based in Eritrea."[47]

At present, the United States has considerably disengaged from Eritrea— even with its geostrategic location for conducting the war on terrorism. In contrast, the US military presence in Djibouti by late 2002 involved 3,200 troops being trained in desert warfare in anticipation of a war with Iraq.[48] By 2004 the abrasiveness of the PFDJ's anti-American rhetoric as well as its refusal to either release US Embassy employees or bring to court the constitutional dissidents held incommunicado since 2001 resulted in a hardening of US policymakers against their most unreliable ally in the Horn. The beginning of a shift of US policy from selective engagement to one of disengagement in Eritrea was finally signaled by the ousting of Eritrea from the African Growth and Opportunity Act (AGOA) and placing its vast remittance network under official scrutiny.[49]

Whither Somalia?

Somalia, after a decade of anarchy, remained a "no man's land" until the preparations for counterterrorism jogged "official" memories that an assessment of US policy toward the collapsed state of Somalia was overdue.[50] The United States began its reengagement with Somalia with a humanitarian intervention to address the conflict-induced famine and dislocation in the country. More recently, Somalia has become an important ally in the US war on terrorism.

Somalia's economy collapsed in the aftermath of the Ogaden War of 1977, fueling preexisting domestic dissatisfaction with the patronage politics of the Barre regime. A number of armed opposition groups were established in this period and increased in the 1980s, providing the impetus for what would later emerge as warlordism in Somalia.[51] Ethiopia's expulsion of the Somali National Movement (SNM) in 1991 led to that organization's confrontation with the regime's troops and the devastation of the northern regions associated with this group. Secession by a portion of the former British Somaliland, which has yet to acquire international recognition after a decade of separate existence, can be traced to the heavy-handed attempt by the government in Mogadishu to retain control. The combination of a massive famine in the countryside and havoc caused by Siad Barre's troops precipitated the decline of his rule. In January 1991, Siad Barre's regime collapsed, but his clan-based loyalist guards continued to fight, further pushing the country into anarchy in which armed marauders established their own zones of rule. By 1992, Somalia's descent into Pyrrhic anarchy was hastened by a split between the two cofounders of the United Somali Congress, due to a unilateral declaration of a provisional government by Ali Mahdi—a step vehemently opposed by Gen. Mohamed Farah Aideed. Somalia's starving population was caught in the crossfire between the two warlords, and an estimated 300,000 died in the sporadic violence while the famine claimed even more lives. It was under such circumstances that humanitarian intervention as a preemptive step to counter the spiraling violence in the region—due to refugees and arms transfers—was introduced as a key element of American policy in the post–Cold War period.

The Bush administration committed itself to Operation Restore Hope (ORH)—a humanitarian intervention—after the UN Security Council passed Resolution 794 on December 3, 1992, authorizing the deployment of 24,000 American troops to secure ports and roads to ensure the delivery of famine aid to Somalis.[52] ORH was envisioned as a stopgap measure to use American troops to secure roads and ports to enable international delivery of food aid to the starving population. Once this objective was met, ORH was intended to be phased out and to be replaced by UN forces whose objectives were to be to facilitate negotiations between the armed groups in order to reestablish state institutions and social order. US disengagement from ORH was to begin after the UN completed training personnel to take over the peacekeeping forces.

American troops landed on the shores of Mogadishu, in a highly publicized humanitarian campaign, on December 9, 1992, and began securing areas for delivery of food aid. Initially, ORH succeeded in meeting its objective of delivering needed supplies, and friendly Somali crowds welcomed US troops until firefights erupted between the warlords who quickly demanded to control the disbursement of the food aid. Thus, in order to deliver the food to the areas controlled by the warlords, the United States and the UN were forced to acknowledge the strongest of the warlords as key political players in a chaotic Somalia. On March 26, 1993, the UN passed Resolution 814 to establish UNISOM II, signaling the beginning of the transition from a purely humanitarian operation to the political phase of seeking to reconcile the key actors.[53] In June, Aideed's forces unleashed a propaganda war, which portrayed continued presence of alien groups as an attempt to recolonize the country, and urged Somalis to resist external meddling. The angry war of words was followed by an ambush of a Pakistani contingent of UNISOM II on June 5, which resulted in the death of twenty-four Pakistanis and the wounding of three Americans and one Italian. The following day, the UN passed Resolution 837 authorizing UNISOM II to launch a military response against Aideed's forces in retaliation for the ambush.[54]

The following four months (June to October 1993), devoted to a manhunt of Aideed and his collaborators, irrevocably altered the original mandate for US reengagement in Somalia based on the motivation of meeting humanitarian needs. With the change of mission, the population no longer welcomed US troops. Differences on how to manage the escalating tensions between UN and US officials also were exacerbated by the lack of coordination between US troops and those of UNISOM. On October 3, 1993, three American helicopters were shot down by Aideed's militia members, killing 18 soldiers and over 300 Somalis.[55] The Clinton administration was forced to end the US-led humanitarian intervention abruptly amidst growing public anger.[56] US troops were evacuated by March 1994, and one year later, the UN followed suit, ending the brief interlude of US reengagement with Somalia.[57]

After ignoring the former Somalia and its problems for almost a decade, the United States has begun some limited reengagement because of its own perceived national interest in combating international terrorism.[58] As an outgrowth of the new attempt to establish relations with Somali leaders that would allow the United States to monitor and engage would-be terrorists, the United States has, since the fall of 2002, been participating in negotiations designed to lead to the reestablishment of an internationally recognized Somali state.[59] Peace talks sponsored by IGAD in 2002, with UN, EU, Arab League, AU, and US backing, continued in the Kenyan town of Eldoret. The talks included not only political elites, but also a record number of women, youth, and civil society organizations. The United States is a signatory to the Eldoret Framework, providing not only observers but also financial assistance for the talks. Given the unstable politics of the Persian Gulf and Middle Eastern countries, the United States now realizes that political stability and peaceful social relations in the Horn are essential to international security.[60]

However, the inclusion of Somalia in the counterterrorist agenda in early 2002 indicates, once again, that the United States seeks engagement without necessarily having a clear picture of the motivations of state and nonstate actors in the Somalia(s). Tellingly, the congressional hearing of February 2002 summarized US goals as follows:

The short-term goal of course is to remove the terrorist threat that might or might not exist in Somalia. . . . A mid-range goal, but one we are starting to work on now, is looking at how Somalia threatens the region and the neighborhood. The third area is . . . long-term challenges and long-term governance issues. Where is Somalia going to be in 4, 5, 6, 10 years from now?[61]

"What is to become of Somalia and Somalis?" was the question asked by the anticolonial Somali religious leader Muhammad Abdille Hassan— dubbed the Mad Mullah by the British more than 100 years ago[62]—and is now being asked by the United States. Although the United States stepped in to fill the vacuum left behind by the Soviet Union in 1977, the emphasis was on short-term access to counter the loss of disengaging in Ethiopia, without replicating the investment of resources that had gone to building a political and economic relationship. The more recent engagement of the United States in the 1990s—the first in the Horn after the Cold War— demonstrated the untested policy of multilateral intervention and the use of force in the fulfillment of humanitarian objectives.

US policymakers' tendency to view US-Somali relations as secondary to its other relations in the Horn has led to a miscalculation of Somalia's importance to the stability of the Horn. The notion that the recalcitrant Somalis (first as "primitive pastoralists," then "irredentists," and lastly, "terrorist-hosting warlords") can only be handled through regional proxies, such as Ethiopia, Djibouti, or Eritrea, must be reassessed to understand the consensus of Somali leaders that anarchy is preferred to subordination to neighboring states.[63] While the attention of the world was riveted on the exodus of frustrated US and UN forces, the northern part of the country quietly seceded from the defunct Somali state, triggering annexationist impulses from Djibouti and Ethiopia countered by Eritrea and Sudan.[64]

Sudan: To Disengage or Reengage?

In contrast to Ethiopia, US policy in the Sudan has historically rested squarely on its utility as a geostrategic base to defend US interests in the Middle East. US policymakers were constantly frustrated in their efforts to end the North-South conflict by Sadiq-al-Mahdi, who implemented sharia law and initiated a rapprochement with Libya. Despite the numerous internationally and regionally sponsored peace initiatives to resolve the North-South conflict, the Khartoum government remained impervious to any US ultimatum or enticement until 2000. Nevertheless the United States maintained a steady but low profile in the efforts to ensure open channels for humanitarian aid supported by a domestic faith-based constituency, which lobbied strongly on behalf of southern Sudanese victims of Khartoum's policy of "arabization and Islamization."

The "blinders" in this part of the Horn were the inability or unwilling-ness of US policymakers to acknowledge the grievances of the non-Arab-ized and non-Islamic communities inhabiting both the North and South. Inadequate US attention to the SPLA leader, John Garang, reflected an unbelievable degree of indifference to the outrage felt by southerners as well as the Nuba and Fur communities, stigmatized by the experience of slavery and treated as second-class citizens. The victims of Afro-Arab racism were united by their desire for socioeconomic and political equality. They were also divided by their religious beliefs that made any idea of rule by a non-Muslim anathema to some. Garang's insistence on a secular and multiethnic, united Sudan did not receive the attention it deserved. Rather, Garang's articulation of these democratic principles—which reflect the emphasis on multi-partyism and secularism—were treated with disbelief both by Northerners and Southerners.[65]

To date, despite the protocols and agreements leading up to the wide-ranging Comprehensive Peace Agreement (December 2004),[66] US policy-makers have emphasized the religious divide while skirting the "racial divide" separating opponents and supporters of the Khartoum regime. Whether it was out of deference to domestic sensitivities or blindness to the existence of an ideology of Afro-Arab supremacy over those populations claiming only Africanness, US policymakers could only reiterate the need for negotiations and humanitarian aid. SPLA's American Christian support-ers appear to be filling the gap by portraying the conflict as both a spiritual and racial struggle for the emancipation of Africans from their bondage to Muslim Arabs. Debates about self-determination and contentious issues such as ownership of oil resources, while looming large in the background, remain muted.

Notwithstanding the Comprehensive Peace Agreement, both the regime in Khartoum and the SPLA and associated allies inside and outside the country must still contend with their domestic and foreign political oppo-nents. The failure of the avowedly Islamic National Islamic Front (NIF) led by the strongman Gen. Omar Bashir, the president of Sudan, and the in-scrutable intellectual Hassan al-Turabi to impose a radical Islam in Sudan has led to social unrest as well as growing dissent and instability. The NIF regime's open support of Iraq during the 1991 Gulf War cost the Sudanese government dearly—both diplomatically and financially. It joined the list of rogue states and its loan applications were rejected—although the closure of the US Embassy in Khartoum in January 1991 was rescinded in March 1991 after the NIF indicated willingness to normalize relations. In response, US policy did not become more proactive and provide direct sup-port for the SPLA. Rather, the United States opted to use its regional allies to encircle it and ostracize it in regional dealings.[67] The older framework of containment put in place to combat the spread of communism in Africa was reconfigured to tackle the new threat to US interests—Islamic fundamentalism. Although the "freezing out" of Sudan by the Ethio-Eritrean alliance worked for five years, the eruption of the border war between the two erstwhile allies led to a rapprochement between Sudanese and Ethiopian leaders, effectively breaking the earlier isolation. The Clinton administration and its "new breed of African policymakers" pursued a policy of isolating the Sudanese regime and rewarding the Ethiopian and Eritrean regimes.[68] The discovery of oil in southern Sudan, where American economic interests coincided with the Bush administration's quest for a diplomatic victory in Africa, led to a pursuit of a dual policy of selective sanctions and economic linkages. The giant of the Horn—which had always taken second place to Ethiopia in US policymakers' hierarchy—thus emerged into the twenty-first century as owner of resources considered valuable by the United States.

The Comprehensive Peace Agreement has provided hope for a peaceful resolution of this long conflict. The agreement has been praised for addressing both parties' primary concerns, laying out the principles agreed to and a framework for a transitional process, and further elaborating on two contentious issues in the negotiations: relations between the state and religion and the right to self-determination for the peoples of southern Sudan.[69] In particular, it acknowledges that Sudan is a multiethnic, multiracial, and multireligious society, providing a legitimate framework for the exercise of freedom in the articulation of diversity in the political and socioeconomic spheres of the New Sudan envisioned in the postconflict period.[70] Equally important, six years following the Comprehensive Peace Agreement, the negotiated peace plan allows for an internationally monitored referendum for southern Sudan to decide on self-determination.[71]

Revenue-sharing was agreed to by the two major participants in the peace process—namely the government of Sudan and the SPLM/A—in May 2004.[72] The identification of the two beneficiaries of the revenue-sharing arrangements—which excluded other political actors, such as the rival groups in Darfur—triggered violent clashes between the Khartoum government and marginalized groups both in the West and East. The National Democratic Alliance, a constellation of opposition groups embracing traditional sectarian parties and armed groups with headquarters in neighboring Eritrea, was excluded as was also the Umma Party, which had withdrawn from the NDA. The armed groups in Darfur—the Sudan Liberation Movement/Army (SLM/A) and the Justice and Equality Movement (JEM)—were mired in their own internecine fighting, which led to the signing of separate peace agreements relating to reforms in the structures of governance.[73] The Abuja talks of July 5, 2005, led to a possible compromise based on the establishment of a "regional autonomy," which would protect minorities' landownership rights. These talks were followed by agreements for reconciliation by the leaders of the SLM/A and JEM.[74]

The key lesson US policymakers learned in Sudan is that unilateral efforts—whether in the military or diplomatic arena—rarely succeed while multilateral efforts, which combine both regional and international mediators, have a better chance of doing so. Only the Sudanese government can determine to adhere to the agreement or renege on it. But its signing of the Comprehensive Peace Agreement provides a basis on which to possibly build a sustainable peace. The issue of choice—a democratic exercise—is the lynchpin of the agreement.

Conclusion and Policy Recommendations

US policy in the Horn (1941–1991) reflects four decades of a "hands-off" policy with "blinders on," except where it was determined that vital US national interests were at stake. For example, to secure a listening post in Eritrea in a worldwide land-based communications network, the United States adopted Ethiopia as a client for more than two decades. Also, when the Soviet Union attempted to establish a beachhead in Ethiopia based on the Brezhnev Doctrine, the United States pursued its encirclement strategy to counter the Soviet Union in the Horn. The latest shift occurred in the fifth decade of US involvement in the Horn, and coincided with the collapse of the Soviet Union. From 1991 to 2001, the United States pursued a new policy of selective reengagement, based on its own perceived strategic needs. This hands-on policy has succeeded in breaking the tradition of unconditional support for repressive client regimes but has yet to be crowned with success.[75]

The United States' inability or unwillingness to either entice or enforce compliance with its ultimatum of "no democracy, no aid" must be urgently examined, amended, or excised if the credibility of US policymakers is to be preserved in the Horn. The question that will be addressed in the near future as the United States embarks on the next phase of its war against terrorism is whether democracy will be a casualty of the new era. To date, it appears that US policymakers are cautiously seeking to maintain a balance between the linkage of democracy and development aid without necessarily sacrificing national interests. However, the United States' declaration of the Sudanese government's brutal repression of the rebellion in Darfur and the targeting of civilians as "genocidal" without necessarily taking the steps required by the Genocide Convention points to another troubling continuity of selective engagement.

The resistance of key actors in the international community—the UN, the AU, and the EU—to this new US role as both a "peacemaker" in one part of the Horn—southern Sudan—while waging a war of unilateral intervention in Iraq indicates that the decade of America's uncontested hegemony is under challenge by both traditional allies and outspoken enemies. How US national interests will be defined globally will thus lead to either the consolidation of the new hands-on policy or its replacement.

The question that the countries of the Horn must ask is: What is in it for us if we engage the United States in the region? Particularly in this era of globalization, avenues have to be found by local policy elites to clearly articulate their interests not only in terms of their individual national interests, but also in terms of regional security needs. The United States should be ready to respond positively to clearly articulated plans to strengthen the African Union as well as IGAD in their capacity to keep the peace in the region, to mediate effectively when disputes occur, and to strengthen democratic institutions and national and regional economies. For the countries of the Horn to be successful in negotiating a fair deal with the United States, they are going to have to be led by a bold, visionary, transparent, and honest leadership class that puts the popular will ahead of individual or narrow group interests.

Notes

1. Peter Schraeder, "Reviewing the Study of US Policy Towards Africa: From Intellectual 'Backwater' to Theory Construction," *Third World Quarterly* 14 (December 1993): 776.

2. Elliot P. Skinner, "Historical Framework Paper" (Washington, DC: National Summit on Africa, 1998).

3. The Horn of Africa comprises the countries of Djibouti, Eritrea, Ethiopia, Somalia, and Sudan.

4. Donald Rothchild, "The Impact of US Disengagement on African Intrastate Conflict Resolution," in *Africa in World Politics: The African State System in Flux,* eds. John W. Harbeson and Donald Rothchild (Boulder: Westview, 2000), pp. 160–187.

5. Harold Marcus, *Ethiopia, Great Britain and the United States 1941–74* (Berkeley: University of California Press, 1983).

6. Edward Korry, "Testimony," in *Hearings Before the US Senate Subcommittee on African Affairs* (Washington, DC: US Government Printing Office, 1976).

7. In keeping with the hierarchical nature of imperial Ethiopia, Harrar Academy served the academic elite of the military, which graduated "gentlemen cadets," and the Holeta Academy included well-trained graduates who would later resent the two-tiered military structure. Mengistu Haile Mariam, who presided over the demise of the ancien régime, was a graduate of the latter.

8. Edmond J. Keller, "United States Foreign Policy on the Horn of Africa: Policymaking with Blinders On," in *African Crisis Areas and U.S. Foreign Policy,* eds. Richard Sklar, Gerald Bender, and James S. Coleman (Berkeley: University of California Press, 1985), pp. 178–193.

9. David Newsom, "Testimony," in *Hearings Before the US Senate Subcommittee on US Security Agreements and Commitments Abroad: Ethiopia* (Washington, DC: US Government Printing Office, 1970).

10. United States Department of Defense (US DOD), *Foreign Military Sales, Foreign Military Construction, and Military Assistance as of 1981* (Washington, DC: US DOD, 1981).

11. George W. Bader, "Testimony," in *Hearings Before the US Senate Subcommittee on US Security Agreements and Commitments Abroad: Ethiopia* (Washington, DC: US Government Printing Office, 1970).

12. Jeffrey Lefebvre, "Moscow's Cold War and Post–Cold War Policies in Africa," in *Africa in the New International Order: Rethinking State Sovereignty and Regional Security,* eds. Edmond J. Keller and Donald Rothchild (Boulder: Lynne Rienner, 1996), p. 208.

13. Marina Ottaway, *Soviet and American Influence in the Horn of Africa* (New York: Praeger, 1982), pp. 50–53.

14. Ibid.

15. Robert D. Gray, "Post-Imperial Ethiopian Foreign Policy: Ethiopian Dependence," *Proceedings from the Fifth International Conference on Ethiopian Studies* (Chicago, 1978), p. 807.

16. Edmond J. Keller, *Revolutionary Ethiopia: From Empire to People's Republic* (Bloomington: Indiana University Press, 1988), p. 204.

17. Colin Legum and Bill Lee, *The Horn of Africa in Continuing Crisis* (New York: Africana, 1979), p. 52.

18. Kenya and Ethiopia had already signed a defense treaty in 1964 with the specific objective of protecting their mutual borders from Somali irredentist claims over the area administered by the British colonial administrators as the Northern Frontier District. Such treaties enabled both Ethiopia and Kenya to come to each other's aid and to maintain control over their permeable borders.

19. Henry Jackson, *From the Congo to SOWETO: US Foreign Policy Towards Africa Since 1960* (New York: William Morrow, 1982).

20. Consecutive issues of *The Military Balance,* International Institute of Security Studies (IISS), *The Military Balance, 1990* (London: International Institute for Strategic Studies, 1977–1989).

21. Terrance Lyons, "The International Context of Internal War: Ethiopia/Eritrea," in *Africa in the New International Order: Rethinking State Sovereignty and Regional Security,* eds. Edmond J. Keller and Donald Rothchild (Boulder: Lynne Rienner Publishers, 1996), p. 87.

22. Authors' fieldnotes: Asmara and Addis Ababa, 1991–1992.

23. Ann Mosley Lesch, *The Sudan: Contested National Identities* (Bloomington: Indiana University Press, 1998), p. 55.

24. Herman Cohen, *Intervening in Africa: Superpower Peacemaking in a Troubled Continent* (New York: St. Martin's Press, 2000).

25. Ibid., p. 59.

26. Gebru Tareke, *Ethiopia: Power and Protest* (Cambridge University Press, 1991), pp. 206–212.

27. John Young, *Peasant Revolution in Ethiopia: The Tigray People's Liberation Front, 1975–1991* (Cambridge: Cambridge University Press, 1997), pp. 152–159.

28. Editorials and articles as well as political cartoons in the privately owned newspapers during 1991–1994 reflected an antipathy to the vision of ethnic federalism and being "ruled" by groups that did not respect the historic unity of Ethiopia.

29. Tareke, *Ethiopia: Power and Protest,* pp. 206–212.

30. Theodore M. Vestal, *Ethiopia: A Post–Cold War African State* (Westport, CT: Praeger Publishers, 1991), pp. 5–7.

31. Edmond J. Keller, "Ethnic Federalism, Fiscal Reform, Development and Democracy in Ethiopia," *Journal of African Political Science* 7 (June 2002): 21–50.

32. Cohen, *Intervening in Africa*, p. 56.

33. For a very instructive study on dictatorships and the "sympathy" for them, see Ronald Wintrope, *The Political Economy of Dictatorship* (Cambridge: Cambridge University Press, 1998).

34. Mohammed O. Abo-Bakr, *Democracy and Political Pluralism in Eritrea* (Cairo: Egyption Office for Publication, 1998).

35. For details see Yohannes Okbazghi, *The United States and the Horn of Africa: An Analytical Study of Pattern and Process* (Boulder: Westview Press, 1997).

36. Field interviews by the authors in January 1998 point to an estimated figure for the democratization project—inclusive of constitutionmaking, civic education, and related activities—that exceeded $2 million during the first five years of independence. These figures are not by any means the most comprehensive due to the excessive secrecy of civil servants who are not accustomed to inquiries of this type from outsiders. Nevertheless, these figures have been corroborated by persons familiar with the democratization program in Eritrea in the 1990s. See also Ruth Iyob, "The Ethiopia-Eritrean Conflict: Diasporic vs. Hegemonic States in the Horn of Africa, 1991–2000," *Journal of Modern African Studies* 38 (December 2000): 651–682.

37. Bereket Habte Selassie, "The Disappearance of the Eritrean Constitution and Its Impact on Current Politics in Eritrea," *News.Asmarino.com* (January 20, 2001, available online at http://news.asmarino.com/Articles/2001/01/bhs-20.asp).

38. Peter Rosenblum, "Irrational Exuberance: The Clinton Administration in Africa," *Current History* 101 (May 2002): 197.

39. Marina Ottaway, *The New African Leaders: Democracy or State Reconstruction?* (Washington, DC: The Brookings Institution, 1999).

40. See *An Evaluation of the June 21, 1992 Elections in Ethiopia* (Washington, DC: African American Institute and the National Democratic Institute, 1992) and Terrance Lyons, "Closing the Transition: The May 1995 Elections in Ethiopia," *Journal of Modern African Studies* 34 (March 1996): 121–143.

41. Collective guilt in the Eritrean context is understood to mean a sense of betrayal by the United Nations, the West, and others in the international community.

42. People's Front for Democracy and Justice, Special Edition, "Interview with President Isaias Afwerki," *Hewyet* (March 1999).

43. Most analytical scholars seem to have been disabused of any hope for democratization in the post-2000 period where human rights violations have continued unabated.

44. PFDJ, "Interview with President Isaias Afwerki."

45. Cohen, *Intervening in Africa*, pp. 41, 54. See also Okbazghi, *The United States and the Horn*, pp. 189–191.

46. Alex P. Kellogg, "War Justifies All: Donald Rumsfeld Courts a Repressive Government in the Horn of Africa," *The American Prospector Online* (December 17, 2002); Judy Sarasohn, "Eritrea Pushes to Get US Base," *Washington Post* (November 20, 2002).

47. "Horn of Africa: US Admits Sending More Troops," *IRIN News.Org* (October 30, 2002, available online at http://www.irinnews.org/report.asp?ReportID=3 0661&SelectRegion=Horn_of_Africa&SelectCountry=HORN_OF_AFRICA).

48. See Sarasohn, "Eritrea Pushes to Get US Base."

49. John Oyuke, "Eritrea Out of AGOA Accord," *The East African Standard* (Nairobi) (April 1, 2004, available online at http://zete.delina.org/runzete.asp? quSri=131).

50. Countless conferences and many prescriptions have been offered but none have yet come to terms that the body politic that was Somalia has, since its infestation by warlords, undergone a transformation so alien to the concept of modern

states that it requires thinking outside the usual alternatives: (1) impose a leviathan, (2) bring about a victory of one warlord, or (3) let the problem be solved by any regional power able and willing to achieve the task of taming the Somali Franken-stein. For different perspectives on the Somali crisis, see Mohamed Sahnoun, *Somalia: The Missed Opportunities* (Washington, DC: United States Institute of Peace, 1994); Terrence Lyons and Ahmed I. Samatar, *State Collapse, Multilateral Intervention and Strategies for Political Reconstruction* (Washington, DC: The Brookings Institution, 1995); and I. W. Zartman, ed., *Traditional Cures for Modern Conflicts: African Conflict "Medicine"* (Boulder: Lynne Rienner Publishers, 1999).

51. The Somali Salvation Democratic Front (SSF) was established in Ethiopia in 1978. The Somali National Movement (SNM) and the United Somali Congress (USC) emerged after 1981.

52. UN Security Council, 3145th meeting, "Resolution 794 [Somalia]" (S/RES/794) (December 3, 1992).

53. UN Security Council, 3188th meeting, "Resolution 814 [Somalia]" (S/RES/814) (March 26, 1993).

54. UN Security Council, 3229th meeting, "Resolution 837 [Somalia]" (S/RES/837) (June 6, 1993).

55. Helen Fogarassy, *Mission Improbable: The World Community in a UN Compound in Somalia* (Lanham, MD: Lexington Books, 1999), pp. 138–140.

56. Edmond J. Keller, "Rethinking African Regional Security," in *Regional Orders: Building Security in a New World,* eds. David Lake and Patrick Morgan (University Park: Pennsylvania State University Press, 1997), p. 310.

57. The cost of this brief reengagement has been estimated to be $1.6 billion and the loss of 151 lives. UN, "Somalia—UNOSOM II: Facts and Figures" (available online at http://www.un.org/Depts/dpko/dpko/co_mission/unosom2factx.html, accessed March 23, 2005).

58. "Somalia: No Proxy Peace," *Africa Confidential* 40 (October 8, 1999): 8.

59. J. Stephen Morrison, "Somalia and Sudan's Race to the Fore in Africa," Center for Strategic and International Studies and the Massachusetts Institute of Technology, *Washington Quarterly* 25 (Spring 2002): 191. A government of Somalia was elected in Kenya in 2005 and is in the process of establishing itself in the country.

60. Ibid.

61. Subcommittee on African Affairs, *Somalia: US. Policy Options* (Washington, DC: US Government Printing Office, 2002), p. 5.

62. These words are attributed to Sheikh Mohamed Abdille Hassan, a religious anticolonial leader who fought against the dismemberment of Somalia. For more details and analyses see Said S. Samatar, *Oral Poetry and Somali Nationalism: The Case of Sayyid Mohammad Abdille Hassan* (Cambridge: Cambridge University Press, 1982) and Abdi Sheikh'-Abdi, *Divine Madness: Mohammed Abdulle Hassan (1956–1920)* (London and New Jersey: Zed Press, 1992).

63. "Somalia: Building Blocks," *Africa Confidential* 40 (September 24, 1999): 7. The need for reassessment of the Somali "problem" as viewed by the realpolitik policymakers of the Cold War years has been pointed out by scholars and policymakers. For analyses on the period 1991 to 1995, see John L. Hirsch and Robert B. Oakley, *Somalia and Operation Restore Hope: Reflections on Peacemaking and Peacekeeping* (Washington, DC: United States Institute of Peace Press, 1995), p. 171. See also Ahmed I. Samatar, ed., *The Somali Challenge: From Catastrophe to Renewal?* (Boulder: Lynne Rienner Publishers, 1994), pp. 137–138.

64. For different perspectives on the unacknowledged Republic of Somaliland, see Gerard Prunier, "Somaliland: Birth of a New Country?" in *The Horn of Africa,*

ed. Charles Gordon (New York: St. Martin's Press, 1994), pp. 64–71; Abdi Samatar, "Warlord Games," *BBC Focus on Africa Magazine* 10 (January–March 1999): 26–27; Adam M. Hussein, "Somalia: A Terrible Beauty Being Born?" in *Collapsed States: The Disintegration and Restoration of Legitimate Authority,* ed. I. William Zartman (Boulder: Lynne Rienner Publishers, 1995), pp. 79–82.

65. For a better understanding of the racial undertones of the conflict and its intentional and unintentional misreadings see Cohen, *Intervening in Africa,* pp. 64–66; John Garang de Mabior and Mansur Khalid, *John Garang Speaks* (London: KTI Ltd., 1987), pp. 91–125; Bona Malwal, "Sudan's Political and Economic Future: A Southern Perspective," in *The Horn of Africa,* ed. Charles Gurdon (New York: St. Martin's Press, 1994), p. 97. The leader of the SPLA is now Salva Kiir, following the death of John Garang in a helicopter crash in southern Sudan in July 2005.

66. The Comprehensive Peace Agreement, signed on December 31, 2004, by the government of Sudan and the Sudan People's Liberation Movement/Army, is the collection of agreements and protocols reached by these two parties from July 2002 until May 2004. These agreements and protocols include the Machakos Protocol (July 2002), the Agreement on Security Arrangements (September 2003), the Agreement on Wealth Sharing (January 2004), the Protocol on Power Sharing (May 2004), the Protocol on the Resolution of the Conflict in Southern Kordofan and the Blue Nile States (May 2004), and the Protocol on the Resolution of the Conflict in the Abyei Area (May 2004). The Comprehensive Peace Agreement also includes the Agreement on Permanent Ceasefire Arrangement and the above protocols' and agreements' implementation modalities.

67. M. Ehasan Ahari, "Rogue States and NMD/TMD: Policies in Search of a Rationale?" *Mediterranean Quarterly* 12 (May 2001): 84–87.

68. Rosenblum, "Irrational Exuberance," pp. 196–197.

69. See "The Conflict in South Sudan and the IGAD Peace Process," *IGAD News,* Intergovernmental Authority on Development (December 2002).

70. See *The Machakos Protocol,* Machakos, Kenya (July 20, 2002), Part C, Articles 61–66.

71. Comprehensive Peace Agreement, January 2005 (available online at http://www.unmis.org).

72. "Sudan: Details of Peace Protocols Signed This Week," *IRINNews.org,* May 28, 2004 (available online at http://www.irinnews.org/report.asp?ReportID=4131&SelectRegion=East_Africa&SelectCountry=SUDAN).

73. International Crisis Group, *The AU's Mission in Darfur: Bridging the Gaps,* Africa Briefing No. 28, Nairobi, Brussels, July 6, 2005.

74. African Union, *Declaration of Principles for the Resolution of the Sudanese Conflict in Darfur, Abuja,* July 5, 2005 (electronic version); "Darfur Rebels Agree to Stop Infighting," *Agence-France Presse,* July 19, 2005, reproduced on Sudan.net (available online at http://www.sudan.net/news/posted/11924.html, accessed July 21, 2005); "Darfur's Rebel Groups Reach Deal," *BBC News,* July 19, 2005 (available online at http://news.bbc.co.uk/go/pr/fr/-/2/hi/africa/4695807.stm, accessed July 21, 2005).

75. The State Department's rebuke of the Eritrean government's incarceration of reformist parliamentarians who demanded the implementation of the constitution ratified in 1997 is an encouraging sign that democracy may still be worth fighting for by citizens of the Horn.

7

Toward Overcoming the Challenges: Policy Recommendations

Dorina A. Bekoe

The countries in East Africa and the Horn face large flows of refugees and weapons stemming from regionalized conflicts, threats of secession and civil conflict by various ethnic groups, and the push for greater democratization by civil society. These factors manifest themselves in an increased number of weapons in private hands, the creation of displaced populations, the adoption of legislation that may curtail freedoms, and pressure for political reform. To address these issues, governments must overcome the challenges of extending their administration, rethinking their policies toward displaced people, and opening their societies. Specifically, governments of East Africa and the Horn must enact policies that foster an effective civil society, develop a holistic approach to ending the illicit trade of firearms, reduce the marginalization of particular ethnic groups, and work with the reengaged United States to broaden democratization in the subregion. As states react to these factors, governments must recognize and reduce the costs to democratic transitions, mitigate the spillover of bad governance, and institute policies for governing in diverse societies. Notably, the problems facing African states are not sui generis—they are also the products of international policies and Africa's entry into the global economy. Consequently, for each of these challenges, resolution lies within the subregion as well as within the international community.

Fostering an Effective Civil Society

After the third wave of democracy swept through Africa in the 1990s, the challenge to new governments and to the societies that they govern remains the consolidation of political reform and breaking away from the past autocratic traditions. In Kenya, Klopp shows the difficulty new regimes encounter in separating from the past because of their need to form partnerships with

127

the former government in order to maintain stability. However, the cooptation of Kenya's old regime by the new government is not unusual or even completely avoidable. A review of democratic transformation in Africa indicates that although civil society has pushed many governments to undertake democratic reform, once in office, governments must manage the state's affairs through incomplete institutions, strong patronage networks, and the personalization of politics. In other words, despite the reform that takes place, it is difficult for new governments to make a clean break with the past. Even new governments, working under new ideologies, find themselves deeply vested in the former systems.[1]

The lesson from Kenya that the National Rainbow Coalition formed partnerships with members of the same government it criticized also illustrates the trade-offs that civil society must make in order to remain viable. There are high costs to such partnerships—in this case, the unaddressed issue of the nearly 350,000 IDPs cited by Klopp—but also potential benefits. For governments facing strong opposition in particular, it presents the possibility of a win-win situation, one where democratization does not mean the ruling party's complete defeat. As such, it provides an opening for civil society to maintain negotiations. Recognizing this in advance can potentially decrease the hostility in the relationship between government and civil society organizations that advocate democratic reform. Chances are that eventually many civil society organizations will reach these conclusions on their own, as the call for democratic reform progresses; however, they are still worth emphasizing. As governments continue to have a monopoly on the use of force and access to policy influence, an understanding—early in the push for democratic reform—by government of the possibility of avoiding a zero-sum game and subsequently by civil society of its room to maneuver may help to move proposals for reform from stalemate to reality. In this regard, it has the potential to decrease the tension and potential violence of maintaining the political status quo as pressure for democratic reform increases.

What useful role can the international community play, given that, through conditionalities, it has been the central promoter of democratization in Africa? International nongovernmental organizations (INGOs) must work to strengthen avenues for information dissemination—such as the print and electronic media—build the capacity of civil society organizations to reach beyond the big cities, and continue to encourage reform of governmental institutions. Klopp ends Chapter 4 on an optimistic note, saying that advocacy for IDPs is beginning to successfully address this and other issues that fall victim to compromises in democratic transitions. Nonetheless, the international advocacy organizations must employ a more focused and less neutral approach to the issues.

Developing a Holistic Approach to Ending Illicit Weapons Trading

The findings in Chapter 2, by Gebrewold and Byrne, provide insight to why existing policies that target the supply of weapons to the subregion have not been able to curb the proliferation of small arms and light weapons. The key, they demonstrate, lies in understanding the demand for firearms and, subsequently, the cultural institutions and structural factors that support their acquisition. Fueling demand are private security concerns, traditional practices, and the lack of opportunities for economic advancement. Governments in the subregion have been unable to fully extend their authority throughout their countries—rendering the borders porous and national institutions weak, while at the same time depriving their citizens of security and economic opportunities. The result, exacerbated by the protracted conflicts in the subregion, has been the perceived need by citizens to arm themselves or to use arms as a means of economic livelihood. Some empirical work by INGOs is increasingly recognizing the need to address the demand for firearms.[2] In fact, case studies show that once individuals experience improvements and predictability in socioeconomic standards *along with* barriers against supply, the primacy of weapons is reduced.[3]

Addressing the demand for weapons also shows the clear need to link security to development even at the communal level. Currently, policymakers and scholars alike link insecurity to underdevelopment with the argument that poorer countries are more prone to civil conflict.[4] The work by Gebrewold and Byrne produces a more precise and tangible link: lack of opportunity, along with uncertainty in the future, increases the perceived need for weapons—a desire easily fulfilled by structural weaknesses such as insecure borders, conflict, and poor institutions. Ironically, the very underdevelopment that drives the demand for small arms is also perpetuated by it, as development cannot occur in a conflict zone.[5]

Addressing demand will require three broad policy approaches. First, the international community can serve as a bridge between governments and civil society organizations. Such linkages are especially important for the rural areas, where government is least present. Second, security-sector reform must be part of broader civil service reforms that work to implement adequate and regular compensation and strong anticorruption provisions. While the renting or selling of service weapons may be explained by the poor compensation received by police, such practices thrive because of poor accountability standards.

Third, governments must consistently take steps to increase the trust level with their citizens. Promises of increased security will likely not be credible from governments that have failed to deliver political and economic goods. Increasing trust between the governments and civil society may be facilitated with the assistance of the international community by continuing with projects such as ensuring free and fair elections, increasing access to education and health care, and investing in community development programs.

Finding Long-Term Solutions for Refugees

A critical challenge for governments in the subregion that must manage large numbers of refugees lies in finding long-term solutions to an issue that many considered a temporary problem. While some of the conflicts in the subregion are of less intensity than others, the fact remains that five of the eight countries (Eritrea, Ethiopia, Somalia, Sudan, Uganda) continue to generate refugees. Consequently, reintegration is not always feasible. Besides the logistical impediments to reintegration, Chapter 3, by Lomo, brings to the fore the increased insecurity of refugee camps through their locations in weakly guarded border towns—a problem related to the failure of state administration—lack of enforcement of human rights, and the limitations they place on mobility. Governments that host refugees, in partnership with international entities such as the UNHCR, must develop long-term and more holistic solutions than are currently employed. Specifically, policies must include the participation of host communities and refugees, work toward integrating refugees with the host community, and take a regional approach in order to consider the impediments in the refugee-generating country.

The international community must be an essential partner in the development of long-term solutions to address the needs of displaced people. Kenya, Tanzania, and Uganda, which bear the bulk of refugees, are themselves underdeveloped and must contend with some internal conflicts (Kenya faces pastoral conflicts; Tanzania must manage electoral violence in Zanzibar; and Uganda, in addition to pastoral conflicts, must fight the Lord's Resistance Army in the North). Requiring these countries to extend access to education, health care, and land to refugees and moving camps to more secure and developed areas are costly and probably unrealistic objectives without the heavy financial and institutional participation of the international community. Furthermore, focusing on development over humanitarian assistance will require institutional changes at the international level—as most funding for refugees falls under the humanitarian rubric.[6] Equally important, the international community must work closely with civil society organizations in refugee-hosting communities to help to dispel misconceptions about refugees and ease integration of refugees into the communities and out of the camps.

Governments in East Africa and the Horn must address refugee policy from a regional perspective. Refugees in Kenya, Tanzania, and Uganda—to mention the most dominant refugee-hosting countries[7]—who hail mainly from Somalia, Sudan, and Burundi, remain there because of continuing insecurity in their countries. It is imperative that the refugee-hosting governments work with refugee-generating countries to bring peace to the region. Much of this is taking place already: the Intergovernmental Authority on Development and the government of Kenya have taken the lead in the Somali peace process; the mediation that resulted in Sudan's Comprehensive Peace Agreement was also spearheaded by IGAD; and the government of Tanzania, along with the African Union, has been instrumental in the peace process in Burundi. These important efforts must be supported financially and logistically by the United Nations, which has the human and operational resources to buttress the efforts of the subregion. The international community has largely withdrawn from Somalia and has only reentered Sudan as a result of the crisis in Darfur. Progress has been made in reintegrating refugees in Burundi,[8] but if the flow of refugees is to stop from the region-at-large, and if they are to be successfully and safely reintegrated, the international community must fully engage in the subregion.

Governing a Multiethnic State

Eritrea, Ethiopia, Somalia, and Sudan face threats to their states by various ethnic groups. In the cases of Sudan and Somalia, these threats developed into full-blown civil wars. While the international media has highlighted the unrest and humanitarian emergency in the Darfur region and the settlement of the civil war between the North and the South, Sudan suffers from ongoing tensions between the government and the Beja in the East and the groups in the Southern Blue Nile, Abyei, and Nuba Mountains—issues also addressed by the protocols in the Comprehensive Peace Agreement.[9] In Somalia, arguably the most challenging of all the states in the subregion with the exception of Somaliland and Puntland, fighting continues among different clan groups, despite recent attempts to establish a government. Eritrea, which won a war of secession against Ethiopia's political and cultural marginalization, has been widely criticized for its oppressive policies against dissenting groups. As Jacquin-Berdal and Mengistu elaborate in Chapter 5, there is one lesson that it must learn from Ethiopia's experience: suppressing political expression will only lead to conflict in the future. Finally, the Ethiopian state continues to be pressured by marginalized groups in Oromia and Somali state.[10] Indeed, the challenge faced by the governments of these countries is how to keep their states intact, reduce the violence waged on the state, and address the grievances by marginalized groups. If the African Union and IGAD are to attain credibility as institutions dedicated to conflict prevention as much as resolution, then they must address these issues directly.

Successfully governing in a multiethnic society also means that the subregional and international institutions must intervene to stop the civil war in Somalia and work harder to consolidate peace in Sudan. IGAD, and Kenya, in particular, have taken the lead in resolving the crises in Sudan and Somalia, but the international community must provide greater support to the region as a whole. Although as mentioned previously, Sudan has received specific attention from the United States due to the war on terrorism and the humanitarian emergency in Darfur—culminating in the authorization of a 10,000-strong UN mission in Sudan,[11] Somalia has been largely forgotten. The African Union simply does not have the capacity to match the intervention of the international community: about 7,700 AU troops have been committed to Darfur (the actual number on the ground is approximately 4,360 as the mission has not fully deployed).[12] Subregional efforts, the most recent being IGAD's decision to deploy a peace support mission to Somalia,[13] are equally problematic due to the interlinkages of conflicts and history which prevent it from credibly mediating conflicts, documented in Chapter 6 by Iyob and Keller and demonstrated by the diffusion of refugees throughout the region and firearms in the region. Thus, the international community's involvement goes beyond the financial assistance that it can bring to negotiations or intervention—it can also bring credibility. Moreover, it is in the interest of the international community, and the United States in particular, to assist failing states—which can become havens for terrorism and other illicit activity.

Benefiting from Reengagement by the United States

The governance challenge for countries that face a reengagement of the United States is to successfully find the balance between nurturing fledging democracies and addressing the very real security threats facing the United States and some countries in the subregion. Although providing security and opening the political space are not mutually exclusive, the fear expressed by many civil society groups in East Africa and the Horn is a repetition of past relationships, where stability has trumped change and as a result kept autocratic rulers in office.[14] Here, the onus does not only lie with the governments of the subregion, but with the United States as well. In this case, governments in Africa and civil society groups should take seriously the Bush administration's doctrine of combating terrorism with democracy.[15] Currently, the Bush administration is present in Djibouti through the establishment of the Combined Joint Task Force–Horn of Africa, which works throughout the Horn of Africa to combat terrorism[16] and is vested in bringing peace to Sudan. These are important opportunities for African countries and NGOs to seek US partnership in consolidating democracy. But as the chapter by Iyob and Keller emphasizes, the lessons of "misreading" the realities on the ground must be fully distilled and incorporated by policymakers in both the Horn and the US, if progress is to occur.

What are those lessons? An important lesson from Iyob and Keller is to understand the developments on the ground with greater certainty. Many governments in the subregion—particularly Eritrea and Ethiopia—seemed to promise reform, but in fact did not undertake the necessary steps to foster democracy. Consequently, the relationship between the United States and a country in the subregion should not be solely with the governing administration, but there should be partnerships with civil society groups and other local organizations. This calls for a closer and more integrated relationship than previously existed. A closer connection to relevant civil society groups will help build a more accurate understanding of the status of a country's democratization progress and other governance challenges. A second lesson is the need for the United States to consistently support democratization efforts. Spotty insistence on democratic conditions sends civil society groups and governments conflicting messages about the US commitment to democracy—critical groups because civil society often leads the efforts for political reform and governments often resist reform. It gives the upper hand to nondemocratic regimes, as they feel no pressure to change.

In the end, if any broad conclusions are to be drawn from the cases in this text, they are that the governance challenges faced by the countries in East Africa and the Horn must be addressed both regionally and internationally. As Richard Joseph noted, Africa's challenges are sufficiently serious that they concern the whole world.[17] The crises faced—refugees and IDP policies, illicit weapons trading, and political participation—are products of events with origins in the region as well as international policies that frame the actions of external countries and organizations. The obstacles to resolving these crises can only be lifted when parties do not act at cross-purposes. In addition, the value of working with organizations on the ground should not be underestimated. In the case of the subregion, civil society organizations can serve as an important asset in addressing the demand for small arms, integrating refugees into host societies, and pushing for democratization.

Notes

1. E. Gyimah-Boadi, "Africa: The Quality of Political Reform," in *Democratic Reform in Africa: The Quality of Progress,* ed. E. Gyimah-Boadi (Boulder: Lynne Rienner Publishers, 2004), p. 22.

2. Tibebe Eshete and Siobahn O'Reilly-Calthrop, "Silent Revolution: The Role of Community Development in Reducing the Demand for Small Arms," *Working Paper* no. 3 (September 2000) (electronic version).

3. Eshete and O'Reilly-Calthrop, pp. 9–10.

4. Paul Collier and Anke Hoeffler, "On the Incidence of Civil War in Africa," *Journal of Conflict Resolution* 46 (February 2002): 13–28.

5. Robert Muggah, "Globalisation and Insecurity: The Direct and Indirect Effects of Small Arms Availability," *IDS Bulletin* 32, no. 2 (2001) (electronic version): 75; Robert Muggah and Peter Batchelor, *"Development Held Hostage": Assessing the Effects of Small Arms on Human Development*, A Preliminary Study of the Socio-Economic Impact and Development Linkages of Small Arms Proliferation, Availability and Use, April 2002, United Nations Development Programme (electronic version).

6. Barbara Harrell-Bond, "Toward the Economic and Social 'Integration' of Refugee Populations in Host Countries in Africa," prepared for the Stanley Foundation conference "Refugee Protection in Africa: How to Ensure Security and Development for Refugees and Hosts," Entebbe, Uganda (November 10–14, 2002) (electronic version), p. 11.

7. UNHCR, *Global Report 2004* (Bucharest: RA Monitorul Oficial, 2005) (electronic version), pp. 165–171, 179–237.

8. Refugees International, "Burundi: Opportunities for the Reintegration of Internally Displaced and Refugees" (available online at http://www.refugeesinternational.org/content/articles/detail/4581/&output=printer, accessed December 7, 2004).

9. International Crisis Group, *Sudan's Other Wars*, Africa Briefing, 25 June 2003 (electronic version); Douglas H. Johnson, *The Root Causes of Sudan's Civil Wars* (Bloomington: Indiana University Press, 2003), pp. 127–142. See also the Comprehensive Peace Agreement, Protocol on the Resolution of the Conflict in Southern Kordofan and the Blue Nile States (May 2004) and Protocol on the Resolution of the Conflict in the Abyei Area (May 2004).

10. Human Rights Watch, "Ethiopia," *World Report 2005* (New York: Human Rights Watch, 2005), electronic version.

11. UN Security Council, 5151st meeting, "Resolution 1590 [on Sudan]" (S/RES/1590/2005) (March 24, 2005) (electronic version).

12. "Darfur: Airlift of Troops for Expanded AU Mission Could Start This Month (US Official)." *Agence France–Presse (AFP)*, June 2, 2005 (available online at http://www.reliefweb.int/rw/rwb.nsf/0/49a32fla30c7c49664925701500053ba2?OpenDocument, accessed July 4, 2005); and UN Security Council, "Monthly Report of the Secretary-General on Darfur," (S/2005/523) (August 11, 2005) (electronic version), paragraph 25.

13. IGAD, "Communiqué of the IGAD Heads of State and Government on Somalia" (January 31, 2005) (electronic version); African Union Peace and Security Council, 24th Meeting, "Communiqué" (PSC/PR/Comm. [XXIV]) (February 7, 2005) (electronic version), paragraph 3.

14. Dorina Bekoe and Paul Omach, *Building Peace in Eastern Africa* (New York: International Peace Academy, 2002), p. 21.

15. US Department of State, "Remarks by the President in Address to the United Nations General Assembly" (September 21, 2004, available online at http://usinfo.state.gov/utils/printpage.html, accessed December 7, 2004).

16. Bruce R. Nardulli, "The U.S. Army and the New National Security Strategy," in *The U.S. Army and the New National Security Strategy,* eds. Lynn E. Davis and Jeremy Shapiro (Arlington, VA: Rand, 2003), p. 39.

17. Richard A. Joseph, "Facing Africa's Predicament: Academe Needs to Play a Stronger Role," *Chronicle of Higher Education* 49 (March 7, 2003) (electronic version).

Acronyms

AGOA	African Growth and Opportunity Act
BICC	Bonn International Center for Conversion
EAC	East African Community
ELM	Eritrean Liberation Movement
ELF	Eritrean Liberation Front
EPDM	Ethiopian People's Democratic Movement
EPLF	Eritrean People's Liberation Front
EPRDF	Ethiopian People's Revolutionary Democratic Front
IDPs	internally displaced people
IGAD	Intergovernmental Authority on Development
IISS	International Institute of Security Studies
ITDG-EA	Intermediate Technology Development Group–East Africa
JEM	Justice and Equality Movement
KANU	Kenya African National Union
LRA	Lord's Resistance Army
MAAG	Military Assistance Advisory Group
NaRC	National Rainbow Coalition
NCCK	National Christian Council of Kenya
NFD	Northern Frontier District
NFP	National Focal Point
NGO	nongovernmental organization
NIF	National Islamic Front
OLF	Oromo Liberation Front
ORH	Operation Restore Hope
PFDJ	People's Front for Democracy and Justice
PGE	Provisional Government of Eritrea
PNDR	Programme of the National Democratic Revolution
PRC	People's Republic of China
RDF	Rapid Deployment Force

RWC	Refugee Welfare Committee
SALW	small arms and light weapons
SLM/A	Sudan Liberation Movement/Army
SNM	Somali National Movement
SPLA	Sudan People's Liberation Army
SPLM/A	Sudan People's Liberation Movement/Army
SRS	self-reliance strategy
SSF	Somali Salvation Democratic Front
TGE	Transitional Government of Ethiopia
TPLF	Tigray People's Liberation Front
UNHCR	United Nations High Commissioner for Refugees
USAID	US Agency for Development
USC	United Somali Congress
WSLF	Western Somali Liberation Front

Bibliography

Aalen, Lovise. "Ethnic Federalism in a Dominant Party State: The Ethiopian Experience: 1991–2000," Report R. Bergen, Norway: Chr. Michelsen Institute, February 2002.

Abdullahi, Ahmednasir. "Ethnic Clashes, Displaced Persons and the Potential for Refugee Creation in Kenya: A Forbidding Forecast." *International Journal of Refugee Law* 9, no. 2 (1997): 196–206.

Abo-Bakr, Mohammed O. *Democracy and Political Pluralism in Eritrea.* Cairo: Egyptian Office for Publication, 1998.

Abraham, Kinfe. *Ethiopia: From Bullets to the Ballot Box: The Bumpy Road to Democracy and the Political Economy of Transition.* Lawrenceville, NJ: Red Sea Press, 1994.

Aden, Ebla Haji. "People with Arms and Grassroots Research: The Case of North-East Kenya." In BICC, *Proceedings from Small Arms and Light Weapons Issues in Uganda: Dynamic, Concepts and Perspectives for Action.* Bonn: BICC, April 2002.

Africa Confidential. "Somalia: No Proxy Peace," 40 (October 8, 1999), p. 8.

African American Institute and the National Democratic Institute. *An Evaluation of the June 21, 1992 Elections in Ethiopia.* Washington, DC: African American Institute and the National Democratic Institute, 1992.

African (Banjul) Charter on Human and Peoples Rights, 27 June 1981. OAU Doc. CAB/LEG/67/3 rev. 5, 21 I.L.M. 58 (1982), entered into force 21 October 1986.

African Rights. "Violence at the Coast: The Human Consequences of Kenya's Crumbling Political Institutions." *Witness* 2 (October/November 1997).

African Union Peace and Security Council. 17th Meeting, *Report of the Chairperson on the Commission on the Situation in Darfur, the Sudan,* 20 October 2004 (electronic version).

Ahari, M. Ehasan. "Rogue States and NMD/TMD: Policies in Search of a Rationale?" *Mediterranean Quarterly* 12 (May 2001): 84–87.

"Another Blow to Land Clash Victims." *The Nation* (Nairobi), May 31, 2004.

Araia, Ghelawdewos. *Ethiopia: The Political Economy of Transition.* Lanham, MD: University Press of America, 1995.

Assembly of the Heads of State and Government. Agreement Establishing the Inter-Governmental Authority on Development (IGAD/SUM-96/AGRE-Doc). Nairobi, 21 March 1996.

Atieno-Odhiambo, E. S. "Hegemonic Enterprises and Instrumentalities of Survival: Ethnicity and Democracy in Kenya." In *Ethnicity and Democracy in Africa*. Edited by Bruce Berman, Dickson Eyoh, and Will Kymlicka. Oxford: James Currey, 2004.

Bader, George W. "Testimony." In *Hearings Before the US Senate Subcommittee on US Security Agreements and Commitments Abroad: Ethiopia*. Washington, DC: US Government Printing Office, 1970.

Bagshaw, Simon, and Diane Paul. "Protect or Neglect? Toward a More Effective United Nations Approach to the Protection of Internally Displaced Persons." Brookings–SAIS Project on Internal Displacement and United Nations Office for the Coordination of Humanitarian Affairs (OCHA), November 2004.

Balsvik, Randi Rønning. *Haile Selassie's Students: The Intellectual and Social Background to Revolution: 1952–1977*. East Lansing: Michigan State University, 1985.

Bekoe, Dorina A., and Paul Omach. *Building Peace in Eastern Africa*. New York: International Peace Academy, 2002.

Bhalla, Nita. "Protests Radicalise Ethiopia's Youths." *BBC News*. 4 May 2001. http://news.bbc.co.uk/2/hi/africa/1312348.stm.

Bonn International Center for Conversion (BICC). "Help Desk for Practical Disarmament." Projects on Small Arms Control. http://www.bicc.de/helpdesk/definition/types.html.

———. *Small Arms in the Horn of Africa: Challenges, Issues and Perspectives*. Brief 23. Bonn: BICC, May 2002.

———. *Gender Perspectives on Small Arms and Light Weapons: Regional and International Concerns*. Brief 24. Bonn: BICC, July 2002.

Brown, Stephen. "Authoritarian Leaders and Multiparty Elections in Africa: How Foreign Donors Help to Keep Kenya's Daniel arap Moi in Power." *Third World Quarterly* 22, no. 5 (2001): 725–739.

———. "Quiet Diplomacy and Recurring 'Ethnic Clashes' in Kenya." In *From Promise to Practice: Strengthening UN Capacities for Prevention of Violent Conflict*. Edited by Chandra Lekha Sriram and Karin Wermester. Boulder and London: Lynne Rienner, 2003.

Calhoun, Craig. "On Ethnic Cleansing in Ethiopia." *Dissent* 46 (Winter 1999): 47.

Canadian International Development Agency. "Governance in Africa." *CIDA, Africa & the G8*. 2002. http://www.acdi-cida.gc.ca/cida_ind.nsf/015451E7CE3F71F85 256BAE007BEC42?OpenDocument (accessed March 11, 2005).

Carothers, Thomas, and Marina Ottaway, eds. *Funding Virtue: Civil Society and Democracy Promotion*. Washington, DC: Carnegie Endowment for International Peace, 2000.

Cater, Charles. *The Regionalization of Conflict and Intervention*. New York: International Peace Academy, 2003.

Chua, Amy. *World on Fire: How Exporting Free Market Democracy Breeds Ethnic Hatred and Global Instability*. New York: Random House, 2003.

Clapham, Christopher. *Transformation and Continuity in Revolutionary Ethiopia*. Cambridge: Cambridge University Press, 1988.

Cohen, Frank S. "Proportional Versus Majoritarian Ethnic Conflict Management in Democracies." *Comparative Political Studies* 30 (October 1997): 607–630.

Cohen, Herman. *Intervening in Africa: Superpower Peacemaking in a Troubled Continent*. New York: St. Martin's Press, 2000.

Cohen, Roberta, and Francis Deng. *Masses in Flight: The Global Crisis of Displacement*. Washington, DC: Brookings Institution, 1998.

Collier, Paul. "Learning from Failure: The International Financial Institutions as Agencies of Restraint in Africa." In *The Self-Restraining State: Power and Accountability in New Democracies.* Edited by Andreas Schedler, Larry Diamond, and Marc F. Plattner. Boulder: Lynne Rienner Publishers, 1999.

Collier, Paul, and Anke Hoeffler. "On the Incidence of Civil War in Africa." *Journal of Conflict Resolution* 46 (February 2002): 13–28.

Commonwealth Observer Group. "The Presidential Parliamentary and Civic Elections in Kenya." London: Commonwealth Secretariat, 1993.

"The Conflict in South Sudan and the IGAD Peace Process." *IGAD News.* Intergovernmental Authority on Development, December 2002.

Connor, Walker. *Ethnonationalism: The Quest for Understanding.* Princeton, NJ: Princeton University Press, 1994.

Co-ordinated Agenda for Action on the Problem of the Proliferation of Small Arms and Light Weapons in the Great Lakes Region and the Horn of Africa. November 2000 (electronic version).

Crisp, Jeff. "Africa's Refugees: Patterns, Problems, Policy Changes." *New Issues in Refugee Research.* Working Paper No. 28. Geneva: Evaluation and Policy Unit, UNHCR, October 2001 (electronic version).

Deng, Francis. Opening Statement by the Representative of the UN Secretary General on Internally Displaced Persons (UNSG/IDP). International Symposium on the Mandate of the UNSG/IDP, Vienna, December 12–13, 2002.

Dreze, Jean, and Amartya Sen. *Hunger and Public Action.* Oxford: Oxford University Press, 1989.

Dumont, Rene. *False Start in Africa.* London: Earthscan Publication, 1988.

East African Standard, Special Reports. September 12, 2004. These reports include "Revenge Mission Fanned the Flames of Ethnic War: Displaced Six Times in 30 Years"; "Huruma Residents Are the Picture of Disillusionment"; "Fourteen Years Later, It's a Hard Life in the Cold"; "Rift Valley MPs Seek Justice for Clashes Victims"; "Reprieve for Squatters as Forest Ban Lifted"; "Kimunya: Internally Displaced Opportunists; It's a Tough Life for the Displaced."

Economic Community of African States. *Protocol on the Free Movement of Persons, Right of Residence and Establishment* (A/P.1/5/79). May 29, 1979.

Economist Intelligence Unit. *Country Profile—Ethiopia.* London: The Economist Intelligence Unit, 1998.

Ellingson, Lloyd. "The Emergence of Political Parties in Eritrea, 1941–1950." *Journal of African History* 18, no. 2 (1977): 261–282.

Eshete, Tibebe. Personal communication. March 2000.

Eshete, Tibebe, and Siobhan O'Reilly-Calthrop. *Silent Revolution: The Role of Community Development in Reducing the Demand for Small Arms.* Working Paper No. 3. September 2000 (electronic version).

———. *Silent Revolution: The Role of Community in Reducing the Demand for Small Arms.* Working Paper No. 3. World Vision, 2003.

Flew, Catherine, and Angus Uruquhart. *Strengthening Small Arms Controls: An Audit of Small Arms Control Legislation in the Great Lakes Region and the Horn of Africa.* SaferAfrica and SaferWorld. February 2004. http://www.saferworld.org.uk/publications/Horn%20narrative%20report.pdf (accessed March 14, 2005).

Fogarassy, Helen. *Mission Improbable: The World Community in a UN Compound in Somalia.* Lanham, MD: Lexington Books, 1999.

Freedom House. *Freedom in the World.* Country Ratings Database. 1972–2003. http://www.freedomhouse.org/ratings/allscore04.xls (accessed March 11, 2005).

———. "Eritrea." *Freedom in the World 2003* (electronic version).

Gagnon, V. P. *The Myth of Ethnic War.* Ithaca, NY: Cornell University Press, 2004.

Garang de Mabior, John, and Mansur Khalid. *John Garang Speaks.* London: KTI Ltd., 1987.

Gellner, Ernest. *Nations and Nationalism.* Ithaca, NY: Cornell University Press, 1983.

Gibson, Samantha. "Aid and Politics in Malawi and Kenya: Political Conditionality and Donor Support to the 'Human Rights, Democracy and Governance' Sector." In *Common Security and Civil Society in Africa.* Edited by Lenmart Wohlgemuth, Samantha Gibson, Stephan Klassen, and Emma Rothchild. Uppsala: Nordiska Africanistitutet, 1999.

Gilkes, Patrick, and Martin Plaut. *War in the Horn: The Conflict Between Eritrea and Ethiopia.* Discussion Paper 82. London: The Royal Institute of International Affairs, 1999.

Gitari, Francis. Akiwumi Commission Nakuru Catholic Diocese.

The Global IDP Project. "Kenya: Tensions Rise as Government Fails to Address Internal Displacement." Norwegian Refugee Council, November 30, 2004.

Government of the Democratic Republic of the Sudan. "Regulation of Asylum Act 1974." *Democratic Republic of the Sudan Gazette* no. 1162, June 15, 1974, section 10(2), pp. 183–186. http://www.unhcr.ch/cgi-bin/texis/vtx/rsd (accessed March 15, 2005).

Government of the Federal Democratic Republic of Ethiopia. *Constitution of the Federal Democratic Republic of Ethiopia.* December 1994.

Government of Kenya. *Report of the Parliamentary Select Committee to Investigate the Ethnic Clashes in Western and Other Parts of Kenya.* Nairobi: Government Printer, 1992.

———. *The Task Force on Truth, Justice and Reconciliation.* Nairobi: Government Printers, 2003.

———. Ministry of Lands. *National Land Policy Formulation Process.* Nairobi: Ministry of Lands, March 2004.

Government of Uganda. "Control of Alien Refugees Act, 1960." 1964 edition, volume 2.

———. "The Constitution of the Republic of Uganda." September 22, 1995.

———. "The Land Act, 1998." *Laws of the Republic of Uganda.* Revised edition. December 2000, IX, p. 4779.

Graduate Institute of International Studies, Geneva. *Small Arms Survey 2003: Development Denied.* Oxford: Oxford University Press, 2003 (electronic version).

Gray, Robert D. "Post-Imperial Ethiopian Foreign Policy: Ethiopian Dependence." In *Proceedings from the Fifth International Conference on Ethiopian Studies.* Chicago, 1978.

Gyimah-Boadi, E. "Africa: The Quality of Political Reform." In *Democratic Reform in Africa: The Quality of Progress.* Edited by E. Gyimah-Boadi. Boulder: Lynne Rienner Publishers, 2004.

Hansard. Parliamentary Debates. July 30, 2003.

Harbeson, John W. "Externally Assisted Democratization: Theoretical Issues and African Realities." In *Africa in World Politics: The African State System in Flux.* 3rd edition. Edited by John W. Harbeson and Donald Rothchild. Boulder: Westview Press, 2000.

Harding, Jeremy. "A Death in Eritrea." *London Review of Books,* July 6, 1995.

Harrell-Bond, Barbara. "Pitch the Tents." *The New Republic* (September 19 & 26, 1994): 15–19.

———. "Toward the Economic and Social 'Integration' of Refugee Populations in Host Countries in Africa." Prepared for the Stanley Foundation conference

"Refugee Protection in Africa: How to Ensure Security and Development for Refugees and Hosts." Entebbe, Uganda, November 10–14, 2002 (electronic version).

Harrell-Bond, Barbara E., and Guglielmo Verdirame. "The Enjoyment of Human Rights by Refugees in Uganda: A Socio-Legal Study." Refugee Studies Centre, University of Oxford, 1998.

Harrell-Bond, Barbara E., Guglielmo Verdirame, Zachary Lomo, and Hannah Garry. *Rights in Exile: A Janus-Faced Humanitarianism.* Oxford: Berghahn Books, 2005.

Henze, Paul B. *Ethiopia and Eritrea in Transition: The Impact of Ethnicity on Politics and Development Opportunities and Pitfalls.* Santa Monica, CA: Rand Corporation, 1995.

Hirsch, John L., and Robert B. Oakley. *Somalia and Operation Restore Hope: Reflections on Peacemaking and Peacekeeping.* Washington, DC: United States Institute of Peace Press, 1995.

"Horn of Africa: US Admits Sending More Troops." *IRINNews.org,* October 30, 2002. http://www.irinnews.org/report.asp?ReportID=30661&SelectRegion=Horn_of_Africa&SelectCountry=HORN_OF_AFRICA.

Horowitz, Donald L. *Ethnic Groups in Conflict.* Los Angeles: University of California Press, 2000.

Hovil, Lucy. "Refugees and the Security Situation in Adjumani District." *Working Paper No. 2.* Refugee Law Project, Makerere University. Kampala, Uganda, 2001.

———. "Free to Stay, Free to Go? Movement, Seclusion and Integration of Refugees in Moyo District." *Working Paper No. 4.* Refugee Law Project, Makerere University. Kampala, Uganda, May 2002.

Hovil, Lucy, and Alex Moorehead. *War as Normal: The Impact of Violence on the Lives of Displaced Communities in Pader District, Northern Uganda. Working Paper No. 5.* Refugee Law Project, Makerere University. Kampala, Uganda, June 2002.

Hoyweghen, Saskia Van. "Mobility, Territoriality and Sovereignty in Post-Colonial Tanzania." *New Issues in Refugee Research.* Working Paper No. 49. Geneva: Evaluation and Policy Unit, UNHCR, October 2001. www.unhcr.ch (accessed March 10, 2005).

Human Rights Watch. *Divide and Rule: State Sponsored Ethnic Violence in Kenya.* New York: HRW, 1993.

———. *Kenya: Old Habits Die Hard.* New York: HRW, 1995.

———. *Failing the Internally Displaced: The UNDP Displaced Persons Program in Kenya.* New York: HRW, 1997.

———. "Eritrea: Release Political Prisoners." September 17, 2003. http://www.hrw.org/press/2003/09/eritrea091703 (accessed December 8, 2004).

———. "Eritrea." *World Report 2005.* New York: Human Rights Watch, 2005 (electronic version).

———. "Ethiopia." *World Report 2005.* New York: Human Rights Watch, 2005 (electronic version).

Hussein, Adam M. "Somalia: A Terrible Beauty Being Born?" In *Collapsed States: The Disintegration and Restoration of Legitimate Authority.* Edited by I. William Zartman. Boulder: Lynne Rienner Publishers, 1995.

Hyden, Goran. "Governance and the Reconstitution of Political Order." In *State, Conflict, and Democracy in Africa.* Edited by Richard Joseph. Boulder: Lynne Rienner Publishers, 1999.

Implementation Plan of the Co-ordinated Agenda for Action on the Problem of the Proliferation of Small Arms and Light Weapons in the Great Lakes Region and the Horn of Africa. November 2000. http://www.smallarmsnet.org/docs.htm.

InDRA Conference Concept Paper. "Refugees and the Transformation of Society: Loss and Recovery." University of Amsterdam, April 1999.

Intermediate Technology Development Group—East Africa. *Conflict in Northern Kenya: A Focus on Internally Displaced.* Nairobi: ITDG, 2003.

———. "Displacements: Resettle Cattle Rustling Victims Too." *Peace Bulletin,* September 2004. http://www.itdg.org/print.php?id-peace5_displacements (accessed February 1, 2005).

———. "Elemi Triangle: A Theatre of Armed Cattle Rustling." *Peace Bulletin,* January 2005. http://www.itdg.org/print.phpd?id=peace6_elemi (accessed February 1, 2005).

Intermediate Technology Development Group—East Africa and United Nations Human Settlements Programme (UN HABITAT). "Crime in Nairobi." Nairobi, December 5, 2000. http://www.unchs.org/press2000/crime_in_nairobi.asp.

International Crisis Group. *Sudan's Other Wars.* Africa Briefing, June 25, 2003 (electronic version).

International Institute of Security Studies (IISS). *The Military Balance.* London: International Institute for Strategic Studies (1977–1989).

Iyob, Ruth. "The Ethiopian-Eritrean Conflict: Diasporic vs. Hegemonic States in the Horn of Africa, 1991–2000." *The Journal of Modern African Studies* 38, no. 4 (2000): 651–682.

Jackson, Henry. *From the Congo to SOWETO: US Foreign Policy Towards Africa Since 1960.* New York: William Morrow, 1982.

Jacobsen, Karen. "Factors Influencing the Policy Responses of Host Governments to Mass Refugee Influxes." *International Migration Review* 30 (Autumn 1996): 655–678 (electronic version).

Johnson, Douglas H. *The Root Causes of Sudan's Civil Wars.* Bloomington: Indiana University Press, 2003.

Joireman, Sandra Fullerton. "Opposition Politics and Ethnicity in Ethiopia: We Will All Go Down Together." *Journal of Modern African Studies* 35, no. 3 (1997): 387–408.

Joseph, Richard A. "Facing Africa's Predicament: Academe Needs to Play a Stronger Role." *Chronicle of Higher Education* 49 (March 7, 2003).

Juma, Monica Kathina. *Unveiling Women as Pillars of Peace: Peace-Building in Communities Fractured by Conflict in Kenya.* An Interim Report for the Management Development and Governance Division, Bureau for Development Policy. UNDP, 2000.

Kagwanja, Peter Mwangi. "Strengthening Local Relief Capacity in Kenya: Challenges and Prospects." In *Eroding Local Capacity: International Humanitarian Action in Africa.* Edited by Monica Kathina Juma and Astri Suhrke. Uppsala: Nordiska AfrikainInstitutet, 2002.

Kahura, Dauti. "Kimunya: Internally Displaced Opportunists." *East African Standard* 11 (September 2004).

Kaiser, John Anthony. *If I Die.* Nairobi: Cana Publishing, 2003.

"Kalenjin Solidarity." *Weekly Review,* September 27, 1991.

Kamungi, Prisca Mbura. "The Current Situation of Internally Displaced Persons in Kenya." *Jesuit Refugee Service,* March 2001.

———. *The Lives and Life-Choices of Dispossessed Women in Kenya.* UNIFEM African Women in Crisis Programme, January 2002.

———. *Kenya's Internally Displaced Persons: Numbers and Challenges.* OCHA Department of Disaster Prevention, Management and Coordination Unit, December 2002.

Kaplan, Robert. "A Tale of Two Colonies." *The Atlantic Monthly,* April 2003, pp. 46–54.

Kebbede, Girma. *The State and Development in Ethiopia.* Atlantic Highlands, NJ: Humanities Press, 1992.

Keller, Edmond J. "United States Foreign Policy on the Horn of Africa: Policymaking with Blinders On." In *African Crisis Areas and U.S. Foreign Policy.* Edited by Richard Sklar, Gerald Bender, and James S. Coleman. Berkeley: University of California Press, 1985.

———. *Revolutionary Ethiopia: From Empire to People's Republic.* Bloomington: Indiana University Press, 1988.

———. "Rethinking African Regional Security." In *Regional Orders: Building Security in a New World.* Edited by David Lake and Patrick Morgan. University Park: The Pennsylvania State University Press, 1997.

———. "Ethnic Federalism, Fiscal Reform, Development and Democracy in Ethiopia." *Journal of African Political Science* 7 (June 2002): 21–50.

Keller, Edmond, and Lahra Smith. "Obstacles to Implementing Territorial Decentralization: The First Decade of Ethiopian Federalism." In *Sustainable Peace: Democracy and Power-Dividing Institutions After Civil Wars.* Edited by Philip Roeder and Donald Rothchild. Ithaca, NY: Cornell University Press, September 2005.

Kellogg, Alan P. "War Justifies All: Donald Rumsfeld Courts a Repressive Government in the Horn of Africa." *The American Prospect Online,* December 17, 2002.

Kenya Human Rights Commission (KHRC). *Ours by Right, Theirs by Might: A Study on Land Clashes.* Nairobi: KHRC, 1996.

———. *Killing the Vote: State Sponsored Violence and Flawed Elections in Kenya.* Nairobi: KHRC, 1998.

Kenya Land Alliance (KLA). *The National Land Policy in Kenya: Addressing Historical Injustices.* Issues Paper no. 2. Nakuru, Kenya: KLA, 2004.

Killion, Tom. "The Eritrean Economy in Historical Perspective." *Eritrean Studies Review* 1 (Spring 1996): 91–118.

———. "Eritrean Workers' Organization and Early Nationalist Mobilization: 1948–1958." *Eritrean Studies Review* 2 (Spring 1997): 1–58.

Klopp, Jacqueline. "Electoral Despotism in Kenya: Land, Patronage and Resistance in the Multi-Party Context." Ph.D. Thesis, Department of Political Science. McGill University, January 2001.

———. "Ethnic Clashes and Winning Elections: The Kenyan Case of Electoral Despotism." *Canadian Journal of African Studies* 35, no. 2 (2001): 473–517.

———. "Civil Society and the State: Partnerships for Peace in the Great Lakes Region." New York: International Peace Academy, June 2004.

Klopp, Jacqueline, and Elke Zuern. "The Politics of Violence in Democratization." Paper presented to the Seminar on Contentious Politics. Columbia University, 2003.

Korellach, Labon. NCCK Peace and Reconciliation Coordinator for Nakuru. Interview. Nakuru, October 25, 2000.

Korry, Edward. "Testimony." In *Hearings Before the US Senate Subcommittee on African Affairs.* Washington, DC: US Government Printing Office, 1976.

La Colonia Eritrea. Manuale d'Instruzione Italiano-Tigrai. Ad uso delle Scuole Indigene per Cura Della Missione Cattolica. Asmara: Tipografia Francescana, 1917.

Law Society of Kenya. *Impunity—Report of the Law Society of Kenya on the Judicial Commission of Inquiry into Ethnic Clashes in Kenya.* Nairobi: Law Society of Kenya, 2000.

Lawyers Committee for Human Rights. *Refugees, Rebels and the Quest for Justice.* 2002.

Lefebvre, Jeffrey. "Moscow's Cold War and Post–Cold War Policies in Africa." In *Africa in the New International Order: Rethinking State Sovereignty and Regional Security.* Edited by Edmond J. Keller and Donald Rothchild. Boulder: Lynne Rienner Publishers, 1996.

Legesse, Asmarom. *The Uprooted: Case Material on Ethnic Eritrean Deportees from Ethiopia Concerning Human Rights Violations.* Report written on behalf of Citizens for Peace in Eritrea. Asmara, Eritrea, July 26, 1998.

———. *The Uprooted—Part Two: A Scientific Survey of Ethnic Eritrean Deportees from Ethiopia Conducted with Regard to Human Rights Violations.* Report written on behalf of Citizens for Peace in Eritrea. Asmara, Eritrea, February 22, 1999.

Legum, Colin, and Bill Lee. *The Horn of Africa in Continuing Crisis.* New York: Africana, 1979.

Lelo, Francis. *A Report on the Health/Medical Needs Assessment of Olenguruone Parish.* Catholic Diocese of Nakuru, 1996.

Lesch, Ann Mosley. *The Sudan: Contested National Identities.* Bloomington: Indiana University Press, 1998.

Lewis, David. "Civil Society in African Contexts: Reflections on the Usefulness of a Concept." *Development and Change* 33, no. 4 (2002).

Lijphart, Arend. *Democracy in Plural Societies: A Comparative Exploration.* New Haven, CT: Yale University Press, 1972.

Lomo, Zachary. "The Role of Legislation in Promoting 'Recovery': A Critical Analysis of Refugee Law and Policy in Uganda." 1998 (unpublished).

Lyons, Terrence. "The International Context of Internal War: Ethiopia/Eritrea." In *Africa in the New International Order: Rethinking State Sovereignty and Regional Security.* Edited by Edmond J. Keller and Donald Rothchild. Boulder: Lynne Rienner Publishers, 1996.

———. "Closing the Transition: The May 1995 Elections in Ethiopia." *Journal of Modern African Studies* 34 (March 1996): 121–143.

Lyons, Terrence, and Ahmed I. Samatar. *State Collapse, Multilateral Intervention and Strategies for Political Reconstruction.* Washington, DC: The Brookings Institution, 1995.

The Machakos Protocol. Machakos, Kenya, July 20, 2002.

MacLean, Lauren Morris. "Mediating Ethnic Conflict at the Grassroots: The Role of Local Associational Life in Shaping Political Values in Côte d'Ivoire and Ghana." *Journal of Modern African Studies* 42, no. 4 (2004): 589–617.

Magenyi, Keffa Karuoya. IDP Coordinator Subukia Zone. "Report on Situational Likia Mau Narok Clashes." October 5, 2004.

Malwal, Bona. "Sudan's Political and Economic Future: A Southern Perspective." In *The Horn of Africa.* Edited by Charles Gurdon. New York: St. Martin's Press, 1994.

Mann, Michael. *The Dark Side of Democracy: Explaining Ethnic Cleansing.* Cambridge: Cambridge University Press, 2005.

Marcus, Harold G. *Ethiopia, Great Britain and the United States 1941–74.* Berkeley: University of California Press, 1983.

———. *A History of Ethiopia.* Berkeley: University of California Press, 2002.

Markakis, John. *National and Class Conflict in the Horn of Africa*. Cambridge: Cambridge University Press, 1987.

———. "Nationalism and Ethnicity in the Horn of Africa." In *Ethnicity and Nationalism in Africa: Constructivist Reflections and Contemporary Politics*. Edited by Paris Yeros. New York: St. Martin's Press, 1999.

Maxted, Julia, and Abebe Zegeye. "Human Stability and Conflict in the Horn of Africa: Part One." *African Security Review* 10, no. 4 (2001): 95–110.

Médard, Claire. "Les Conflits 'Ethniques' au Kenya: Une Question de Votes ou de Terres?" *Afrique Contemporaine* 180 (October/December 1996): 62–74.

———. "Dispositifs Électoraux et Violences Ethniques: Réflexions Sur Quelques Strategies Territoriales de Régime Kényan." *Politique Africaine* 70 (June 1998): 32–39.

Médecins Sans Frontières (MSF). "Learn More About Shelter." MSF-USA: Refugee Camp Project. http://www.refugeecamp.org/leanmore/shelter/index.htm (accessed March 18, 2005).

Mengistu, Aida. "Eritrea and Ethiopia: Uneasy Peace." *The World Today* 57 (May 2001): 9–11.

Mkapa, Benjamin, President of Tanzania. Annual National Congress of Chama cha Mapinduzi (CCM). Dodoma, October 28, 2002.

Mkutu, Kennedy. "Pastoral Conflicts and Small Arms: The Kenya-Uganda Border Region." *SaferWorld,* November 2003, p. 11 (electronic version).

Monga, Celestin. *The Anthropology of Anger*. Boulder: Lynne Rienner Publishers, 1996, pp. 27–29.

Morrison, J. Stephen. "Somalia and Sudan's Race to the Fore in Africa." *The Washington Quarterly* 25 (Spring 2002): 191–205.

Mousseau, Demet Yalcin. "Democratizing with Ethnic Divisions: A Source of Conflict?" *Journal of Peace Research* 38 (2001): 547–567.

Muggah, Robert. "Globalisation and Insecurity: The Direct and Indirect Effects of Small Arms Availability." *IDS Bulletin* 32, no. 2 (2001) (electronic version).

Muggah, Robert, and Peter Bachelor. *Development Held Hostage: Assessing the Effects of Small Arms on Human Development*. New York: United Nations Development Program, April 2002.

Mutumba, Richard. "Congo Refugees a Threat—MP." *The New Vision* (Uganda), September 27, 2002, p. 4.

The Nairobi Declaration on the Problem of the Proliferation of Illicit Small Arms and Light Weapons in the Great Lakes Region and the Horn of Africa. Nairobi, March 15, 2000. Reproduced by SaferAfrica. http://www.saferafrica.org/DocumentsCentre/Books/Matrix/NairobiDeclaration.asp (accessed November 22, 2004).

The Nairobi Protocol for the Prevention, Control and Reduction of Small Arms and Light Weapons in the Great Lakes Region and the Horn of Africa. Nairobi, April 21, 2004. Reproduced by Smallarmsnet. http://www.smallarmsnet.org/docs/saaf12.pdf.

Nardulli, Bruce R. "The U.S. Army and the New National Security Strategy." In *The U.S. Army and the New National Security Strategy*. Edited by Lynn E. Davis and Jeremy Shapiro. Arlington, VA: Rand, 2003.

National Council of Churches of Kenya (NCCK). *Cursed Arrow: A Report of Organized Violence Against Democratic Kenya*. Nairobi: Church House, 1992.

———. "Press Release." February 12, 1992.

———. *Deception, Dispersal and Abandonment*. Nairobi: NCCK, 1995.

Negash, Tekeste. *No Medicine for the Bite of a White Snake: Notes on Nationalism and Resistance in Eritrea, 1890–1941*. Uppsala: Uppsala University Press, 1986.

Negash, Tekeste, and Kjetil Tronvoll. *Brothers at War: Making Sense of the Eritrean-Ethiopian War.* Oxford: James Currey, 2000.

Newsom, David. "Testimony." Hearings Before the US Senate Subcommittee on US Security Agreements and Commitments Abroad: Ethiopia. Washington, DC: Government Printing Office, 1970.

Norwegian Refugee Council. *Internally Displaced People: A Global Survey.* London: Earthscan Publications, 2002.

———. *Profile of Internal Displacement: Kenya.* November 30, 2004.

Nowrojee, Binafer. "UN and African Regional Responsibility to Provide Human Rights Protection to the Internally Displaced: Learning Lessons from the Experience of UNDP in Kenya." *Refugee Survey Quarterly* 18, no. 1 (1999).

Office of the Prime Minister/UNHCR. "Strategy Paper, Self Reliance for Refugee Host Areas in Moyo, Arua, and Adjumani Districts, 1999/2003." 1999.

Ogata, Sadako. United Nations High Commissioner for Refugees. Speech at Makerere University Main Hall, August 1998.

Okbazghi, Yohannes. *The United States and the Horn of Africa: An Analytical Study of Pattern and Process.* Boulder: Westview Press, 1997.

Organization of African Unity. Convention Governing the Specific Aspects of Refugee Problems in Africa. September 10, 1969 (electronic version).

———. *Bamako Declaration of an African Common Position on the Illicit Proliferation, Circulation and Trafficking of Small Arms and Light Weapons.* Bamako, December 2000. http://www.saferafrica.org/DocumentsCentre/Books/Matrix/BamekoDeclaration.asp.

Orvis, Stephen. "Kenya Civil Society: Bridging the Urban-Rural Divide." *Journal of Modern African Studies* 41, no. 2 (2003): 247–268.

Ottaway, Marina. *Soviet and American Influence in the Horn of Africa.* New York: Praeger, 1982.

———. *The New African Leaders: Democracy or State Reconstruction?* Washington, DC: The Brookings Institution, 1999.

Oyugi, Cyrus Samuel King'ori, Mohamed Tabia, Keffa Magenyi, Irene Wambui, and Ndung'u Wainaina. "A Joint Statement by Survivors of Ethnic Clashes." A preparatory conference to precede the launch of a national survivors network for the internally displaced persons (IDPs) in Kenya. Kasarani, Kenya, September 26–28, 2003. http://www.db.idpproject.org/Sites/idpSurvey.nsf/16F3 E57093335B82c1256F4E0053A0EB/$file/IDPs+National++Conference+Report ++Sept++2003.doc.

Oyuke, John. "Eritrea Out of AGOA Accord." *The East African Standard* (Nairobi), April 1, 2004. http://zete.delina.org/runzete.asp?quSri=131.

Pastoral Letter of the Catholic Bishops of Kenya. *A Call to Justice, Love and Reconciliation.* Nairobi: St. Paul Publications, 1992.

Péninou, Jean-Louis. "Guerre Absurde Entre l'Ethiopie et l'Erythrée." *Le Monde Diplomatique,* July 1998, p. 15.

People's Front for Democracy and Justice. Special Edition. "Interview with President Isaias Afwerki." *Hewyet,* March 1999.

Plaut, Martin. "Political Turmoil in Ethiopia and Eritrea." *BBC News,* June 5, 2001. http://news.bbc.co.uk/2/hi/africa/1371175.stm.

"Proliferation and Impact of Small Arms in Garissa, Kenya." Community workshop cohosted by SALIGAD, Pastoralists' Peace and Development Initiative, and OXFAM. Garissa, Kenya, June 2000.

Prunier, Gerard. "Somaliland: Birth of a New Country?" In *The Horn of Africa.* Edited by Charles Gordon. New York: St. Martin's Press, 1994.

Randi Balsvik, Rønning. *Haile Selassie's Students: The Intellectual and Social Background to Revolution: 1952–1977.* East Lansing: Michigan State University, 1985.

"Refugees a Threat—Defence." *The New Vision* (Uganda), September 8, 2002, p. 4.

Refugees International. "Burundi: Opportunities for the Reintegration of Internally Displaced and Refugees." December 1, 2004. http://www.refugeesinternational. org/content/aricles/detail/4581/&output=printer (accessed December 7, 2004).

Reilly, Ben, and Andrew Reynolds. "Electoral Systems and Conflict in Divided Societies." *Papers on International Conflict Resolution No. 2.* Committee on International Conflict Resolution, Commission on Behavioral and Social Sciences and Education, National Research Council. Washington, DC: National Academy Press, 1999.

Republic of Kenya. *Report of the Parliamentary Select Committee to Investigate the Ethnic Clashes in Western and Other Parts of Kenya.* Nairobi: Government Printer, 1992.

Republic of Kenya, Ministry of Lands and Housing. *National Land Policy Formulation Process.* Nairobi: Ministry of Lands and Housing, March 2004.

Republic of Uganda. *Control of Alien Refugees Act, 1960,* section 11(a).

Rogge, John. *The Internally Displaced Population in Kenya, Western and Rift Valley Provinces: A Need Assessment and a Program Proposal for Rehabilitation* Report prepared for UNDP. Nairobi, October 1993.

Rosenblum, Peter. "Irrational Exuberance: The Clinton Administration in Africa." *Current History* 101 (May 2002): 195–204.

Rotberg, Robert I., and Deborah L. West. "The Good Governance Problem: Doing Something About It." *The World Peace Foundation,* July 2004.

Rothchild, Donald. "The Impact of US Disengagement on African Intrastate Conflict Resolution." In *Africa in World Politics: The African State System in Flux.* Edited by John W. Harbeson and Donald Rothchild. Boulder: Westview, 2000.

"The Rwanda Emergency: Causes, Responses, Solutions?" *Journal of Refugees Studies* 9, no. 3 (1996).

Sahnoun, Mohamed. *Somalia: The Missed Opportunities.* Washington, DC: The United States Institute of Peace, 1994.

Saihou, Saidy. Interview with the author, April 2002.

Sakataka, William. Interview with the author. Adjumani, Uganda, August 1998.

Samatar, Abdi. "Warlord Games." *BBC Focus on Africa Magazine* 10, no. 1 (January–March 1999): 26–27.

Samatar, Ahmed I., ed. *The Somali Challenge: From Catastrophe to Renewal?* Boulder: Lynne Rienner Publishers, 1994.

Samatar, Yasin. "The Eldoret Consensus: Implementation of the Major Outcomes of the Somali Peace and Reconciliation Conference." *School of Diplomacy and International Relations,* December 1, 2002.

Santiso, Carlos. "Good Governance and Aid Effectiveness: The World Bank and Conditionality." *The Georgetown Public Policy Review* 1 (Fall 2001): 1–22 (electronic version).

Sarasohn, Judy. "Eritrea Pushes to Get US Base." *Washington Post,* November 20, 2002.

Schraeder, Peter. "Reviewing the Study of US Policy Towards Africa: From Intellectual 'Backwater' to Theory Construction." *Third World Quarterly* 14 (December 1993): 775–787.

Selassie, Bereket Habte. "The Disappearance of the Eritrean Constitution and Its Impact on Current Politics in Eritrea." *News.Asmarino.com,* January 20, 2001. http://news.asmarino.com/Articles/2001/01/bhs-20.asp.

Sen, Amartya. *Poverty and Famines: An Essay on Entitlement and Deprivation.* Oxford: Oxford University Press, 1981.

Senior Protection Officer, Directorate of Refugees, Ministry of Disaster Preparedness and Refugees, Office of the Prime Minister. Discussion with the author. Kampala, October 2002.

Shaw, Robert, and Wamuyu Gatheru, eds. *Our Problems, Our Solutions: An Economic and Public Policy Agenda for Kenya.* Nairobi: Institute of Economic Affairs, 1998.

Sisk, Timothy D. *Power Sharing and International Mediation in Ethnic Conflicts.* Washington, DC: United States Institute of Peace, 1996.

Skinner, Elliot P. "Historical Framework Paper." Washington, DC: National Summit on Africa, 1998.

Small Arms Survey 2003. *Development Denied.* Oxford: Oxford University Press, 2003.

Smith, Anthony D. *National Identity.* London: Penguin, 1991.

Snyder, Jack. *From Voting to Violence: Democratization and Nationalist Conflict.* New York: W.W. Norton & Co., 2000.

"Somalia: Building Blocks." *Africa Confidential.* 40 (September 24, 1999), p. 7.

Strategic Survey 1977. International Institute for Strategic Studies. London, 1977.

Subcommittee on African Affairs. *Somalia: US. Policy Options.* Washington, DC: US Government Printing Office, 2002.

"Sudan: Details of Peace Protocols Signed This Week." *IRINNews.org,* May 28, 2004. http://www.irinnews.org/report.asp?ReportID=41318&SelectRegion=East_Africa&SelectCountry=SUDAN.

Tareke, Gebru. *Ethiopia: Power and Protest.* Cambridge: Cambridge University Press, 1991.

Teferra, Daniel. *Social History and Theoretical Analyses of the Economy of Ethiopia.* Lewiston, NY: Edwin Mellen Press, 1990.

Thoolen, Hans. Report of the Roundtable Conference on the Self-Reliance Strategy for Refugee Hosting Areas in Arua, Moyo and Adjumani Districts, June 11, 1999.

Twesigomwe, Carlos. Interview published in *Your Rights* (a publication of the Uganda Human Rights Commission) 3 (January 2000): 8–12.

UNDP (United Nations Development Programme). *Human Development Report 2002.* New York: United Nations Development Programme, 2003.

———. "Somalia–UNOSOM II: Facts and Figures." http://www.un.org/Depts/dpko/dpko/co_mission/unosom2factx.html (accessed March 23, 2005).

UNDP and Government of Kenya. *Country Programme Action Plan 2004–2008.* Nairobi: UNDP, 2004.

UN General Assembly. Universal Declaration of Human Rights. Res/217A(III), December 10, 1948.

———. "Eritrea: Report of the United Nations Commission for Eritrea; Report of the Interim Committee of the General Assembly on the Report of the United Nations Commission for Eritrea." A/Res/5/390A, December 2, 1950.

———. Convention on the Rights of the Child. A/RES/44/25, November 20, 1989 (entered into force September 2, 1990).

———. "Report of the Panel of Governmental Experts on Small Arms." A/52/298, Annex, August 27, 1997.

———. "Report of the Group of Governmental Experts on Small Arms." A/54/258, August 19, 1999.

———. "United Nations Conference on the Illicit Trade in Small Arms and Light Weapons in All Its Aspects, 9–20 July 2001." A/CONF.192/SR.1, July 27, 2001.

UNHCR (United Nations High Commissioner for Refugees). International Covenant on Economic, Social, and Cultural Rights, 1966 (entered into force January 1976).

———. "Personal Protection of Refugees." Executive Committee Conclusions No. 72 (XLIV), 1993.

———. Convention and Protocol Relating to the Status of Refugees. Published as UNHCR/PI/CONV-UK1.PM5/AUGUST 1996.

———. *Global Appeal 2005.* Bucharest: RA Monitorul Oficial, 2004 (electronic version).

UNOCHA (United Nations Office for the Coordination of Humanitarian Affairs). *Affected Populations in the Horn of Africa.* Nairobi: OCHA Regional Support Office for Central and East Africa, May 31, 2004.

UN Security Council. 3145th meeting, "Resolution 794 [Somalia]." S/RES/794, December 3, 1992.

———. 3188th meeting, "Resolution 814 [Somalia]." S/RES/814, March 26, 1993.

———. 3229th meeting, "Resolution 837 [Somalia]." S/RES/837, June 6, 1993.

———. "Monthly Report of the Secretary-General on Darfur." S/2005/523. August 11, 2005 (electronic version).

United Republic of Tanzania. The Refugees Act, 1998, November 1998.

United States Department of Defense. *Foreign Military Sales, Foreign Military Construction, and Military Assistance as of 1981.* Washington, DC: USDOD, 1981.

United States Department of State. "Remarks by the President in Address to the United Nations General Assembly," September 21, 2004. http://usinfo.state.gov/utils/printpage.html (accessed December 7, 2004).

Uppsala Conflict Data Program. Established by the Department of Peace and Conflict Research at Uppsala University. http://www.pcr.uu.se/database/index.php.

USAID (United States Agency for International Development). "Office of Democracy and Governance." http://www.usaid.gov/our_work/democracy_and_governance/technical_areas/dg_office/gov.html (accessed March 12, 2005).

———. "Democracy and Governance in Djibouti." http://www.usaid.gov/our_work/democracy_and_governance/regions/afr/djibouti.html (accessed March 11, 2005).

———. "Democracy and Governance in Ethiopia." http://www.usaid.gov/our_work/democracy_and_governance/regions/afr/ethiopia.html (accessed March 11, 2005).

———. "Democracy and Governance in Somalia." http://www.usaid.gov/our_work/democracy_and_governance/regions/afr/somalia.html (accessed March 11, 2005).

———. "Democracy and Governance in Sudan." http://www.usaid.gov/our_work/democracy_and_governance/regions/afr/sudan.html (accessed March 11, 2005).

———. "Promoting More Transparent and Accountable Governance Institutions." *USAID Democracy and Governance Program.* http://www.usaid.gov/our_work/democracy_and_governance/technical_areas/governance (accessed March 17, 2005).

Uvin, Peter. *Aiding Violence: The Development Enterprise in Rwanda.* West Hartford, CT: Kumarian Press, 1998.

———. "Ethnicity and Power in Burundi and Rwanda: Different Paths to Mass Violence." *Comparative Politics* 31, no. 3 (1999).

Van Damme, Wim. "Do Refugees Belong in Camps? Experiences from Goma and Guinea." *The Lancet* 346 (August 5, 1995): 360–363.

Varshney, Ashutosh. *Ethnic Conflict and Civil Life.* New Haven, CT: Yale University Press, 2002.

Vestal, Theodore M. *Ethiopia: A Post–Cold War African State.* Westport, CT: Praeger Publishers, 1991.

Wa Mutua, Makau. "The Interaction Between Human Rights, Democracy and Governance and the Displacement of Populations." *International Journal of Refugee Law* (Special Issue/July 1995).

Weiss, Taya. "A Demand-Side Approach to Fighting Small Arms Proliferation." *African Security Review* 12 (2003) (electronic version).

Werker, Eric. "Refugees in Kyangwali Settlement: Constraints on Economic Freedom." *Working Paper No. 7.* Refugee Law Project, Makerere University, Kampala, Uganda, December 2002.

Whittaker, Reg. "Refugees: The Security Dimension." *Citizenship Studies* 2, no. 3 (1998): 413–434 (electronic version).

Wintrope, Ronald. *The Political Economy of Dictatorship.* Cambridge: Cambridge University Press, 1998.

Woldemikael, Tekle Mariam. "Political Mobilization and Nationalist Movements: The Case of the Eritrean People's Liberation Front." *Africa Today,* 2nd Quarter, 1991, pp. 31–43.

World Bank Institute. *Governance Indicators: 1996–2002.* http://www.worldbank. org/wbi/governance/govdata2002 (accessed March 11, 2005).

Young, John. *Peasant Revolution in Ethiopia: The Tigray People's Liberation Front, 1975–1991.* Cambridge: Cambridge University Press, 1997.

Zakaria, Fareed. *The Future of Freedom.* New York: W.W. Norton & Co., 2003.

Zartman, I. W., ed. *Traditional Cures for Modern Conflicts: African Conflict "Medicine."* Boulder: Lynne Rienner Publishers, 1999.

Zeratsion, Ghidey. "The Ideological and Political Causes of the Ethio-Eritrean War: An Insider's View." Paper submitted for the International Conference on the Ethio-Eritrean Crises. Amsterdam, July 24, 1999.

Zewde, Bahru. *A History of Modern Ethiopia 1855–1991.* 2nd edition. Oxford: James Currey; Athens: Ohio University Press; Addis Ababa: Addis Ababa University Press, 2001.

The Contributors

Dorina A. Bekoe is Africa specialist and program officer in the Research and Studies Department at the US Institute of Peace in Washington, D.C. Prior to this position, she was in the Africa Program at the International Peace Academy in New York. Her research interests include development, peacebuilding, and conflict resolution. She has published on peacebuilding in Liberia, the New Partnership for Africa's Development, and the African Peer Review Mechanism.

Siobhan Byrne currently lives in Jerusalem, where she conducts research related to her thesis on identity politics in deeply divided societies. She was a member of the SALIGAD team at the Bonn International Center on Conversion in 2002, a project on small arms and light weapons in the member states of the Intergovernmental Authority on Development (IGAD).

Kiflemariam Gebrewold is former director of the Bonn International Center on Conversion's SALIGAD team, a project on small arms and light weapons in the member states of the Intergovernmental Authority for Development (IGAD). He has worked in West-East Africa and the Horn of Africa for ten years for German aid agencies and published extensively on topics such as smart sanctions, small arms and child soldiers, mercenaries, and crisis prevention. Currently he is associated with AIDA Consultants/ Germany and working on, among others topics, disarmament, demobilization, and reintegration issues in southern Sudan.

Ruth Iyob is associate professor of political science and a fellow of the Center for International Studies at the University of Missouri, St. Louis. She served as the director and senior policy adviser of the Africa Program of the International Peace Academy from 2004 to 2005. Her research has focused on understanding the complex factors at play that have fuelled long-standing conflicts in postcolonial Africa. Her publications include books and chapters on nationalism, liberation politics, democratization, citizenship, US-African foreign policy, and Afro-Arab and Euro-African relations in the postcolonial world.

Dominique Jacquin-Berdal is lecturer in the Department of International Relations at the London School of Economics. Her research interests include the Horn of Africa, war in Africa, nationalism, and ethnicity. She is the author of *Nationalism and Ethnicity in the Horn of Africa* (Edward Mellen Press, 2002) and coauthor, with Martin Plaut, of *Unfinished Business: Ethiopia and Eritrea at War* (The Red Sea Press, 2005).

Edmond J. Keller is professor of political science at UCLA and director of the UCLA Globalization Research Center–Africa. He specializes in comparative politics with an emphasis on Africa. He is the author of *Education, Manpower and Development: The Impact of Educational Policy in Kenya* (1980) and *Revolutionary Ethiopia: From Empire to People's Republic* (1988), and coeditor, with Donald Rothchild, of *Africa in the New International Order: Rethinking State Sovereignty and Regional Security* (1996).

Jacqueline M. Klopp is assistant professor of international and public affairs and director of the economic and political development concentration at Columbia University's School of International and Public Affairs. She is currently working with Kang'ethe Mungai and the Network of Internally Displaced in Kenya to build a Regional IDP Resource and Research Center based in Nairobi.

Zachary Lomo is director of the Refugee Law Project in the Faculty of Law at Makerere University in Kampala, Uganda. He has written extensively about the issues facing refugees in eastern Africa, focusing particular attention on international law and human rights.

Aida Mengistu works in New York as an advocacy officer for the United Nations Office for the Coordination for Humanitarian Affairs (OCHA), focusing on advocacy campaigns and outreach to draw attention to forgotten and acute humanitarian crises. From September 2003 to May 2005, she worked with OCHA-Sudan as a reporting and information officer for the Darfur crisis. Prior to OCHA, she was a senior program officer with the International Peace Academy.

Index

About This Publication

Both the obstacles to governance and the opportunities for democratization confronted in East Africa—with its geostrategic importance, porous borders, governments heavily dependent on foreign aid, and some of Africa's longest-running conflicts—provide valuable insights into how good governance policies can be implemented effectively throughout the developing world. *East Africa and the Horn* explores these regional constraints and opportunities, focusing on issues of civil society, the ubiquitous trade in small arms and light weapons, large numbers of refugees, tensions around national identity, and the legacy of US policy.

The authors also underscore the need for even peaceful countries in the region to proactively address potentially destabilizing issues in neighboring states.

Dorina A. Bekoe is Africa specialist and program officer in the Research and Studies Department at the US Institute of Peace, where she works on conflict management and resolution, new institutional norms, and peace accord implementation.

The International Peace Academy

The International Peace Academy (IPA) is an independent, international institution dedicated to promoting the prevention and settlement of armed conflicts between and within states through policy research and development.

Founded in 1970, the IPA has built an extensive portfolio of activities in fulfillment of its mission:

- Symposiums, workshops, and other forums that facilitate strategic thinking, policy development, and organizational innovation within international organizations.
- Policy research on multilateral efforts to prevent, mitigate, or rebuild after armed conflict.
- Research, consultations, and technical assistance to support capacities for peacemaking, peacekeeping, and peacebuilding in Africa.
- Professional-development seminars for political, development, military, humanitarian, and nongovernmental personnel involved in peacekeeping and conflict resolution.
- Facilitation in conflict situations where its experience, credibility, and independence can complement official peace efforts.
- Outreach to build public awareness on issues related to peace and security, multilateralism, and the United Nations.

The IPA works closely with the United Nations, regional and other international organizations, governments, and nongovernmental organizations, as well as with parties to conflicts in selected cases. Its efforts are enhanced by its ability to draw on a worldwide network of government and business leaders, scholars, diplomats, military officers, and leaders of civil society.

The IPA is a nonprofit organization governed by an international Board of Directors. The organization is funded by generous donations from governments, major philanthropic foundations, and corporate donors, as well as contributions from individuals and its Board members.

International Peace Academy Publications

Available from Lynne Rienner Publishers, 1800 30th Street, Boulder, Colorado 80301 (303-444-6684), www.rienner.com.

The Democratic Republic of Congo: Economic Dimensions of War and Peace, Michael Nest, with François Grignon and Emizet F. Kisangani (2006)

East Africa and the Horn: Confronting Challenges to Good Governance, edited by Dorina A. Bekoe (2006)

Profiting from Peace: Managing the Resource Dimensions of Civil War, edited by Karen Ballentine and Heiko Nitzschke (2005)

Western Sahara: Anatomy of a Stalemate, Erik Jensen (2005)

Exploring Subregional Conflict: Opportunities for Conflict Prevention, edited by Chandra Lekha Sriram and Zoe Nielsen (2004)

West Africa's Security Challenges: Building Peace in a Troubled Region, edited by Adekeye Adebajo and Ismail Rashid (2004)

War Economies in a Regional Context: Challenges of Transformation, Michael Pugh and Neil Cooper, with Jonathan Goodhand (2004)

The UN Security Council: From the Cold War to the Twenty-First Century, edited by David M. Malone (2004)

The United Nations and Regional Security: Europe and Beyond, edited by Michael Pugh and Waheguru Pal Singh Sidhu (2003)

The Political Economy of Armed Conflict: Beyond Greed and Grievance, edited by Karen Ballentine and Jake Sherman (2003)

From Promise to Practice: Strengthening UN Capacities for the Prevention of Violent Conflict, edited by Chandra Lekha Sriram and Karin Wermester (2003)

The Chittagong Hill Tracts, Bangladesh: On the Difficult Road to Peace, Amena Mohsin (2003)

Peacekeeping in East Timor: The Path to Independence, Michael G. Smith, with Moreen Dee (2003)

From Cape to Congo: Southern Africa's Evolving Security Challenges, edited by Mwesiga Baregu and Christopher Landsberg (2003)

Ending Civil Wars: The Implementation of Peace Agreements, edited by Stephen John Stedman, Donald Rothchild, and Elizabeth M. Cousens (2002)

Sanctions and the Search for Security: Challenges to UN Action, David Cortright and George A. Lopez, with Linda Gerber (2002)

Ecuador vs. Peru: Peacemaking Amid Rivalry, Monica Herz and João Pontes Nogueira (2002)

Liberia's Civil War: Nigeria, ECOMOG, and Regional Security in West Africa, Adekeye Adebajo (2002)

Building Peace in West Africa: Liberia, Sierra Leone, and Guinea-Bissau, Adekeye Adebajo (2002)

Kosovo: An Unfinished Peace, William G. O'Neill (2002)

From Reaction to Conflict Prevention: Opportunities for the UN System, edited by Fen Osler Hampson and David M. Malone (2002)

Peacemaking in Rwanda: The Dynamics of Failure, Bruce D. Jones (2001)

Self-Determination in East Timor: The United Nations, the Ballot, and International Intervention, Ian Martin (2001)

Civilians in War, edited by Simon Chesterman (2001)

Toward Peace in Bosnia: Implementing the Dayton Accords, Elizabeth M. Cousens and Charles K. Cater (2001)

Sierra Leone: Diamonds and the Struggle for Democracy, John L. Hirsch (2001)

Peacebuilding as Politics: Cultivating Peace in Fragile Societies, edited by Elizabeth M. Cousens and Chetan Kumar (2001)

The Sanctions Decade: Assessing UN Strategies in the 1990s, David Cortright and George A. Lopez (2000)

Greed and Grievance: Economic Agendas in Civil War, edited by Mats Berdal and David M. Malone (2000)

Building Peace in Haiti, Chetan Kumar (1998)

Rights and Reconciliation: UN Strategies in El Salvador, Ian Johnstone (1995)